Contractor's Guide To The Building Code

Jack M. Hageman

Craftsman Book Company
6058 Corte Del Cedro, Carlsbad, CA 92008

Acknowledgements

The author expresses his thanks to the International Conference of Building Officials and to the International Association of Plumbing and Mechanical Officials for their assistance and permission to use charts, tables and quotes from their respective books, the *Uniform Building Code* and the *Uniform Plumbing Code.*

All portions of the Uniform Building Code, except where otherwise noted, are reproduced from 1982 Edition, Copyright 1982, with the permission of the publisher, the International Conference of Building Officials.

Portions of the Uniform Plumbing Code are reproduced with the permission of the publisher, the International Association of Plumbing and Mechanical Officials.

The interpretation and comments listed herein are solely the responsibility of the author and should bear no reflection on either the publishers of the Uniform Building Code, the Uniform Plumbing Code, or the publishers of this book.

Library of Congress Cataloging in Publication Data

Hageman, Jack M.
  Contractor's guide to the building code.

  Includes index.
  1. Building laws—United States. I. Title.
KF5701.H34   1983   343.73'07869   83-5247
ISBN 0-910460-91-4   347.3037869

© 1983 Craftsman Book Company
Fourth Printing 1986

Cartoons by John R. Hageman

Contents

Cuz it says so in ʧᴇ ʙꝏᴋ .

1
Why Do I Need a Permit?

If you're in the construction business, you're going to have building code problems. Every contractor has had an inspector hold up his job or delay a permit until some minor discrepancy is handled just the way the code requires. From your standpoint, following the code is only an annoying and expensive necessity. But the building department, and probably the owner or architect that set your project in motion, regard the code as a good defense against poor practice that might otherwise plague generations of occupants of the building you erect.

No matter what your viewpoint, the building code is a fact of life that every builder must deal with. Your objective, and mine in writing this book, is to make following the code as simple, painless and inexpensive as possible.

Every construction contract you sign assumes that you will build according to the code. You aren't going to get paid until what you build has passed inspection. It's no defense that your estimate didn't include what the inspector demands. You're assumed to know the code and build every project accordingly.

Unfortunately, knowing the code isn't easy. The building code is a complex law intended to be enforced rather than read and understood. The code book itself doesn't have a good index. Related subjects are covered in widely separated sections. Some hard-to-understand sections refer to sections that are even harder to follow. The code seems to grow larger and more complex every time it's revised. There are exceptions, within exceptions, within other exceptions. A lawyer used to handling intricate tax problems would feel right at home with the building code.

But you can't spend a career mastering the building code. At least you shouldn't. Your job is building, not nitpicking. As a builder you need to know only enough to stay out of trouble and avoid expensive mistakes. This book will help. You also need the code itself, of course. The manual you are now reading isn't the code, so don't try to quote from it to your building inspector. Instead, use it as your answer book on code problems. Go to the chapter or section in this book that addresses the problem you're having. Read enough so you have some background on what the code demands. Then go to the code itself if necessary to sort out the fine details. Use the index in this manual to direct you to the code sections that apply to your situation. This publication should save you hours of valuable time and prevent expensive mistakes.

A word about the code itself is in order here. The code we are talking about is the 1982 edition of the Uniform Building Code as published by the International Conference of Building Officials in Whittier, California. The I.C.B.O. is a non-profit organization founded in 1922. About 1600 city and county building departments and state agencies all across the U.S. belong to the I.C.B.O. and participate in drafting and approving the model code. Many other organizations, companies and private individuals participate in the code drafting and revising process. The I.C.B.O. also sponsors research in the field of building safety.

Every three years the code or its revisions are republished as a recommendation—a recommendation to the 1600 building department members of the I.C.B.O. Each county or city then decides if it will adopt the revision as a regulation for that community. Most routinely do. The model code that the I.C.B.O. publishes is a very well researched and highly persuasive document. But many communities change some sections, delete others or add material they feel is important. Thus the code in force in your community may not be exactly like the most recent code published by the I.C.B.O.

Be aware that there are two other "standard" building codes in the U.S. The B.O.C.A. in Chicago and the Southern Building Code Congress also offer model codes. These have been adopted by many communities east of the Mississippi. But the I.C.B.O. code is the most widely adopted. And the differences between the three major model codes are becoming less significant. After all, what is good building practice west of the Mississippi should also be good practice east of the Mississippi.

You need a copy of the current building code in force when you do business. Some bookstores sell the U.B.C. and you can buy it from the I.C.B.O., 5360 South Workman Mill Road, Whittier, California 90601 (213-699-0541). But every building department that really wants to help contractors follow the code should sell it right over the counter at every building department office. Only your building department has the official version enforced in your community. If the inspector can't supply one, have him refer you to a convenient source. The building department expects you to know and follow the code; expect them to furnish a copy to you at reasonable cost.

No matter how carefully you build and how knowledgeable you are about the code, you're going to have an occasional dispute with an inspector. Let me offer some advice. I've stood on the inspector's side of the counter through many disputes with contractors and have heard most of the arguments. You're not going to win very many direct confrontations with a building department. But there's a lot you can do to get them to see your side of the argument.

First, understand that the building department holds all the best cards. They can make any builder's life very unpleasant and cost him a lot of money. They have the full power of government behind them and can use it effectively if necessary to compel compliance on your part. But they would usually prefer to have your voluntary cooperation.

Adopt this attitude toward the building department and inspectors you deal with: "You have a job to do. I have a job to do. Together we're going to put up a building that both you and I as professionals in the construction industry will be proud of." The more you think of building officials as implacable adversaries, the more likely they will become just that.

In a dispute with the building department, you have one big advantage. The inspector didn't make the rules and can't write the code to fit your situation. He can only enforce the code as it is written. *An inspector can require anything the code demands. But that's all!* He's on very shaky ground if he insists on something that isn't in the code book. That's why you need a copy of the code. If a dispute arises, have the inspector cite the specific section and words involved. Then read those words yourself in your copy of the code. If that code section doesn't support the inspector's position, you're going to win the point. The building department can require only what's in the book. Nothing more. Of course, inspectors make a living by knowing the code. They probably know it much better than you ever will. But they can be wrong! Don't be afraid to request reference to a specific code section, read that section, and form your own opinion of what is required. If the inspector is wrong and can't be persuaded to change his mind, there's a perfectly good appeal process available to every contractor. More on that later in this chapter.

Inspectors know that they can't enforce what the code doesn't require. But remember that highly experienced inspectors and plans examiners wrote the code. It gives inspectors room to maneuver and compromise where compromise may be in the best interest of everyone concerned. Every experienced contractor has heard an inspector say that the code *actually* requires this or that, "but it will be O.K. if you handle it this way."

That inspector is relaxing his interpretation of the code. But probably not out of generosity. He wants your cooperation on some other point that may not be covered so clearly by the exact letter of the code. Thus you're usually better off cooperating when an inspector complains about some minor point that is vague or omitted in the code. If you demand strict interpretation of code sections, your inspector may demand the same. And he can cite more sections that can be enforced strictly than you ever thought possible. The point is worth emphasizing: Cooperation is going to save you more money than confrontation.

Sometimes you're going to have a code issue so important that no easy alternative is possible. You have to take it up with the building department. Before going through the appeal procedure explained in this chapter, request a meeting with one of the senior inspectors or the "Building Official." Offer to meet early in the morning before the inspectors start their field work. Be sure both the inspector involved and his supervisor can be at this meeting. Prepare your case very carefully. Show that the code doesn't really require what you are being asked to do or point out an alternative that will save money and is just as good. Above all, demonstrate that you are a conscientious, professional, cooperative contractor interested in quality construction. Invite a compromise on the issue in dispute. More than likely you'll get one if any legitimate compromise is possible.

But don't expect any inspector to waive a clear code requirement just to save you money or trouble, especially if you're asking for special treatment other contractors don't receive. Code protection is too valuable to waive on a whim. If you've traveled in other countries where codes are non-existent or not enforced, you know how important building codes are. And be aware that cities and counties are liable for the mistakes their building departments make. Owners of defective buildings have recovered substantial sums from municipal governments that did not enforce the building code they adopted. Every building official knows the importance of the code he administers.

Purpose of the Code
Several points are worth mentioning before we begin careful examination of code sections. One of these is the purpose of the code. Section 102 makes it clear that health, safety and protecting property are the primary aims of the code:

The purpose of this code is to provide minimum standards to safeguard life or limb, health, property and public welfare by regulating and controlling the design, construction, quality of materials, use and occupancy, location and maintenance of all buildings and structures within this jurisdiction and certain equipment specifically regulated herein.

Notice the words "minimum standards" in the first sentence. You can build to higher standards. Nearly every building you put up will include far more than the code requires. But it also must include everything in the code.

That's an important point in Section 102 if you ever have to dispute some code interpretation. Argue that what you want to do protects health, safety and property as well or better than what the code requires.

Can I Use That Material?

The building code doesn't demand that you use only the methods and materials it lists. Section 105 states the following:

The provisions of this code are not intended to prevent the use of any material or method of construction not specifically prescribed by this code, provided any alternate has been approved and its use authorized by the building official.

"Building official" is the title of the senior man in the building department office. He may require proof that the method or material conforms to the intent of the code. If you're thinking about using a new method or material, something that hasn't had much use in your area, check with the building official beforehand.

For example, earth sheltered structures are being built in some areas. Many inspectors throw up their hands at inspecting earth sheltered buildings. Why? Because they're not adequately covered in the code. This is an area where you have to look at the intent of the code and not the literal meaning. Many inspectors don't have the experience or the time to make such evaluations.

Some less experienced inspectors may look at something, consult their code book, then look up wide-eyed and say: "I can't find it in the book, so you can't use that material or do it that way." Fortunately, that isn't what the code says. Section 105 allows use of *any* material or method that is approved by the building department in your community, even if it isn't approved in the code itself.

"That's fine," you say. "But how can I get approval for what I want to do?" Section 204 is titled "Board of Appeals." This section says that you have the right to appeal any inspector's decision.

In order to determine the suitability of alternate materials and methods of construction and to provide for reasonable interpretations of this code, there shall be and is hereby created a Board of Appeals consisting of members who are qualified by experience and training to pass upon matters pertaining to building

construction. The building official shall be an ex-officio member and shall act as secretary of the board. The Board of Appeals shall be appointed by the governing body and shall hold office at its pleasure. The board shall adopt reasonable rules and regulations for conducting its investigations and shall render all decisions and findings in writing to the building official with a duplicate copy to the appellant.
The key phrase here is that the board members "are qualified by experience and training." So even if the inspector lacks construction knowledge, the people you are appealing to will have it. Furthermore, if what you are trying to do with your material is controversial, the inspector may want you to take this route to get the opinions of other experts.

When is a Permit Needed?
Section 301 (a) tells you when you'll need a building permit:

It shall be unlawful for any person, firm or corporation to erect, construct, enlarge, alter, repair, move, improve, remove, convert, or demolish any building or structure . . . without first obtaining a separate permit.

That's pretty broad language. Almost any type of construction, no matter how minor, needs a building permit. Section 301 (b) exempts certain types of work. Most important in these exemptions are small out-buildings such as playhouses, small walls and fences and finish work like painting and paperhanging. Everything else needs a permit.

Figure 1-1 shows a typical building permit. Permit fees are set by the county or city. They're calculated to pay most of the costs of the building department. (That way, tax money doesn't support your building department.) Those who use the services pay for them. Figure 1-2 shows the permit fees recommended by the Uniform Building Code. This fee schedule was probably used when the code was adopted in your community. But check with your local department to be sure.

Demolition of Buildings
You must have a permit to remove or demolish a building. This usually involves a small fee which covers the cost of issuing the permit. A copy of every permit issued goes to the Tax Assessor. This lets him know you are about to make some changes which may change your tax status. Since you are paying taxes on all of the buildings and improvements on your property, removing one decreases your taxes.

BUILDING DEPARTMENT

CITY OF KENNEWICK, WASHINGTON

P. O. Box 6108
210 West 6th Avenue
Phone: (509) 586-4181, Ext. 23

1. Recorded Owner	2. Location of Property	3. Owners Address (If Different Than 2)

4. LEGAL DESCRIPTION

Lot	Block	Tract	Plat

5. Use Zone	6. Fire Zone	7. Occupancy

8. Required Inspections		9. Estimated Value
Foundations		

BUILDING PERMIT

11. Date Issued

12 Expiration Date

8681

13. TYPE OF PERMIT

Building	☐	Street	☐
Plumbing	☐	Street Cut	☐
Sidewalk	☐	Mechanical	☐

THIS PERMIT MUST BE POSTED IN PLAIN VIEW
FOR OBSERVATION FROM THE STREET.

Frame

Lath and Drywall

Plumbing

Mechanical

Street or Walk

Final

10. FEES —
Building

Plumbing

Street Walk

Mechanical

Plan Check

Total

14. CLASS OF WORK:		17. TYPE OF CONSTRUCTION		20. PLUMBING		
New ☐	Alteration ☐	Fire Resistive ☐		Bath Tubs ___	Grease Traps ___	
Addition ☐	Repair ☐	Semi-Fireproof ☐		Showers ___	Floor Drains ___	
Move ☐	Demolish ☐	Heavy Timber ☐		Lavatories ___	Urinals ___	
15. Building Size		Ordinary Masonry ☐		Kitchen Sinks ___	Drink Fountain ___	
		Frame ☐		Laundry Trays ___	Dental Lav. ___	
___ X ___		Unprotected Metal ☐		Auto Washer ___	Swim Pool ___	
16. Lot Size		18. Plans Submitted ☐		Water Closets ___	Miscellaneous ___	
		Plot Plan Submitted ☐		Water Heaters ___	Total Units ___	
___ X ___		Site Plan Approval ☐				

21. SET BACKS	Front	Rear	Left	Right	22. Height	23. No. Stories	24. No. Families

25. MECHANICAL	Heating	Air Conditioning	Miscellaneous

26. Description of Work

27. Bldg. Cont.	29. Street & Walk Cont.
28. Plbg. Cont.	30. Mechanical Cont.
31. Bldg. Cont. State License No.	If no number please explain on attached sheet.

32. Engineering Data		
Field Book No. ___	I certify no work will be done except as described above or on accompanying plans. All work will be performed in compliance with all codes and ordinances of the City of Kennewick, and as summarized on back of permit.	All work must be inspected prior to concealment.
Page No. ___		
Date		This department must have 24 hours notice for all inspections.
Sidewalk Constructed ☐	Applicant's Signature ___	
Power of Attorney ☐	Building Inspector ___	

Figure 1-1   Typical Building Permit

TABLE NO. 3-A—BUILDING PERMIT FEES

TOTAL VALUATION	FEE
$1.00 to $500.00	$10.00
$501.00 to $2,000.00	$10.00 for the first $500.00 plus $1.50 for each additional $100.00 or fraction thereof, to and including $2,000.00
$2,001.00 to $25,000.00	$32.50 for the first $2,000.00 plus $6.00 for each additional $1,000.00 or fraction thereof, to and including $25,000.00
$25,001.00 to $50,000.00	$170.50 for the first $25,000.00 plus $4.50 for each additional $1,000.00 or fraction thereof, to and including $50,000.00
$50,001.00 to $100,000.00	$283.00 for the first $50,000.00 plus $3.00 for each additional $1,000.00 or fraction thereof, to and including $100,000.00
$100,001.00 and up	$433.00 for the first $100,000.00 plus $2.50 for each additional $1,000.00 or fraction thereof

Other Inspections and Fees:

1. Inspections outside of normal business hours . . . . $15.00 per hour
   (minimum charge—two hours)

2. Reinspection fee assessed under provisions of
   Section 305 (g) . . . . $15.00 each

3. Inspections for which no fee is specifically
   indicated . . . . $15.00 per hour
   (minimum charge—one-half hour)

4. Additional plan review required by changes, additions
   or revisions to approved plans . . . . $15.00 per hour
   (minimum charge—one-half hour)

From the Uniform Building Code, ©1982, ICBO.

Figure 1-2   Building Permit Fees

Posting the Permit

Always post the building permit on the site. The law requires certain inspections which must be signed off by the inspector. This is your guarantee that he has been there and approved the job to that point. If your job does not pass the inspection, the inspector will leave a *Notice of Non-Compliance* or a *Correction Notice* explaining what you have to correct before you can proceed. (See Figure 1-3.)

Many people think that work inside of a building does not require a permit. If they're doing work exempted by the code, such as replacing kitchen cabinets, that assumption is correct. However, any remodeling or renovation other than the exempt items does require a permit.

CITY OF KENNEWICK
INSPECTION DEPARTMENT

CORRECTION NOTICE

IMPORTANT: Call for re-inspection when items are completed.
DO NOT cover until approved.

PROJECT ADDRESS   *4321 ANNY PLACE*

COMMENTS

① *FOOTING INSUFFICIENT DEPTH*
MUST DBE BELOW FROSTLINE

② *BACKFILL UNDER FOOTING*
NOT ADEQUATELY SETTLED

DO NOT REMOVE

FINAL INSPECTION REQUIRED ON ALL BUILDINGS BEFORE OCCUPANCY.

DATE *11-18-82* SIGNED _____
BUILDING INSPECTOR

Figure 1-3   Correction Notice. The name of these
will vary with different jurisdictions but the
message is the same -- "No more work until correction is made."

This brings up an unusual sidelight. During my travels around my city, going about my inspections, I would occasionally see construction rubble piled near a back door, in a driveway or under a carport. This almost always meant that work of some kind was going on inside the structure. If, after checking with the office, I found out there was no permit issued for work at that location, I would have a little talk with the occupant and remind him a permit was needed.

I tried not to be heavy-handed in my dealings with people and it usually paid off. Most people responded very well to this kind of treatment. However, never realizing that it was their pile of rubble that attracted me, many of them would ask, "Who finked on me?"

Right of Entry

Section 202 (c) gives the building official his authority to make any necessary inspections:

Whenever necessary to make an inspection to enforce any of the provisions of this code, or whenever the building official or his authorized representative has reasonable cause to believe that there exists in any building or upon any premises any condition or code violation which makes such building or premises unsafe, dangerous or hazardous, the building official or his authorized representative may enter such building or premises at all reasonable times to inspect the same or to perform any duty imposed upon the building official by this code, provided that if such building or premises be occupied, he shall first present proper credentials and request entry; and if such building or premises be unoccupied, he shall first make a reasonable effort to locate the owner or other persons having charge or control of the building or premises and request entry. If such entry is refused, the building official or his authorized representative shall have recourse to every remedy provided by law to secure entry.

This right of entry is seldom needed. And it isn't nearly as ferocious as it sounds. Most people are cooperative, and building inspectors use this right judiciously.

Required Inspections

A permit always requires some sort of inspection. The inspection depends on the scope of the job. It varies from a simple drive-by to see if the obvious has been completed, as in the case of a re-roof, to twelve or sixteen highly technical inspections. For most residential and small commercial work, there are five required inspections, set forth in Section 305 (e).

1. Foundation inspection: This is made after the trenches have been excavated, the forms erected, and all the materials for the foundation delivered. Concrete supplied from a central mixing plant (commonly called "transit mixed") doesn't have to be on the site during inspection.

2. Concrete slab or under-floor inspection: This is made after all in-slab or under-floor building service equipment, conduit, piping accessories and their ancillary equipment items are in place, but before any concrete is poured or floor sheathing installed, including the subfloor.

3. Frame inspection: This is made after the roof, all framing, fire blocking and bracing are in place; after all pipes, chimneys and vents are complete; and after the rough electrical, plumbing and heating wires, pipes and ducts are approved.

4. Lath and/or gypsum board inspection: This is made after all lathing and gypsum board, interior and exterior, is in place, but before any plastering is applied or before gypsum board joints and fasteners are taped and finished.

5. Final inspection. This is made after finish grading, when the building has been completed and is ready for occupancy.

If an inspection shows that the project is not acceptable, a correction notice is issued and another inspection scheduled before the project can continue. Such a re-inspection may require an additional fee. Some projects, such as large shopping malls and multi-story buildings, often require a full-time inspector on the job. This inspector's salary is paid by the owner either directly or through his contractor. In most jurisdictions new construction requires a *Certificate of Occupancy* when complete.

The Inspector Doesn't Like The Way You Did It
Occasionally, an inspector finds a job that could be done better using a different method. He may offer advice, and probably will. But his advice isn't binding unless it's supported by either the Uniform Building Code or a local ordinance. He can stop the job for safety reasons, but he must have the code to back him up. If something isn't in the code, he can't enforce it. You have the right to ask him to show you the relevant section of the code. Then you still have the right to appeal his decision.

Figure 1-4 The inspector can seldom rule on *craftsmanship*. This chimney, a prefabricated metal chimney is installed legally, the furring is installed legally, but . . .

Building inspectors are often pretty good craftsmen themselves. It may be to your advantage to heed their advice. But an inspector isn't really inspecting the craftsmanship of your building unless it's set forth in his adopted ordinance. Craftsmanship is a judgment decision, and who says either of you has the final word in judging? However, if the craftsmanship weakens the structure or makes it unsafe, the inspector will probably consider it. But he must be prepared to back up his words.

I've often used a little charm to get shoddy work improved. I once visited a house where the trim around a split entry stairway had been butted in square, without mitering. I mentioned this to the contractor and he jumped on me about exceeding my authority. "Besides," he added, "who will ever know?"

"Everyone will," I assured him, "because I'm the biggest tattle-tale in town and I can hardly wait to tell everyone you do this type of work."

When I returned later, all the corners had been neatly mitered.

His Nibs will see you now.

2

How Do I Get a Permit?

If you are simply replacing worn-out shingles, getting a permit should only involve going down to the building department and paying for one. However, if you are doing a bigger job, like constructing a new residence or a small commercial building, there's a lot more involved.

Are Plans Needed?

The first thing you need is a complete set of plans and specifications for your project. Whether or not these have to be drawn by an architect or engineer varies with jurisdictions. U.B.C. Section 302(b) states the following:

Plans, engineering calculations, diagrams and other data shall be submitted in one or more sets with each application for a permit. The building official may require plans, computations and specifications to be prepared and designed by an architect or engineer licensed by the state to practice as such.

The code allows several exemptions. These vary from jurisdiction to jurisdiction. Find out what the requirements are in your area. The code isn't clear on the subject, but most inspectors use a variation of the following rule of thumb: Get plans for all new construction; on remodel work the scope of the project will determine the need for plans. Small or minor work may only require simple sketches.

If the code required submission of plans for all permits, even the construction of fences and private garages would require expensive architectural drawings.

Many inspectors request plans for remodel work. Usually this is to check that the applicant has adequately researched the job. He should know that by ripping out a certain partition, he isn't removing a vital bearing wall. Believe me, it happens. Check with your inspector to find out when plans are needed for remodel work.

But what about new construction? To get a permit for new construction you'll need three items:

1. Plans
2. Specifications
3. Engineering data and notes to back up items shown on the plans or the accompanying specifications

Plans or Specifications—Which is First?

Plans are a graphic representation, or working drawings, to show what is being built and how. *Specifications* detail information not given on the plans. Your plans might show an exterior door as a 3'0" x 6'8" opening. The specifications would describe it as *solid core, exterior grade, two-light, left-hand swing.* There is only room for so much detail on the drawings; the rest of the information is in the specifications. Sometimes the specifications, or specs, are listed on one sheet of the plans. Or they may be contained in a book of a hundred pages or more.

There's been much litigation on the importance of plans over specifications, or vice versa. For us, the plans and specs, as a whole, are sufficient. Whether or not specific items appear in all working drawings is of little concern, so long as they do appear someplace and do not contradict other portions. No fragment of the plans or specs takes precedence over other fragments. The document must be considered as a whole.

The plans, often referred to as *blueprints* or *prints,* must contain the following information:

1. Plot plan
2. Foundation plan

3. Floor plan
4. Roof plan
5. Elevations
6. Sections, details, etc.

Plans are usually divided into the following areas:

1. Architectural
2. Structural
3. Electrical
4. Plumbing
5. Mechanical (includes refrigeration, heating and ventilation, etc.)

Those are the divisions you'll find on large, complex drawings. For smaller projects, such as most homes, the structural, electrical and mechanical features may be included in the architectural drawings.

Most of the information on the plans is clear and easily understood. One item however, needs clarification. That's the plot plan. It is very critical, particularly for those living in urban areas.

The Plot Plan

The plot plan is usually regulated by the zoning ordinance, which is separate from the building code. Always study the ordinance before you begin any project. Are you allowed to build a duplex dwelling unit on your lot? What are the building set-backs from the property lines? How much of the lot area can be covered with buildings? Are there any height restrictions? These are just a few of the questions you should be asking yourself. They are among the issues the inspector will consider.

Many people, even contractors, have little knowledge of zoning ordinances. Often they'll try to get a permit for something the zoning ordinance doesn't allow. If they've owned the property for a while they should be aware of the zoning and any recent changes.

On the other hand, if they've recently purchased the property, they may be unaware of all the details of the zoning ordinance.

Zoning Laws

Most building departments enforce zoning laws. Zoning is what they consider first when approached for a permit. In general, the zoning ordinance divides the community into four areas:

1. *Residential*   — Where we live.
2. *Commercial* — Where commerce is conducted.

3. *Industrial* — Where goods are produced.
4. *Agricultural* — Where food is produced.

Usually there are several variations in each category. This is where a working knowledge of the zoning ordinance is very helpful. *Don't rely on visual consideration to determine the zone.* Just because there's a commercial building next door doesn't guarantee that your client can put one on his lot. The zone line might run right down the property line. If your client wants to put up a commercial building he may have to reclassify his lot.

You can usually build "up" but you can't build "down." *Residential* is the highest use and *agricultural* is the lowest. You could, therefore, in most cases, build a residence in a *commercial* zone but you couldn't build a commercial building in a *residential* zone.

This rule also applies to variations within the zones. If, for example, there are three variations in a *residential* zone—R-1 for single family residences, R-2 for duplex residences, and R-3 for multi-family residences—a single-family residence could usually be built in an R-2 or R-3 zone. An apartment house, however, could not be built in an R-1 or R-2 zone.

The building inspector or the planning department in the jurisdiction where you intend to build can tell you what is allowed at any particular site. Although zoning can be changed, it is time consuming.

What the Inspector Looks At
Near the front of the U.B.C. is a simple outline inspectors often use for plan checking. This is reproduced in Figure 2-1. We'll be considering each of these points in the next few chapters. The first, however, is discussed below.

Types of Occupancy
Occupancy refers to the use or type of activity to which a proposed building will be put. *Occupant Load* refers to the number of people who will be occupying the space. The difference in these terms is slight but very important.

There are seven main categories or "groups" of occupancy. These are shown in U.B.C. Table No. 5-A (Figure 2-2). Several categories are broken down into sub-categories. Generally, occupancies are arranged by the degree of hazard in a building. The main thing to remember is that all buildings are classified.

EFFECTIVE USE OF THE UNIFORM
BUILDING CODE

The following procedure may be helpful in using the Uniform Building Code:

1. Classify the building:

   A. **OCCUPANCY GROUP:** Determine the occupancy group which the use of the building most nearly resembles. See the '01 sections of Chapters 6 through 12. See Section 503 for buildings with mixed occupancies.

   B. **TYPE OF CONSTRUCTION:** Determine the type of construction of the building by the building materials used and the fire resistance of the parts of the building. See Chapters 17 through 22.

   C. **LOCATION ON PROPERTY:** Determine the location of the building on the site and clearances to property lines and other buildings from the plot plan. See Table No. 5-A and '03 sections of Chapters 18 through 22 for exterior wall and wall opening requirements based on proximity to property lines. See Section 504 for buildings located on the same site.

   D. **FLOOR AREA:** Compute the floor area of the building. See Table No. 5-C for basic allowable floor area based on occupancy group and type of construction. See Section 506 for allowable increases based on location on property and installation of an approved automatic fire-sprinkler system. See Section 505 (b) for allowable floor area of multistory buildings.

   E. **HEIGHT AND NUMBER OF STORIES:** Compute the height of the building, Section 409, from grade, Section 408, and for the number of stories, Section 420. See Table No. 5-D for the allowable height and number of stories based on occupancy group and type of construction. See Section 507 for allowable story increase based on the installation of an approved automatic fire-sprinkler system.

   F. **OCCUPANT LOAD:** Compute the occupant load of the building. See Section 3302 (a) and Table No. 33-A.

2. Verify compliance of the building with detailed occupancy requirements. See Chapters 6 through 12.

3. Verify compliance of the building with detailed type of construction requirements. See Chapters 17 through 22.

4. Verify compliance of the building with exit requirements. See Chapter 33.

5. Verify compliance of the building with detailed code regulations. See Chapters 29 through 43, Chapters 47 through 54, and Appendix.

6. Verify compliance of building with engineering regulations and requirements for materials of construction. See Chapters 23 through 29.

From the Uniform Building Code, ©1982, ICBO.

Figure 2-1   Outline for Simplified Plan Checking

TABLE NO. 5-A—WALL AND OPENING PROTECTION OF OCCUPANCIES BASED ON LOCATION ON PROPERTY

TYPES II ONE-HOUR, II-N AND V CONSTRUCTION: For exterior wall and opening protection of Types II One-hour, II-N and V buildings, see table below. Exceptions to limitation for Types II One-hour, II-N and Type V construction, as provided in Sections 709, 1903 and 2203 apply. For Types I, II-F.R., III and IV construction, see Sections 1803, 1903, 2003 and 2103.

GROUP	DESCRIPTION OF OCCUPANCY	FIRE RESISTANCE OF EXTERIOR WALLS	OPENINGS IN EXTERIOR WALLS
A See also Section 602	1—Any assembly building with a stage and an occupant load of 1000 or more in the building	Not applicable (See Sections 602 and 603)	
	2—Any building or portion of a building having an assembly room with an occupant load of less than 1000 and a stage 2.1—Any building or portion of a building having an assembly room with an occupant load of 300 or more without a stage, including such buildings used for educational purposes and not classed as a Group E or Group B, Division 2 Occupancy	2 hours less than 10 feet, 1 hour elsewhere	Not permitted less than 5 feet Protected less than 10 feet
	3—Any building or portion of a building having an assembly room with an occupant load of less than 300 without a stage, including such buildings used for educational purposes and not classed as a Group E or Group B, Division 2 Occupancy	2 hours less than 5 feet, 1 hour less than 40 feet	Not permitted less than 5 feet Protected less than 10 feet
	4—Stadiums, reviewing stands and amusement park structures not included within other Group A Occupancies	1 hour less than 10 feet	Protected less than 10 feet
B See also Section 702	1—Gasoline service stations, garages where no repair work is done except exchange of parts and maintenance requiring no open flame, welding, or use of flammable liquids		
	2—Drinking and dining establishments having an occupant load of less than 50, wholesale and retail stores, office buildings, printing plants, municipal police and fire stations, factories and workshops using material not highly flammable or combustible, storage and sales rooms for combustible goods, paint stores without bulk handling Buildings or portions of buildings having rooms used for educational purposes, beyond the 12th grade, with less than 50 occupants in any room	1 hour less than 20 feet	Not permitted less than 5 feet Protected less than 10 feet

(Continued on next page)

Figure 2-2 Categories of Occupancy

TABLE NO. 5-A—Continued
TYPES II ONE-HOUR, II-N AND V ONLY

GROUP	DESCRIPTION OF OCCUPANCY	FIRE RESISTANCE OF EXTERIOR WALLS	OPENINGS IN EXTERIOR WALLS
B (Cont.)	3—Aircraft hangars where no repair work is done except exchange of parts and maintenance requiring no open flame, welding, or the use of highly flammable liquids Open parking garages (For requirements, See Section 709.) Heliports	1 hour less than 20 feet	Not permitted less than 5 feet Protected less than 20 feet
	4—Ice plants, power plants, pumping plants, cold storage and creameries Factories and workshops using noncombustible and nonexplosive materials Storage and sales rooms of noncombustible and nonexplosive materials	1 hour less than 5 feet	Not permitted less than 5 feet
E See also Section 802	1—Any building used for educational purposes through the 12th grade by 50 or more persons for more than 12 hours per week or four hours in any one day 2—Any building used for educational purposes through the 12th grade by less than 50 persons for more than 12 hours per week or four hours in any one day 3—Any building used for day-care purposes for more than six children	2 hours less than 5 feet, 1 hour less than 10 feet[1]	Not permitted less than 5 feet Protected less than 10 feet[1]
H See also Sections 902 and 903	1—Storage, handling, use or sale of hazardous and highly flammable or explosive materials other than flammable liquids [See also Section 901 (a), Division 1.]	See Chapter 9 and the Fire Code	
	2—Storage, handling, use or sale of Classes I, II and III-A liquids; dry cleaning plants using Class I, II or III-A liquids; paint stores with bulk handling; paint shops and spray-painting rooms and shops [See also Section 901 (a), Division 2.]	4 hours less than 5 feet, 2 hours less than 10 feet, 1 hour less than 20 feet	Not permitted less than 5 feet Protected less than 20 feet
	3—Woodworking establishments, planing mills, box factories, buffing rooms for tire-rebuilding plants and picking rooms; shops, factories or warehouses where loose combustible fibers or dust are manufactured, processed, generated or stored; and pin-refinishing rooms		
	4—Repair garages not classified as a Group B, Division 1 Occupancy		

[1]Group E, Divisions 2 and 3 Occupancies having an occupant load of not more than 20 may have exterior wall and opening protection as required for Group R, Division 3 Occupancies.

(Continued on next page)

Figure 2-2 (continued)   Categories of Occupancy

		1 hour less than 60 feet	Protected less than 60 feet
H (Cont.)	5—Aircraft repair hangars		
I See also Section 1002	1—Nurseries for the full-time care of children under the age of six (each accommodating more than five persons) Hospitals, sanitariums, nursing homes with nonambulatory patients and similar buildings (each accommodating more than five persons)	2 hours less than 5 feet, 1 hour elsewhere	Not permitted less than 5 feet Protected less than 10 feet
	2—Nursing homes for ambulatory patients, homes for children six years of age or over (each accommodating more than five persons)	1 hour	
	3—Mental hospitals, mental sanitariums, jails, prisons, reformatories and buildings where personal liberties of inmates are similarly restrained	2 hours less than 5 feet, 1 hour elsewhere	Not permitted less than 5 feet, protected less than 10 feet
M[2]	1—Private garages, carports, sheds and agricultural buildings (See also Section 1101, Division 1.)	1 hour less than 3 feet (or may be protected on the exterior with materials approved for 1-hour fire-resistive construction)	Not permitted less than 3 feet
	2—Fences over 6 feet high, tanks and towers	Not regulated for fire resistance	
R See also Section 1202	1—Hotels and apartment houses Convents and monasteries (each accommodating more than 10 persons)	1 hour less than 5 feet	Not permitted less than 5 feet
	3—Dwellings and lodging houses	1 hour less than 3 feet	Not permitted less than 3 feet

[2]For agricultural buildings, see Appendix Chapter 11.

NOTES: (1) See Section 504 for types of walls affected and requirements covering percentage of openings permitted in exterior walls.

(2) For additional restrictions, see chapters under Occupancy and Types of Construction.

(3) For walls facing streets, yards and public ways, see Part IV.

(4) Openings shall be protected by a fire assembly having a three-fourths-hour fire-protection rating.

Figure 2-2 (continued)   Categories of Occupancy

From the Uniform Building Code, ©1982, ICBO.

The term *occupancy,* as used in building codes, refers to the way in which buildings are used. It also refers to how the safety of persons and property is affected by the hazards resulting from such uses. This term is further broken down into *normal* and *abnormal* uses or occupancies, though not necessarily for permit purposes.

Normal occupancy deals with the number and distribution of people and their practices within buildings. It also refers to the kind, amount and arrangement of materials, goods or merchandise commonly used or stored in buildings, and with ordinary industrial processes.

Abnormal occupancy covers special uses which create extraordinary hazards.

Occupancy is Based On Degree of Hazard

Most local building codes regulate occupancies. However, it would be difficult to write a description of each building or building use in a town. Therefore, many codes generalize, combining the different occupancies into similar groups having similar characteristics insofar as such characteristics relate to possible life or property hazards.

Hazards must be considered in determining occupancy. Top priority always goes to occupant safety. In large groups of people there is greater danger of catastrophe than in small groups. In an emergency everyone wants out at the same time and will rush to the same exit and fight and climb over each other to escape while a second exit is largely ignored. A large, disorganized group takes longer to evacuate than a smaller one. Therefore, in addition to more exits, the building must be able to resist structural failure for a longer period of time. Fire resistance requirements are geared for saving lives rather than property.

The fundamental considerations in setting up occupancy group ratings are life hazards first and then property hazards. Let us first examine the following life hazards.

Common hazards: People are the greatest common hazard. Man is his own worst enemy. He smokes, works, gathers in groups, makes things, uses flammable liquids, and fills rooms with highly combustible materials. In short, man creates most of his own hazards. And, when the fat hits the fire, he panics and creates additional hazards.

Day and night occupancies: These are broken down into two categories—where man works and where man sleeps. The work environment can be very hazardous depending on the type of work involved, the size of the work groups, and the materials used and produced.

Night occupancy can be equally serious. A fire can frequently make great headway before it is discovered.

Night occupancies pertain to resting or sleeping. They include hotels, dormitories and apartment houses.

Dwelling occupancies: Unlike night occupancies, dwelling occupancies refers to one- and two-family residences. More deaths occur each year in one- and two-family dwellings than in any other type of occupancy. But since these deaths are usually the result of many fires involving one or two casualties, the hazards involved in a dwelling occupancy are considered much less than those in an occupancy where a large number of people are gathered.

Commercial and industrial hazards: In considering commercial and industrial occupancies, the uses vary considerably. Generally, they're determined by actual or potential hazardous conditions. Particularly important is the storage of combustible substances or the presence of especially hazardous materials or production processes.

Where the number of people per unit of floor area is relatively small and those present are familiar with potential hazards and the means of exit in an emergency, personal hazards are reduced. In other words, where you have a group familiar with their surroundings such as in an industrial occupancy, for example, the hazards would be less than for strangers in a commercial occupancy.

The type of construction is greatly influenced by the degree of hazard. The classification or grouping of occupancies together with the minimum fire and safety precautions and protective facilities for a building or a particular type of construction, helps determine the placement, maximum size, and height above grade of usable rooms or spaces. Relating the type of construction of a building to the occupancy or use correlates safety and economy.

Height and Area Hazards

How do height and area pose hazards? Hazards to life increase as building height increases, especially when the height is above that at which fire department personnel and equipment can readily operate. On the other end of the scale, basement fires present additional problems. Most basements are difficult to get into and even more difficult to escape. Fire fighters approach basement fires with extra caution.

Area means a space at one-story level which is entirely segregated and enclosed by adequate fire-resistive barriers. If there are no separating barriers, the area would be the entire floor space of the structure at a certain floor level.

The greater the area, the greater the risk of material and human loss, and the greater the difficulty of reaching the center of the fire.

Hazards in General

Let's review the different types of hazards found in most occupancies.

- Normal and abnormal hazards based on the nature of the occupancy.
- Height and area hazards.
- Spread of fire due to air currents, dirt and lint, combustible decorations and draperies, combustible finishes, trim and the structure itself.
- Fire-resistive qualities of material.
- Toxic and heated gases.
- Unprotected openings.
- Lack of adequate separation between areas.
- Exposure, or lack of separation between buildings.

These are the hazards you'll run into most often. But there's one other very vital hazard. It's one that we've talked about, and when mixed with any one of the eight above, it can really be volatile. This hazard is *Man*. In any decision on hazards, the inspector will consider the number of people a building normally houses.

Occupancy Groups

In the 1982 Edition of the Uniform Building Code, the traditional seven groups were spread out to comprise 24 sub-groups. Let's go through the list briefly to see how the major groupings are made. Remember, the first place always goes to the highest hazard.

A — Assembly
B — Business, including offices, factories, mercantile and storage.
E — Educational
H — Hazardous
I — Institutional
M — Miscellaneous Structures
R — Residential

You'll have to squeeze every building in town into one of these seven groupings. However, the U.B.C. has provided sub-groups to help you break down the list. Let's take each group by itself, add the sub-groups, and set-up the general requirements for each. U.B.C. Table No. 5-A (Figure 2-2) describes each type of occupancy.

Group A Occupancies
Where people assemble in large numbers for entertainment, deliberation, worship, to await transportation or for dining, the hazards are considered to be the greatest. Therefore, they constitute the first category. Group A is further broken down into five sub-groups, determined first by the occupant load and second by the activity.

The first sub-group is the most hazardous occupancy; the last sub-group is the least hazardous. This means hazard to human life. Remember, the higher the human load, the higher the hazard.

Why were *educational* and *office* buildings excluded? Familiarity with surroundings reduces occupancy hazard. Usually, *Group A,* will be occupied by people who are not completely familiar with the building they occupy.

Note in U.B.C. Table No. 5-A that buildings with stages have the highest hazards. This is due to the generally high occupancy on the stage and in the fly gallery. Theaters have changed considerably during the last few decades. You won't find fly galleries in drive-in theaters or most new motion picture theaters, nor will you find a proscenium wall.

A *fly gallery* is a narrow raised platform at the side of the theater stage from which the flying scenery lines are operated. A *proscenium wall* is the wall that separates the stage from the auditorium and provides the arch that frames it.

Group A-4 covers stadiums, reviewing stands, and amusement park structures not included with other Group A occupancies. These are not included under Group M (Miscellaneous Structures) because Group M is only for buildings of low human occupancy.

Group B Occupancy

Group B is referred to as the "Mercantile Group" because it covers most commercial stores and small factories. It makes up the core of most small cities and many of the larger ones.

This grouping of four sub-groups has several surprises. Again, look at U.B.C. Table No. 5-A (Figure 2-2).

The first surprise comes under the B-2 sub-group. The last sentence is the kicker:

Buildings or portions of buildings having rooms used for educational purposes, beyond the 12th grade, with less than 50 occupants in any room.

Why is this provision located here when the other educational buildings come under a more restrictive section? The answer is that there are fewer than fifty people in a room and they are beyond the 12th grade. The group is smaller and old enough to react rationally in an emergency.

These establishments include the small business college and the beauty college. There is a fine line between commercialism and education. For instance, what about the beauty colleges that use their commercial outlet for training of beauticians?

The code can't cover all eventualities nor all the uses. Therefore, these groupings are designed to cover the more common ones.

The second surprise in this group is the B-4 section. In the old code this was a separate use and was the area where the hard-to-define items were placed. Ice plants, cold storage, power and pumping stations and any other facilities not using combustible or flammable materials are in this group. These uses usually have an extremely low occupant load and a very low hazard operation.

Group E Occupancies

Group E occupancies are commonly referred to as eight-to-five educational buildings. As indicated in Group E-3, they can be for day-care uses also. Here, the three sub-groups are concerned more with type of occupants.

Group E-3, of course, is for day-care centers. Notice that it is based on a scale of six children to one adult. The idea is that one baby sitter should be able to control six children to the extent that fire safety is not such a big risk. Also, it allows a babysitter to care for fewer than six children in an average residence with little other supervision.

This doesn't mean a capable person couldn't take care of seven or eight children. It just means that a standard was needed, and having no technical basis for one, an arbitrary figure was used. This occurs frequently in the building code and is one of the reasons for the appeal process. Unless there is a technical or scientific reason for a particular figure, an arbitrary one will be used.

Group H Occupancy

"H" stands for Hazardous. Why isn't it closer to the top of the list? Occupancies are based on risk to humans and on human loads. Most of the sub-groups in Group H have a relatively low human load.

H-4 is for repair garages and H-5 is for aircraft repair hangars. Why should aircraft repair have a lesser rating than automotive repair? Repair garages are relatively smaller, with more flammable or combustible material stored closer together. Hangars are larger, with fewer people and better opportunity for fire control.

Group I Occupancies

Group I concerns persons under close supervision or restraint due to discipline, health or age. The three sub-groups generally indicate the degree of supervision.

The big items here are the first two. I-1 covers children under the age of six and non-ambulatory patients in hospitals or nursing homes. These are contrasted with ambulatory patients and children over the age of six. It makes sense that the lesser restriction should cover those better able to respond and follow directions in an emergency.

Technically, either of these groups can come and go somewhat at will. Then why aren't the prisoners or other restrained persons at the top of the list? They couldn't, we presume, get out if they wanted to. Look at the right hand column of Group I, U.B.C. Table No. 5-A, *Permitted in Types I and II-FR only*. Due to the nature of their restraint, prisoners are required to be housed in the most fire resistive construction the code covers. Those types of construction will be detailed in Chapter Four.

Group M Occupancies

This is probably the least regulated occupancy group. There are only two sub-groups, Group M-1 for private garages, carports, sheds, and agricultural buildings; and Group M-2 for fences over six feet high, tanks, and towers.

Group R Occupancies

This is where we live. Group R takes care of hotels, motels, apartments, condominiums and private residences. There are only two sub-groups here, generally, multi-family and single-family structures.

R-2 is one of those open-ended zoning categories. We've listed the two common groups of residential structures. Although the two groups seem quite closely related, they are still miles apart. That way, if the code people decide there should be an intermediate group due to possible combinations of risks not currently known, there would be a place for it.

Remember the so-called *night* and *dwelling* occupancies? The typical night occupancy referred to hotels, dormitories and large multiple dwellings. Single-family residences are under Group R-3, along with lodging houses.

Then why are lodging houses listed under residences and not under hotels?

Turn to the definition section in Chapter Four of the U.B.C. Here we find that a hotel is any building containing six or more guest rooms while a lodging house is any building containing not more than five guest rooms. Again we can see that the degree of hazard is determined by the number of occupants.

Summary

While those are the general classifications of occupancy, some areas seem to overlap while other areas don't appear to be covered adequately. If you're getting ready to put up a building, find out what it will be used for. Meeting the occupancy requirements can have a great effect on the cost of the proposed structure.

A few paragraphs back we examined the difference between the hotel and the lodging house. On the surface they appear to be similar, but the difference for code purposes lies in the definitions which are based on the number of lodgers. Very often in the administration of the building code, as in any law, a fine point may be based strictly on a definition. Hotels and motels are a good example. In the eyes of the building code there is no difference between them, but most planners and zoning officials insist that motels must have room access directly to the outside while hotels do not have to meet such a requirement.

Now that we have determined the occupancy group for your building, the next step is to pursue the concept of density and how it is determined.

3
Determining Occupancy Loads and Other Related Problems

We've mentioned how hazard determines occupancy. But we've only touched the surface of this vital subject. *Hazard* is going to follow us all through the book. The building codes revolve around hazard. Without hazard there would be little need for building codes. If you read up on the history of the building codes, you'll see that the original codes, dating back to Babylonian times, were based on hazard.

Yet, in spite of its importance, hazard is only one aspect of occupancy determination. You will remember that in many occupancy restrictions we kept running into *occupancy load*. How is occupancy load determined for any given area?

Computing Occupancy Loads

Determining occupancy load involves more than just figuring out how many people can squeeze into a given area. The primary consideration is the number of people who can normally be expected to use the space safely for its designed purpose.

There are two people who should be especially interested in this. First, of course, is the owner. He's the one who will be using the property. He has to know how many people can use his restaurant, factory, or shop.

The other interested party is the building inspector. He must know how many people will occupy a site and what their normal activity will be. Then he can determine the type of occupancy and, in many cases, the type of construction needed for the facility.

An important reference is U.B.C. Table No. 33-A, *Minimum Egress and Access Requirements,* reproduced in Figure 3-1. Mark the spot well. Of all the charts and tables in the U.B.C., this will be the most useful. It's the table the inspector normally uses to determine the average occupancy of any given area. Column 1 describes the use, Column 2 describes the number of occupants for which two or more exits are required, and Column 3, the one we'll probably use most, lists the number of square feet normally allotted to one person in any particular usage. In this chapter we'll be dealing mainly with Columns 1 and 3.

The 1982 Edition has retitled Column 3. Instead of listing it as the "Square feet per occupant" it now lists it as the "Occupant Load Factor." The effect is the same and for this book we'll still continue thinking of it as square footage because that is what it still means.

Footage Often Indicates Activity
The square footage allowed per occupant in Column 3 varies from a minimum of seven square feet to a maximum of 500 square feet. Generally, the square footage allowed indicates the type of activity in an area. For example, the first item on the list is *Aircraft Hangars (No Repair).* Normally, hangars are large and spacious (square feet per occupant is 500). On the other hand, in *Auction Rooms,* the second item, people usually stand shoulder to shoulder. Here, the minimum amount of space is seven square feet per occupant.

How did we arrive at such an odd figure as *seven square feet* per occupant? Seven square feet is assumed to be the normal amount of space a standing person needs to move and act normally. For example, if you were to stand in a closet two and one-half feet wide by three feet long, you probably wouldn't be too uncomfortable. You might not like the darkness or the lack of fresh air, but otherwise you could tolerate it pretty well.

TABLE NO. 33-A—MINIMUM EGRESS AND ACCESS REQUIREMENTS

USE[1]	MINIMUM OF TWO EXITS OTHER THAN ELEVATORS ARE REQUIRED WHERE NUMBER OF OCCUPANTS IS AT LEAST	OCCU-PANT LOAD FACTOR[9]	ACCESS BY MEANS OF A RAMP OR AN ELEVATOR MUST BE PROVIDED FOR THE PHYSICALLY HANDICAPPED AS INDICATED[3]
1. Aircraft Hangars (no repair)	10	500	Yes
2. Auction Rooms	30	7	Yes
3. Assembly Areas, Concentrated Use (without fixed seats) Auditoriums Bowling Alleys (Assembly areas) Churches and Chapels Dance Floors Lodge Rooms Reviewing Stands Stadiums	50	7	Yes[3] [4]
4. Assembly Areas, Less-concentrated Use Conference Rooms Dining Rooms Drinking Establishments Exhibit Rooms Gymnasiums Lounges Stages	50	15	Yes[3] [10]
5. Children's Homes and Homes for the Aged	6	80	Yes[5]
6. Classrooms	50	20	Yes[11]
7. Dormitories	10	50	Yes[5]
8. Dwellings	10	300	No
9. Garage, Parking	30	200	Yes[6]
10. Hospitals and Sanitariums— Nursing Homes	6	80	Yes
11. Hotels and Apartments	10	200	Yes[8]
12. Kitchen—Commercial	30	200	No
13. Library Reading Room	50	50	Yes[3]
14. Locker Rooms	30	50	Yes
15. Mechanical Equipment Room	30	300	No
16. Nurseries for Children (Day-care)	7	35	Yes

[1]Refer to Sections 3320 and 3321 for other specific requirements.
[2]Elevators shall not be construed as providing a required exit.
[3]Access to secondary areas on balconies or mezzanines may be by stairs only, except when such secondary areas contain the only available toilet facilities.
[4]Reviewing stands, grandstands and bleachers need not comply.

Figure 3-1 Minimum Egress and Access Requirements

USE[1]	MINIMUM OF TWO EXITS OTHER THAN ELEVATORS ARE REQUIRED WHERE NUMBER OF OCCUPANTS IS AT LEAST	OCCU-PANT LOAD FACTOR[9]	ACCESS BY MEANS OF A RAMP OR AN ELEVATOR MUST BE PROVIDED FOR THE PHYSICALLY HANDICAPPED AS INDICATED[3]
17. Offices	30	100	Yes[5]
18. School Shops and Vocational Rooms	50	50	Yes
19. Skating Rinks	50	50 on the skating area; 15 on the deck	Yes[3]
20. Stores—Retails Sales Rooms			
Basement	7	20	Yes
Ground Floor	50	30	Yes
Upper Floors	10	50	Yes
21. Swimming Pools	50	50 for the pool area; 15 on the deck	Yes[3]
22. Warehouses	30	300	No
23. Lobby Accessory to Assembly Occupancy	50	7	Yes
24. Malls (see Appendix Chapter 7)			
25. All others	50	100	

[5]Access to floors other than that closest to grade may be by stairs only, except when the only available toilet facilities are on other levels.

[6]Access to floors other than that closest to grade and to garages used in connection with apartment houses may be by stairs only.

[7]See Section 3303 for basement exit requirements.

[8]See Section 1213 for access to buildings and facilities in hotels and apartments.

[9]This table shall not be used to determine working space requirements per person.

[10]Access requirements for conference rooms, dining rooms, lounges and exhibit rooms that are part of an office use shall be the same as required for the office use.

[11]When the floor closest to the grade offers the same programs and activities available on other floors, access to the other floors may be by stairs only, except when the only available toilet facilities are on other levels.

From the Uniform Building Code, ©1982, ICBO.

Figure 3-1 (continued) Minimum Egress and Access Requirements

There's more to it than that, however. I mentioned that the seven-foot area would be a space two and one-half feet by three feet. But in practice, this space also includes sufficient area for aisles, hallways, furniture and machines.

You'll note as you look down the list in U.B.C. Table No. 33-A that there are two types of assembly areas. One is for *concentrated use* and the other is for *less concentrated use*. The major difference is that the former refers to occupancies without fixed seats, while the latter pertains to those with seating. A seated person must have at least 15 square feet of space.

Computing the Size of Your Building

Once you know how many people will be using the building, multiply that number by the square footage allowed for each person as given in U.B.C. Table No. 33-A. This will give you the total number of square feet required.

The figure in the book is the *minimum size* for that occupancy. You may build larger than the minimum—as large as the owner's wallet will allow—but you may not build smaller.

You should become familiar with these figures. The building inspector is going to use them in computing the capacity of the building. The fire marshal is going to use them when he puts up his capacity signs. It's also important to understand *use.* You may think that you're erecting a *Stadium*, which requires seven square feet of space per occupant. But if the inspector says you have a *Gymnasium,* you'll have to provide twice as much space.

Computing Building Size for Mixed Occupancies

Many buildings house different occupancy groups. If you are building, designing, or merely thinking about building such a structure, you must go through the same steps required for a single occupancy building—only they must be repeated several more times. Schools are a good example, having auditoriums, gymnasiums, vocational shops, classrooms, libraries and administrative offices. Each has its own footage requirements, as shown in U.B.C. Table No. 33-A.

Let's say that our building will house a lodge with a membership of 250 people. On dance night there may be as many as 400 people in the building. They want a dining room to accommodate 150 persons at a time and a bar that will hold another 100. There will be a kitchen staff of four. The library, or reading room, will be open to the members and normally will serve about ten people at a time.

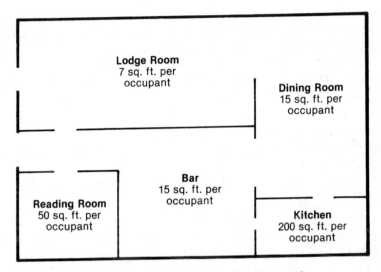

Figure 3-2   Sketch of Lodge Example

How much room should you provide? For the moment, let's assume that other features such as fire resistance and type of construction have been taken care of. What we're after now is the amount of space the building will require.

Find *Lodge Rooms* in U.B.C. Table No. 33-A (Figure 3-1). The table tells us that lodge rooms require seven square feet per occupant. With a membership of 250 multiplied by 7, we find that the main lodge room must be 1750 square feet, approximately 35 feet wide by 50 feet long. (This measurement is for illustration only. The configuration is up to the owner.)

The other areas will be calculated as follows:

Dance Floor: 400 people x 7 square feet equals 2,800 sq. ft.

Dining Room: 150 people x 15 square feet equals 2,250 sq. ft.

Bar: 100 people x 15 square feet equals 1,500 sq. ft.

Reading Room: 10 people x 50 square feet equals 500 sq. ft.

Kitchen: 4 people x 200 square feet equals 800 square feet.

As you can see, the building will have to contain 9600 square feet.

So what happens if this is more space than the lodge feels they can afford? Do a little juggling. Have the design changed a bit. By making minor adjustments, you can still give your client quite a lot of room.

The lodge hall, for instance, can be combined with the dance floor to eliminate 1750 square feet. This means that a lodge meeting and a dance couldn't be held at the same time. If this were an "adults only" dining operation they may consider combining the bar and the dining room. They could even eliminate the reading room. But the kitchen space should not be tampered with. In fact, I'd be surprised if a kitchen staff of four could operate in only 800 square feet, considering all the sophisticated kitchen equipment in use today. But I would be inclined to go along with the recommendations of kitchen consultants who will probably be involved in designing the kitchen, so long as they provide at least 200 square feet per person.

If the membership figures are correct and the estimates of dining and dancing are also correct, the figures we've just determined are final. Depending on exiting and other features, however, the building could be constructed in two or even three stories to add more room.

Occupancy or Occupant Load?
What we've just done was determine the occupant load for one building use. *Do not interpret this as a method of establishing occupancy.* We did that in the last chapter. *Occupancy* is the type of business or operation being performed; *occupant load* is the normal number of people using the premises while business or operations are being conducted.

Mixed Occupancy and Different Ownerships
Let's consider what we'd have to do for a project involving several different ownerships operating cooperatively. In this case we'd have to approach the situation from a slightly different angle.

Let's break down the different operations and establish them as separate uses. Let's say, for instance, that the Loyal Order of Hose Handlers has a lodge room in this building. In another area, perhaps on another floor, we have the Romp and Stomp Ballroom. In a third area, maybe on the ground floor, is the Greasy Spoon Restaurant and Taphouse.

The lodge room would be an assembly room, probably without a stage, although it could easily have one. It houses less than 300 people. U.B.C. Table No. 5-A (Chapter Two, Figure 2-2) tells us that it is either group A-2.1 or A-3. But beware! This is one of the things that can cost you a lot of money. Group A-2.1 is listed as having "an occupant load of 300 *or more* without a stage"; Group A-3 is listed as having "an occupant load of *less than* 300 without a stage." It doesn't seem like much of a difference until you come to the type of construction allowed. As indicated in U.B.C. Table No. 5-B (Figure 3-3), Group A-2.1 is not permitted in Type II-N, III-N or V-N construction, but Type A-3 may be placed in those categories. This difference can really add to construction costs. (Types of construction will be discussed in detail in the next chapter.)

Using the magic number of "300" as an occupant load may be an arguing point. You may be better off to reduce your square footage by a few feet and come up with an occupant load of 299. On a building 30 feet wide, that may only amount to reducing the length by a few inches.

Now, assume the dance hall has a stage. Since it will have over 300 occupants, the hall must be put in an A-1 grouping. The bar/restaurant with less than 300 occupants is back in the A-3 grouping.

Several paragraphs back I mentioned types of construction. Because you have an A-1 grouping (the dance hall) in your building, you must have Type I construction throughout the entire building. This is an important consideration when mixing occupancies because by leaving out the dance hall you could go to a lesser (and less expensive) type of construction.

Area Separation
Area separation is usually defined as a fire-resistive separation between two distinct areas, designed to reduce the rapid spread of fire from one area to another. It is usually referred to in hourly terms. In other words, a one-hour fire-resistive area separation means that the adjacent area will be protected for a minimum of one hour.

Will we need an area separation in our building? U.B.C. Table No. 5-B (Figure 3-3) says no, but let's look at it. For mixed occupancies within the Group A occupancy group there is no required separation except the usual partitions requested by the occupants or required by the type of construction. This depends on the location, area, and height of the building, and a few other considerations, but not occupancy.

TABLE NO. 5-B—REQUIRED SEPARATION IN BUILDINGS OF MIXED OCCUPANCY
(In Hours)

	A-1	A-2	A-2.1	A-3	A-4	B-1	B-2	B-3	B-4	E	H-1	H-2	H-3	H-4-5	I	M²	R-1	R-3
A-1		N	N	N	N	4	3	3	3	N	4	4	4	4	3	1	1	1
A-2			N	N	N	3	1	1	1	N	4	4	4	4	3	1	1	1
A-2.1				N	N	3	1	1	1	N	4	4	4	4	3	1	1	1
A-3					N	3	N	1	N	N	4	4	4	4	3	1	1	1
A-4						3	1	1	1	N	4	4	4	4	3	1	1	1
B-1							1	1	1	4	2	1	1	1	4	1	3¹	N
B-2								1	1	1	2	1	1	1	2	1	1	N
B-3									1	1	2	1	1	1	4	1	1	N
B-4										1	2	1	1	1	4	N	1	1
E											4	4	4	4	1	1	1	1
H-1												1	1	1	4	4	4	4
H-2													1	1	4	1	3	3
H-3														1	4	1	3	3
H-4-5															4	1	3	3
I																1	1	1
M²																	1	1
R-1																		N
R-3																		

Note: For detailed requirements and exceptions, see Section 503.

¹The three-hour separation may be reduced to two hours where the Group B, Division 1 Occupancy is limited to the storage of passenger motor vehicles having a capacity of not more than nine persons. This shall not apply where provisions of Section 702 (a) apply.

²For agricultural buildings, see also Appendix Chapter 11.

From the Uniform Building Code, ©1982, ICBO.

Figure 3-3 Required Separation in Buildings of Mixed Occupancy

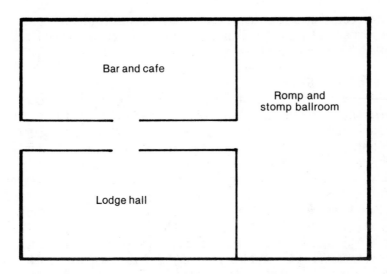

Figure 3-4 Common Hall to Various Occupancies

Access Between Occupancies

Related to area separation is *access between occupancies*. For example, could we have access from one separate area to another without having to go out to the street and come back through another door?

One way of doing this would be to have the areas separated by a common hallway with direct outside access. (See Figure 3-4.) You could use this hallway to go from the dining room or the bar to the dance hall. However, either it must be short so it won't create an additional hazard by its length, or it must have enough doors to allow adequate exit to the outside. This is also controlled by the code and will be discussed later.

The idea isn't new. Enclosed shopping malls have been doing this for years. Although nearly all house the same occupancy group, most provide access to a common enclosed "hallway."

Since we are on the subject of aisles, halls, and getting in or out of a building, it might be a good time to bring up *vomitories*. Vomitories have been around a long time and are not what you may think. You may have one in your church, theater, auditorium or gymnasium. The dictionary says this is an entrance piercing the banks of aisles of a theater or auditorium. In practice, it's an interior court into which a number of hallways might enter. Examples are a hallway in a shopping mall or a cluster of businesses opening into a central court.

Occupancy—Restrictive Requirements

Now, what about some of the more restrictive requirements of the different occupancy groups we discussed a few minutes ago? These requirements can alter the shape, size and capacity of a proposed building. In some cases there may be trade-offs (if you do this then you can enlarge that, and that sort of thing). Up to this point we've been dealing mostly in generalities. From here on things may get a little sticky.

Buildings or parts of buildings classed in Group A-1 must be Type I or Type II-FR construction. They can't exceed the area and height limits specified in Section 505, 506, or 507. These sections encompass U.B.C. Tables Nos. 5-A, 5-B, 5-C, and 5-D, and govern the gross floor area and the heights of buildings for this group. They also allow for certain increases for such items as automatic sprinkler systems.

Is this good or bad? That depends on what you want to do. Let's take a closer look. U.B.C. Table No. 5-A is shown in Figure 2-2 (Chapter Two), Table 5-B, is shown in Figure 3-3 and Tables 5-C and 5-D are shown in Figures 3-5 and 3-6.

Group A-1, you will recall, is "Any assembly building with a stage and an occupant load of 1000 or more in the building." Remember that we're working with gross floor area and that most of the occupants will be seated. At 15 square feet per occupant for 1000 occupants, we'll need a gross floor area of 15,000 square feet. This isn't exceptional for a grand ballroom in some of the larger hotels. Even a skating rink could be larger than that (using nominal figures, about 100' x 150'). Type I construction is about the most fire resistive the code calls for and will be expensive to build. Will it be worth it? That's up to you, the owner and his banker.

The code also says that if the main floor slopes, the slope can't exceed one in five. Also, the building must front directly on or have access to a public street at least 20 feet wide, and the main assembly floor must be located at or near ground level. The code also requires you to furnish light and ventilation by windows or skylights with an area at least one-eighth the total floor area, one half of which must be openable.

TABLE NO. 5-C—BASIC ALLOWABLE FLOOR AREA FOR BUILDINGS ONE STORY IN HEIGHT[6]
(In Square Feet)

OCCUPANCY	TYPES OF CONSTRUCTION								
	I	II			III		IV	V	
	F.R.	F.R.	ONE-HOUR	N	ONE-HOUR	N	H.T.	ONE-HOUR	N
A-1	Unlimited	29,900	Not Permitted						
A) 2-2.1	Unlimited	29,900	13,500	Not Permitted	13,500	Not Permitted	13,500	10,500	Not Permitted
A) 3-4	Unlimited	29,900	13,500	9,100	13,500	9,100	13,500	10,500	6,000
B) 1-2-3[1]	Unlimited	39,900	18,000	12,000	18,000	12,000	18,000	14,000	8,000
B-4	Unlimited	59,900	27,000	18,000	27,000	18,000	27,000	21,000	12,000
E	Unlimited	45,200	20,200	13,500	20,200	13,500	20,200	15,700	9,100
H) 1-2[2]	15,000	12,400	5,600	3,700	5,600	3,700	5,600	4,400	2,500
H) 3-4-5	Unlimited	24,800	11,200	7,500	11,200	7,500	11,200	8,800	5,100
I) 1-2	Unlimited	15,100	6,800	Not Permitted	6,800	Not Permitted	6,800	5,200	Not Permitted
I-3	Unlimited	15,100	Not Permitted[3]						
M[4]	See Chapter 11								
R-1	Unlimited	29,900	13,500	9,100[5]	13,500	9,100[5]	13,500	10,500	6,000[5]
R-3	Unlimited								

[1]For open parking garages, see Section 709.
[2]See Section 903.
[3]See Section 1002 (b).
[4]For agricultural buildings, see also Appendix Chapter 11.
[5]For limitations and exceptions, see Section 1202 (b).
[6]For multistory buildings, see Section 505 (b).

From the Uniform Building Code, ©1982, ICBO.

N—No requirements for fire resistance
F.R.—Fire resistive
H.T.—Heavy Timber

Figure 3-5 Allowable Floor Area for Buildings One Story in Height

TABLE NO. 5-D—MAXIMUM HEIGHT OF BUILDINGS

OCCUPANCY	TYPES OF CONSTRUCTION								
	I	II			III		IV	V	
	F.R.	F.R.	ONE-HOUR	N	ONE-HOUR	N	H.T.	ONE-HOUR	N
MAXIMUM HEIGHT IN FEET	Unlimited	160	65	55	65	55	65	50	40
MAXIMUM HEIGHT IN STORIES									
A-1	Unlimited	4	Not Permitted						
A) 2-2.1	Unlimited	4	2	Not Permitted	2	Not Permitted	2	2	Not Permitted
A) 3-4	Unlimited	12	2	1	2	1	2	2	1
B) 1-2-3[1]	Unlimited	12	4	2	4	2	4	3	2
B-4	Unlimited	12	4	2	4	2	4	3	2
E[2]	Unlimited	4	2[2]	1	2[2]	1	2[2]	2[2]	1
H-1	Unlimited	2	1	1	1	1	1	1	1
H) 2-3-4-5	Unlimited	5	2	1	2	1	2	2	1
I-1	Unlimited	3	1	Not Permitted	1	Not Permitted	1	1	Not Permitted
I-2	Unlimited	3	2	Not Permitted	2	Not Permitted	2	2	Not Permitted
I-3	Unlimited	2	Not Permitted[3]						
M[4]	See Chapter 11								
R-1	Unlimited	12	4	2[5]	4	2[5]	4	3	2[5]
R-3	Unlimited	3	3	3	3	3	3	3	3

[1] For open parking garages, see Section 709.
[2] See Section 802 (c).
[3] See Section 1002 (b).
[4] For agricultural buildings, see also Appendix Chapter 11.
[5] For limitations and exceptions, see Section 1202 (b).

N—No requirement for fire resistance
F.R.—Fire Resistive
H.T.—Heavy Timber

From the Uniform Building Code, ©1982, ICBO.

Figure 3-6   Maximum Height of Buildings

Plumbing Requirements

Plumbing requirements of the U.B.C. are quite light for the general public, but provisions are more specific where the handicapped are involved. Several items, however, are worthy of note. You must provide, in an approved location, at least one lavatory for each two water closets for each sex and at least one drinking fountain for each floor level. This is a rather strange requirement because the U.B.C. does not cover water closets in Group A occupancies. For this you must consult your plumbing code. In the Uniform Plumbing Code the requirements would be as follows:

| Water Closets | | Urinals | Lavatories |
Males	Females		
4 − 401 to 600	4 − 201 to 400	4 − 401 to 601	3 − 401 to 750
Over 400, add 1 fixture for each additional 500 males and one for each 300 females.		Over 600, 1 for each additional 300 males.	Over 750, 1 for each additional 500 persons.

From the Uniform Plumbing Code, ©1982, IAPMO

Before anyone yells "Foul!" because of the difference in the two codes, let's correct the discrepancies. In the first place, the Uniform Building Code is created by one group and the Uniform Plumbing Code by another. If you're in an area that uses only the U.B.C. and not the U.P.C., go by the requirements of the U.B.C. Otherwise, the more restrictive of the two would apply. Therefore, although the U.B.C. says you need only half as many lavatories as water closets, the UPC states quite clearly that for 1000 occupants you would need five water closets for the men and six for the ladies, The difference is that the men would have urinals. Likewise, you would need four lavatories for each sex, but the building code only calls for three for the men and three for the ladies.

Sprinklers and Exits

These are two items that will be discussed in greater detail in later chapters. Automatic fire-extinguishing systems and standpipes are covered in Section 3802. Exiting is covered in Chapter 33 of the U.B.C.

Group A occupancies, you will remember, have five major subgroups. Division 1, 2 and 2.1 occupancies are not allowed in buildings without at least one-hour fire-resistive protection. This is spelled out in U.B.C. Table No. 5-C (Figure 3-5). Let's take a look at this table and discuss how it could affect your building plans.

Type of Construction Versus Occupancy
U.B.C. Table 5-C has columns showing the type of construction allowed in various occupancies and the allowable square footage. The column at the left of the chart gives the occupancy. The other columns give the square footage of floor area allowed for any of these occupancies for the type of construction shown. These types of construction will be discussed in the next chapter. But for now, all you need to know is that there are five main types of construction and that these are determined by safety. Type I is the most fire resistive; Type V is the least. As I said, we'll get into them in more detail later.

Building Height Versus Type of Construction
Take a look at U.B.C. Table No. 5-D (Figure 3-6). This shows how the type of construction governs the height of a building. I suppose you could read it like this: If you want to build this high, this is what you have to do for this particular occupancy.

Type I construction, which is about as incombustible as you can get, has no height limitations. Type II construction may go to 160 feet with *Fire Resistive* (F.R.) construction. All lesser types range between 40 feet and 65 feet high. To further confuse you, note that below the height limitation in feet is *Maximum Height in Stories*. Also notice that in some instances there are certain occupancies that are nót allowed in some types of construction regardless of height or area. This is very important to remember.

The use of "N" in these charts means there are *No Requirements* for fire resistance. Unless otherwise noted, this applies to any of the U.B.C.'s charts.

Allowable Area Increases
You might think that U.B.C. Tables Nos. 5-C and 5-D are too restrictive. Well, they may be, but there is some relief in sight. For instance, there are several ways to increase the basic allowable floor area. One is to use a higher type of construction. In many

cases this is necessary and is frequently desirable, but it might be too expensive. In that case, there's an item in the code that might help you. I call it *spacial separation*. It refers to allowing more space around your building to protect it from fires coming from adjacent buildings. This also protects adjacent buildings from fires originating in your building.

One very good way of increasing allowable floor area is by installing automatic sprinkler systems. But this is limited to certain occupancies and certain conditions. And it's going to be expensive.

Increasing space allowances is a matter of balancing one method against another to see which is best for you. Let's see what the U.B.C. has to say about it:

Section 506(a) General. The floor areas specified in Section 505 (referring to Table 5-C) *may be increased by one of the following:*

1. Separation on two sides. Where public space, streets, or yards more than 20 feet in width extend along and adjoin two sides of the building, floor areas may be increased at a rate of 1¼ percent for each foot by which the minimum width exceeds 20 feet, but the increase shall not exceed 50 percent.

2. Separation on three sides. Where public space, streets or yards more than 20 feet in width extend along and adjoin three sides of the building, floor areas may be increased at a rate of 2½ percent for each foot by which the minimum width exceeds 20 feet, but the increase shall not exceed 100 percent.

3. Separation on all sides. Where public space, streets or yards more than 20 feet in width extend on all sides of a building and adjoin the entire perimeter, floor areas may be increased at a rate of 5 percent for each foot by which the minimum width exceeds 20 feet. Such increases shall not exceed 100 percent, except for buildings not exceeding two stories in height of Group B, Division 4 Occupancy and one-story buildings housing aircraft hangars and as further limited in Section 902(b) for aircraft repair hangars.

It goes on to state that any one- or two-story buildings in Group B and Group H, Division 5 occupancies can't be limited if provided with an approved automatic sprinkler system and surrounded by public space at least 60 feet wide. And there's more. The next paragraph says that the area of Group B, Division 4 occupancies in a one-story Type II, Type III One-hour, or Type IV building can be unlimited if the building is surrounded by a public space at least 60 feet wide. In Section 506(c) you'll find another item that might encourage you to install a sprinkler system:

The area specified in Section 505 may be tripled in one-story buildings and doubled in buildings of more than one story if the building is provided with an approved automatic sprinkler system throughout.

This means that if you have a Type V One-hour building, you would normally be allowed 10,500 square feet in an R-1 occupancy (hotels, apartments). If you were to install an automatic sprinkler system, you could increase this to 31,500 square feet. This is better than you'd get if you went with Type II F.R. construction. But there's more to it than that. Let's take a look.

Compounding Area Computation
A moment ago I mentioned that you could increase the area in your building if it is surrounded by yards and streets, what I call spacial separation. Let's go back to the 10,500-square-foot building mentioned earlier. By providing sprinklers we found that you could increase that footage to 31,500, provided it was all on one story. Now let's assume that this building has a 50-foot-wide street on one side. Going back to Section 506(a) you'll find that the area can be increased again at the rate of 1¼ percent for each foot the minimum width exceeds 20 feet. But the increase can't exceed 50 percent.

This amounts to a substantial increase in the size of your building. Let's figure it out:

10,500 x 1¼% x 30' x 3 (for sprinklers) = 43,311 square feet.

The question that usually arises here is which should you figure first, the percent increase gained by the separation or the tripling for the sprinklers? Let's try it this way:

10,500 x 30' x 1¼% x 3 = 43,312

The difference is the result of rounding off the decimals. Otherwise the effect is the same. Oh yes, about the 30 feet on a 50-foot street—the additional footage was based on a width excess of 20 feet.

Let's go over this once more. This time let's assume that instead of a separation on just one side, there will be a separation on all sides. Remember, the code says that we use a five percent increase for each foot of sideyard by which the minimum width exceeds 20 feet. For our purposes we'll also assume that the yards are all 50 feet wide.

10,500 x 30' x 5% x 3 = 96,075 square feet.

This is probably more of an increase than you planned on. You can use any or all of it, if you desire. The main thing is that you must figure out which is best for you—more space around the building, if available, or installing an automatic sprinkler system to get as much space as you need.

Maximum Height of Buildings and Increases

Adding sprinklers to a building increases its allowable height. The maximum height and number of stories of every building depends on its occupancy and construction. Limits are set forth in U.B.C. Table No. 5-D.

If completely sprinklered, a building may be increased in height by one story. But this increase is *not* allowed if you have already computed the increase in floor area based on the sprinklers. Sorry about that.

Towers, spires and steeples that are part of the building and not used for habitation or storage are limited in height only by structural design if constructed of noncombustible material. If they're constructed of combustible material, they can't exceed 20 feet above the height limitations in U.B.C. Table No. 5-D.

Elevators and High-rise Buildings

While we're discussing building height and area, I'd like to mention several hazards posed by elevators in high-rise buildings.

In the spring of 1972 following the San Fernando earthquake, a report was issued about elevator troubles in multi-story buildings resulting from the earthquake. It seems that all that shaking caused the cables and counterweights to bang around quite a bit in the elevator shafts, rendering many elevators inoperable even though there was little structural damage. In a five- to ten-story building this might be little more than a nuisance. But can you imagine what it would be like in a 30-story building?

Also, automatic elevators have proved troublesome in high-rise fire fighting. Why?

Most modern elevators have automatic controls. Unfortunately, the automatic controls respond to heat. Elevators can be very useful in taking fire-fighters and their equipment to higher floors. Fire fighters are usually instructed to leave the car at either the floor above or below the fire. This way they are not exposed to a sudden burst of heat or flame as soon as the door is opened.

However, because they respond to heat, the automatic controls will take the elevator directly to the floor of the fire and open the doors automatically. You can imagine what the consequences of that might be.

Also, fire fighters may not be able to signal a car. If the fire is close enough to the shaft, the heat may stop the car, forcing the fire fighters to haul their equipment up many flights of stairs to get to the fire.

Group B Area Requirements

Generally, Group B area requirements are quite lenient. And since more buildings outside the downtown area are surrounded by parking areas and streets (spacial separation), allowable increases are generally in order. Allowable heights are also lenient. Although U.B.C. Table No. 5-A (Figure 2-2 in Chapter 2) allows a B-1 occupancy in a Type V-N building (frame, with no fire-resistive construction) of 6,000 square feet, Section 1102 limits service stations to noncombustible or one-hour fire-resistive construction. Storage garages must have floors protected against saturation.

Storage areas larger than 1,000 square feet in wholesale and retail stores must be separated from the sales area with one-hour separation walls unless the building is to be sprinklered. Then the allowable area may be increased.

Attic Separations

One thing that you'll find quite common in this section of the code is that the attics must be divided by area separations if they exceed 3,000 square feet and are constructed with combustible materials. However, if the attic is to be sprinklered, the allowable area may be increased.

These separations are very important. Two serious motel fires in 1980 were aggravated by openings cut into the area separations by plumbers and electricians.

These separations must be constructed of gypsum wallboard (sheetrock) at least 1/2-inch thick, 1-inch-thick tight-fitting wood, 3/8-inch-thick plywood, or other approved noncombustible material with adequate support. Protect any openings in attic separations by installing self-closing doors. And be sure all wiring, plumbing or ductwork is protected.

Exiting

Exiting from store buildings is an old problem. It's mostly a matter of store owners not wanting to give up any interior space. Exit doors must swing in the direction of egress (the way out). They must not swing over the public right of way. That means all exit doors on commercial buildings built to the property line must be recessed. Many property owners are reluctant to do so because it robs them of space inside the store. On new construction this isn't too much of a problem because it can be incorporated into the design of the building. The problem, therefore, is replacing of doors on existing buildings.

This problem is related to another: exiting from basements in Group B occupancies. All basements in Group B occupancies are supposed to have two exits, one of which must open to the outside. But many older buildings aren't designed this way. And many owners of new buildings are reluctant to meet this requirement.

It's possible to get around this by having the basement stairs end near the rear door so that exiting will not be impeded. But check with the inspector. He'll be the one granting final approval.

Group B-4 is probably the most liberal of all the occupancies regarding building height, area, exiting and other requirements. Usually this is due to the normally low human load in these buildings and the abundance of space around them.

How Much Remodeling is Acceptable?

Most builders are not aware of the extent to which the building code covers remodel work. So far we've been talking about new construction. But what about remodeling?

One of the first questions the inspector may ask is why you intend to remodel. If you're merely upgrading the property and there will be no change in occupancy, there's no problem. But, if there'll be another tenant who, by the nature of his business, will change the occupancy, there may be a few problems. The different occupancy may require basic changes in the building that weren't anticipated. Essentially, you would have to go back to the basic question of occupancy determination. Therefore, let's assume you are only upgrading the premises.

If your city adopted the U.B.C. without amendment, the following sections would apply:

Section 104(a) General. *Buildings and structures to which additions, altera-tions or repairs are made shall comply with all requirements of this code for new facilities except as specifically provided for in this section. See Section 1210 for provisions requiring installation of smoke detectors in existing Group R, Division 3 Occupancies.*

(b) Additions, Alterations or Repairs. Additions, alterations or repairs may be made to any building or structure without requiring the existing building or struc-ture to comply with all the requirements of this code provided the addition, alteration or repair conforms to that required for a new building or structure. Ad-ditions, alterations or repairs shall not cause an existing building or structure to become unsafe or overloaded. Any building so altered, which involves a change in use or occupancy, shall not exceed the height, number of stories or area permitted for new buildings. Any building plus new additions shall not exceed the height, number of stories, and area specified for new buildings.

Alteration or repairs to an existing building or structure which are nonstruc-tural and do not adversely affect any structural member or any part of the building or structure having required fire resistance may be made with the same materials of which the building or structure is constructed.

Exception: *The installation or replacement of glass shall be as required for new installations.*

(c) Existing Occupancy. Buildings in existence at the time of the adoption of this code may have their existing use or occupancy continued, if such use or oc-cupancy was legal at the time of adoption of this code, provided such continued use is not dangerous to life.

Any change in the use or occupancy of any existing building or structure shall comply with the provisions of Sections 307 and 502 of this code.

The owner may be remodeling his building to bring it up to code standards. Or, he may be doing it for economic reasons, such as obtaining favorable insurance rates and coverage. In that case, I recommend that the building inspector go through the place with you, pointing out all areas of non-compliance. You are not bound, however, to restore the building unless the inspector finds something hazardous.

Group E Occupancies

This group covers schools. The trend today is toward larger, con-solidated schools. Usually larger contracting firms get these jobs, but not always. The line between a small and large contractor might be based entirely on the scope of the work. There's also the possibility of several smaller firms banding together to form a con-sortium.

Usually, plans for new construction of schools are examined thoroughly before you get to the construction stage. The state and even the federal people will go over the plans with a fine tooth comb. The local building department will give them another review. All the general contractor has to do is follow the plans. However, there is still the chance that small contractors will be called upon for remodel work in and around certain schools as well as for construction of certain private schools. Therefore, let's take a look at the requirements.

Group E occupancies (the educational group) may be any type of construction. Of course, they are still governed by U.B.C. Tables Nos. 5-C and 5-D (Figures 3-5 and 3-6), in which the area or height controls the type of construction. It should be noted, though, that generally all areas for the first and second grades as well as areas for kindergarten students cannot be located above the first floor.

This might be interesting to remember when dealing with day care centers. Often these centers are in existing buildings; you may even be called upon to convert a basement for their use. Consult the local building inspector or fire marshal before getting too far advanced in your plans.

Group E occupancies are one of the few places in the building code that specify a definite number of water closets, urinals and lavatories. The plumbing code, however, does list requirements for different types of occupancies, so all groups are covered.

Section 805 states:

Water closets shall be provided on the basis of the following ratio of water closets to the number of students:
  Elementary schools . . .Boys-1 to 100, Girls-1 to 35 Secondary schools . . Boys-1 to 100, Girls-1 to 45
  In addition, urinals shall be provided for boys on the basis of 1 to 30 in elementary and secondary schools.
  There shall be provided at least one lavatory for each two water closets or urinals, or at least one drinking fountain on each floor for elementary and secondary schools.

Group E Exiting
All exit doors serving areas of more than 50 occupants must swing outward and must be equipped with panic hardware. This requirement for swing of doors is a good one and is a generally accepted rule of thumb.

This is a good place to bring up the requirements for school corridors. Section 3319(e) requires that a corridor in a Group E, Division 1 occupancy must be the width required by Section 3303, plus 2 feet. No corridor may be less than 6 feet wide. This is the section where the width of exits is discussed and which states that a corridor may be only 44 inches wide. Seems like a contradiction, doesn't it? If a corridor can't be less than 6 feet wide, how can you have a 44-inch-wide corridor? This makes it sound as though you could have a 44-inch corridor feeding into a 6-foot exit, but that isn't so. Section 3302(b) states that the total width of exits in feet can't be less than the total occupant load served divided by 50. This raises two very important points: (1) We're talking about schools, so the rule of 6-foot exit (and corridors) must apply; (2) even when you think you've found the answer, read further. Your answer may not be complete.

Can the corridor be reduced by so-called "natural" barriers? Yes, but very little. Section 3305(d) states:

(d) Projections. The required width of corridors shall be unobstructed.

Exception: *Handrails and doors, when fully opened, shall not reduce the required width by more than 7 inches. Doors in any position shall not reduce the required width by more than one-half. Other nonstructural projections such as trim and similar decorative features may project into required width 1½ inches on each side.*

A future chapter will cover in detail how exit widths are determined. But I would like to mention one other requirement. The maximum distance required to get out of the building must not exceed 150 feet for unsprinklered buildings and 225 feet for sprinklered buildings.

Groups I and H

Group I occupancies (the institutional group) must have approved fire alarm systems. Audible alarms can be used in non-patient areas, but visible alarms may be used in patient areas. The last thing a heart patient needs is a false alarm to rouse him out of a deep sleep.

Again stringent exiting, height, area, and construction requirements apply. This is because of the nature and habits of the occupants of most institutions.

The Group H occupancies (hazardous) covers special hazards. These include areas where highly flammable materials are stored, processed or used. This grouping also includes highly combustible manufacturing. See U.B.C. Table No. 9-A (Figure 3-7) for *Exempt Amounts of Hazardous Materials, Liquids and Chemicals.* There are a few special provisions regarding construction. The walls must be of at least one-hour fire-resistive construction and surrounded by public space, streets, or yards at least 60 feet wide. If cars or airplanes are stored, repaired, or operated, the floor surfaces must be non-combustible.

Height is also important. If the building is over 95 feet high, the structural frame must be of at least four-hour fire-resistive construction. In the next chapter we'll go into more detail about fire-resistiveness and how to build it into a building.

Another item that strikes fear into the hearts of many developers is the *space* required around a building. This really isn't a very big problem. I mentioned that a street 60 feet wide would serve as part of the open space. In most cities that's the normal width of a street, so in most cases one side would be taken care of. Further, most zoning ordinances require a certain amount of off-street parking for most businesses. That provides even more open space.

Like a lot of requirements that are taken care of automatically, some of these items are put in the book "just in case." One item, however, should be considered and must be provided. That is exhaust ventilation.

Exhaust Ventilation
Exhaust ventilation is stringently controlled in Group H occupancies, especially if there are vehicles operating nearby. The fan system must be capable of changing the air every fifteen minutes. The exhaust ventilation must be taken from a point at or near floor level.

This would be a requirement in your own garage if you were in the practice of idling your car for any length of time. But you're hardly likely to go to the expense of putting in an exhaust system when all you need to do is open your garage door.

Before leaving Group H occupancies, I should mention that doors which are part of an automobile ramp enclosure must be equipped with automatic closing devices.

TABLE NO. 9-A—EXEMPT AMOUNTS OF HAZARDOUS MATERIALS, LIQUIDS AND CHEMICALS

MATERIAL	MAXIMUM QUANTITIES
1. Flammable liquids[1]	
Class I-A	30 gal.[2]
Class I-B	60 gal.[2]
Class I-C	90 gal.[2]
2. Combustible liquids[1]	
Class II	120 gal.[2]
Class III-A	250 gal.[2]
3. Combination flammable liquids[3]	120 gal.[2]
4. Flammable gases	3000 cu. ft. at one atmosphere of pressure at 70°F.
5. Liquefied flammable gases	60 gal.
6. Flammable fibers—loose	100 cu. ft.
7. Flammable fibers—baled	1000 cu. ft.
8. Flammable solids	500 lbs.
9. Unstable materials	No exemptions
10. Corrosive liquids	55 gal.
11. Oxidizing material—gases	6000 cu. ft.
12. Oxidizing material—liquids	50 gal.
13. Oxidizing material—solids	500 lbs.
14. Organic peroxides	10 lbs.
15. Nitromethane (unstable materials)	No exemptions
16. Ammonium nitrate	1000 lbs.
17. Ammonium nitrate compound mixtures containing more than 60% nitrate by weight	1000 lbs.
18. Highly toxic material and poisonous gas	No exemptions
19. Smokeless powder	20 lbs.[4]
20. Black sporting powder	1 lb.[5]

[1]The quantities of alcoholic beverages in retail sales or storage uses are unlimited, provided the liquids are packaged in individual containers not exceeding 4 liters.

    The quantities of medicines, foodstuffs and cosmetics, containing not more than 50 percent by volume of water-miscible liquids and with the remainder of the solution not being flammable, in retail sales or storage occupancies are unlimited when packaged in individual containers not exceeding 4 liters.

[2]Quantities may be increased by 100 percent in areas which are not accessible to the public. In buildings where automatic fire-extinguishing systems are installed, the quantities may be increased 100 percent in areas accessible to the public.

[3]Containing not more than the exempt amounts of Class I-A, I-B or I-C flammable liquids.

[4]Quantities of smokeless powder may be increased to a maximum of 100 pounds, providing those amounts exceeding 20 pounds are stored in an approved Class II magazine as specified in the Uniform Fire Code.

[5]Quantities of black sporting powder may be increased to a maximum of 5 pounds, providing said amount is stored in an approved Class II magazine as specified in the Uniform Fire Code.

From the Uniform Building Code, ©1982, ICBO.

Figure 3-7 Exempt Amounts of Hazardous Materials

Heliports and Helistops
Heliports and helistops are controlled under Group B occupancies, not Group H as you might think. Apparently this is because they are primarily outdoor operations and are usually considered part of the commercial area. In spite of their outdoor activities, however, requirements regarding their operation are stringent.

Even if you live in a small town, you may be called upon to build a helistop or even the more sophisticated heliport. The local hospital might need one. And many crop dusters are now using helicopters in their business. So don't discount them.

It's important to understand the difference between a heliport and a helistop, or landing pad. According to the definition section of the U.B.C., a heliport is any area where helicopters can be completely serviced, while a helistop is only for taking on or discharging passengers. A heliport, therefore, is subject to far more restrictions, because there will be flammable materials present.

The landing pad, or helistop, beside the local hospital would have very few restrictions. But if the pad were on the roof of the hospital, you'd have to calculate the additional weight into the roof load. However, you would not be able to add fuel or do any service work up there. A simple concrete pad with adequate clearance would suffice for a helistop.

Group M Occupancies
Group M is where we've lumped together all the miscellaneous structures that aren't considered under the other categories. These are assumed to have limited human occupancy and, therefore, relatively light impact on human safety.

About the only major restriction here is that private garages are limited to 1,000 square feet. If a garage exceeds this limitation it must be put into another occupancy group and more restrictive construction might be required. But don't panic. Just think how large that garage would have to be. The standard double garage is usually about 24 x 30 feet, which is fairly large by any standard, and that's only 720 square feet.

Group M-1 structures, the agricultural buildings, are described in Chapter 11 of the Appendix to U.B.C. Occupancy and type of construction are spelled out in U.B.C. Tables Nos. 11-A and 11-B. (See Figure 3-8).

TABLE NO. 11-A—BASIC ALLOWABLE AREA FOR A GROUP M, DIVISION 3 OCCUPANCY, ONE STORY IN HEIGHT AND MAXIMUM HEIGHT OF SUCH OCCUPANCY

	I	II			III & IV		V	
		F-R	1-Hour	N	1-Hour or Type IV	N	1-Hour	N
Allowable Area[1]	Unlimited	60,000	27,100	18,000	27,100	18,000	21,100	12,000[1]
Maximum Height in Stories[2]	Unlimited	12	4	2	4	2	3	2

[1]See Section 1108 for unlimited area under certain conditions.
[2]For maximum height in feet, see Chapter 5, Table No. 5-D.

TABLE NO. 11-B— REQUIRED SEPARATIONS BETWEEN GROUP M, DIVISION 3 AND OTHER OCCUPANCIES (In Hours)

Occupancy	A	E	I	H	B-1	B-2	B-3	B-4	R-1	R-3	M
Rating	4	4	4	4	4	1	1	1	1	1	N

From the Uniform Building Code, ©1982, ICBO.

Figure 3-8   Occupancy and Type of Construction

Group R - The Residential Occupancy

Group R, the residential occupancy, is one of the two occupancies with which most people will be concerned, although smaller communities must also deal with Group M, which covers agricultural buildings. The other main group will be Group B, or business and commercial buildings.

Group R-1 controls hotels, motels, apartment houses, convents and monasteries. Until you get into occupant load situations where you'll be housing large groups, the usual construction restrictions are quite liberal.

I think you'll see a gradual decline in the difference between *hotel* and *motel*. The hotel, or inn, has a long history. Nearly every country has them in one form or another. But the motel is a fairly recent invention, dating back only about fifty or sixty years to the "cabin camps" of the early auto era. Gradually the difference between hotels and motels has decreased to the point where they're now practically the same.

This is also explained in the definitions chapter of the U.B.C. Here, you'll find a hotel listed as:

Any building containing six or more guest rooms intended or designed to be used, or which are used, rented or hired out to be occupied, or which are occupied for sleeping purposes by guests.

A little further along in the definitions we find that motels:

Shall mean hotel as defined in this code.

In apartments, every sleeping room below the fourth floor must have an openable window or exterior door to permit emergency exit or rescue. The window must have at least five square feet of openable area with a minimum dimension of 22 inches. The sill must be no more than 48 inches above the floor.

There are two main reasons for this. One lies in the code itself. First, the line is drawn at the fourth floor because that is as high as the ladders of most fire trucks can reach. The other reason is that under the code, you must use either Type I or Type II construction above the fourth floor. By using the more fire-restrictive type of construction plus the other requirements, fire danger will be reduced considerably.

A few other restrictions are noteworthy. Corridors serving 30 or more people as determined by U.B.C. Table No. 33-A, (Figure 3-1), must be of one-hour fire-resistive construction. All doors leading into this corridor must be solid core; there can be no louvers, grilles, or transoms unless they are protected by a fire shutter controlled by a 135 degree fusible link. The corridor can't have a dead-end length over 20 feet long.

Panic Leaping From Second Stories
Fire safety is important. Much of the building code is based on it. Many people don't know that they're quite safe even if they have to jump from the second story. But is jumping really the answer? A far more comfortable alternative is *dropping* from the second floor.

In Figure 3-9 I've tried to dramatize my point. If you're standing on a second floor balcony, your eye level is approximately 16 feet above the first floor, which we'll assume to be close to grade level. The eye level dimension is critical because it tells your brain how high up you are. The balcony railing is about 13 feet above grade. If there was a fire behind you and you were hanging from the balcony railing, you'd find that your feet would be only about 6 feet above grade—a relatively short drop to the ground.

These dimensions will vary from person to person and building to building. But the distance is less if you drop from a hanging position than if you jumped from the building.

Dwelling Requirements
Group R-3 occupancies are dwellings and are probably the least restricted of all occupied buildings. Most of the requirements are just common sense. For example, living, dining and sleeping rooms are required to have windows. These windows must open directly to the outside, but they can open to a roofed porch if it has a ceiling height of at least 7 feet and is 65% open on the longer side. It, too, must open directly to the outside.

Required windows must have a total area of at least 10% of the floor area of the room or at least ten square feet. Bathrooms must have windows at least three square feet in area, half of which is openable. Baths without windows must have mechanical ventilation direct to the outside air.

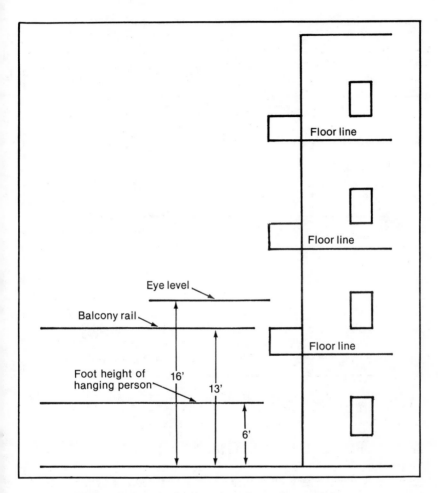

Figure 3-9 Panic Leaping from Second Story

If your house is new and has wood sash, it's probably openable. If your house is old and has been painted several times, the windows may not be openable. However, if you're using aluminum sash, they probably aren't painted shut.

A room with a water closet must be separated from food preparation or storage rooms by a tight fitting door. The code used to read that they couldn't open into such an area, and although this restriction has been relaxed, I still think it's a good idea.

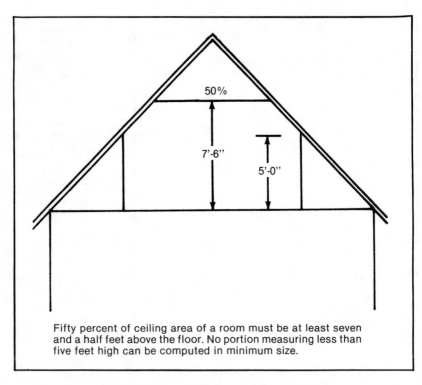

Fifty percent of ceiling area of a room must be at least seven
and a half feet above the floor. No portion measuring less than
five feet high can be computed in minimum size.

Figure 3-10   Relative Ceiling Heights

Possibly, a few of you grew up on farms where the toilet was out
beyond the woodshed and the bathtub was brought in on Saturday
night and placed in front of the kitchen stove. Well, no more. The
code says that every dwelling unit must have a water closet,
lavatory, and either a bathtub or shower, and the kitchen must
have a sink. These fixtures must be provided with hot and cold
running water.

The code gives standard height and area requirements. Your
ceiling can't be less than 7'6'' for at least 50% of the area, and no
part can be less than 5 feet. (See Figure 3-10.) One room must have
at least 150 square feet of area; bedrooms must be at least 70
square feet. No room (except a kitchen) may be less than 7 feet at
any dimension. A water closet compartment must be at least 30 inches wide and have a space at least 24 inches in front of the water
closet.

Attached Garages

An attached garage must have a one-hour fire-resistive separation between it and the house. And door openings into the house must be solid core with a self-closing device. No garage can open directly into a sleeping room.

The separation requirement between the garage and the residence may seem a little ridiculous. A recent survey disclosed that four out of five fires began, not in the garage as often suspected, but in the house. That brings up an interesting question: "What are they trying to protect—the car or the house?"

The other requirement—the self-closing, solid core door—deserves a comment or two. This is to protect people inside the house from carbon monoxide coming from an auto idling in the garage, even with the garage door open.

Consider, for instance what might happen on a cold day. You open the garage door and start your car. The rest of the family is asleep and you're not aware that the wind is blowing gas fumes into your house. This could be fatal. That's why you must have a door with a self-closing device.

Don't blame the building inspector for this requirement. It's in the code and it's a good regulation. The code has many worthy items; the problem is often a matter of follow-up. The inspector can make you install protective devices such as smoke alarms, but he can't require you to maintain them. However, most people do.

Smoke alarms are required by code in residential units. Many states have laws requiring them in all new residential units. But there's no law requiring regular maintenance. That's where the program comes apart.

4

Types Of Construction and Fire Resistance

In the last chapter we discussed the different occupancy groups and their influence on the construction requirements of buildings. In this chapter we'll look into the ways that types of construction influence the occupancy of a building.

To have a certain occupancy usage in a building, there are certain types of construction we must adhere to and some we must avoid. These are given in U.B.C. Table No. 17-A, shown in Figure 4-1.

Buildings Classified by Construction
In addition to being classified by occupancy, buildings are classified by type of construction, according to U.B.C. Table No. 17-A. If a building doesn't entirely conform to a type of construction for a certain classification—we're speaking of minimums, not maximums—it must be placed into a lower classification. The entire building would be limited to the restrictions of the lower type. We'll discuss this in greater detail later in the chapter.

The code doesn't require any building to conform to a higher classification than the minimum requirements for occupancy, height, and area. But a higher type of construction may be used. It

TABLE NO. 17-A—TYPES OF CONSTRUCTION—FIRE-RESISTIVE REQUIREMENTS
(In Hours)
For Details see Chapters under Occupancy and Types of Construction and for Exceptions see Section 1705.

| BUILDING ELEMENT | TYPE I | TYPE II | | | TYPE III | | TYPE IV | | TYPE V | |
| | | NONCOMBUSTIBLE | | | | | COMBUSTIBLE | | | |
	Fire-Resistive	Fire-Resistive	1-Hr.	N	1-Hr.	N	H.T.	N	1-Hr.	N
Exterior Bearing Walls	4 Sec. 1803 (a)	4 1903 (a)	1	N	4 2003 (a)	4 2003 (a)	4 2103 (a)		1	N
Interior Bearing Walls	3	2	1	N	1	N	1		1	N
Exterior Nonbearing Walls	4 Sec. 1803 (a)	4 1903 (a)	1	N	4 2003 (a)	4 2003 (a)	4 2103 (a)		1	N
Structural Frame[1]	3	2	1	N	1	N	1 or H.T.		1	N
Partitions – Permanent	1[2]	1[2]	1[2]	N	1	N	1 or H.T.		1	N
Shaft Enclosures	2	2	1	1	1	1	1		1	N
Floors	2	2	1	N	1	N	H.T.		1	N
Roofs	2 Sec. 1806	1 1906	1 1906	N	1	N	H.T.		1	N
Exterior Doors and Windows	Sec. 1803 (b)	1903 (b)	1903 (b)	1903(b)	2003 (b)	2003 (b)	2103 (b)		2203	2203

N—No general requirements for fire resistance. H.T.—Heavy Timber.

[1]Structural frame elements in the exterior wall shall be protected against external fire exposure as required for exterior bearing walls or the structural frame, whichever is greater.

[2]Fire-retardant treated wood (see Section 407) may be used in the assembly, provided fire-resistance requirements are maintained. See Sections 1801 and 1901, respectively.

From the Uniform Building Code, ©1982, ICBO.

Figure 4-1   Fire-Resistive Requirements for Types of Construction

might be advisable for insurance reasons to go to a higher classification. But you must build to at least the minimum code standards and U.B.C. Table No. 17-A. Buildings may be divided by fire walls and each area considered separately. However, these separations must be complete from the foundation to the roof, and they must meet minimum standards to be classified as fire walls.

Chapter 17 in the U.B.C. gives the general code restrictions that apply to various types of construction. Tighter restrictions are found in the following chapters of the code:

Chapter 18—Type I Fire Resistive Buildings
Chapter 19—Type II Buildings
Chapter 20—Type III Buildings
Chapter 21—Type IV Buildings
Chapter 22—Type V Buildings

The general restrictions, however, are listed and then excepted for certain occupancy groups. For instance, consider Sections 1703 and 1704:

Section 1703. Usable space under the first story shall be enclosed except in Groups R, Division 3 and M Occupancies, and such enclosure when constructed of metal or wood shall be protected on the side of the usable space as required for one-hour fire resistive construction. Doors shall be self-closing, of noncombustible construction or solid wood core, not less than 1¾ inches in thickness.
Section 1704. Roof coverings shall be as specified in Section 3202 (b).

Fire Resistance Determines Type of Construction
Notice in U.B.C. Table No. 17-A that the fire resistance of certain building elements determines the type of construction to be used. These elements are the exterior and interior bearing walls, exterior nonbearing walls, structural frame, permanent partitions, shaft enclosures, floors, roofs, exterior doors and windows.

Table 17-A is kind of sneaky. It lists everything that must be done to build a certain fire resistiveness into a building and thereby establish the type of construction. But what if you slack up on one little item? Let's say, for instance, that you're building a 15-story apartment building, Type I. Checking U.B.C. Table No. 5-D (Chapter Three, Figure 3-6) you'll find that in a Type II building you're limited to 12 stories for an apartment building. Therefore, you'll have to use Type I construction.

Maybe by reducing the roof from a two-hour fire resistive construction to one-hour you could save a few bucks. After all, a one-hour roof is pretty safe. So you draw up your specifications and then find the building inspector shaking his head. What went wrong?

The inspector has noted that if one segment or element of Table 17-A is reduced, the whole structure is automatically reduced one grade. Although you have a fine building, if you insist on going with the one-hour roof, he can only let you build a 12-story apartment building.

You have to make a choice. Are you going to build a two-hour roof, or are you going to reduce your building to 12 stories? In the long run the loss of the three additional floors might be greater than spending a few extra dollars for the higher type roof. Weigh all sides before deciding. But remember, *whenever one element of the building is reduced in grade, then the whole building must be classified in a lower grade.*

It's possible to have a four-hour exterior bearing wall, three-hour structural frame, and two-hour floors—all elements of a Type I building—and still wind up with a Type V building because the rest of the elements did not measure up to the requirements of U.B.C. Table No. 17-A.

Roof Structures
This is another item that could be tricky. Generally, you'll find that skylights, penthouses, and roof structures must have the same construction as the rest of the building and be the same distance from the property lines. Furthermore, any roof structure used for housing anything other than mechanical equipment must be considered as an additional story.

The construction details of the above items are covered fully in other chapters. But their use is still a matter of the type of construction you wish to use. In other words, if you're building a frame building of Type V construction, the skylight must be of at least Type V construction.

Fire-Retardant Materials
Fire-retardant-treated wood may be used in non-bearing partitions. However, this brings up some problems. There are two types of fire-retardant-treated wood. One is where the wood has been

Figure 4-2   Both are residential buildings, but due to the nature of their occupancies they must be classified separately both by occupancy and type of construction.

subjected to pressure impregnation of the retardant. The other is where the retardant has been sprayed or painted on. Both are acceptable, and this is where the problem arises.

The inspector considers "acceptable" to mean when the material is applied based on the manufacturer's recommendations.

"Acceptable" does *not* mean when the user applies the material the way he thinks it should be applied. There's a vast difference between the two.

It's usually a matter of economics and what some people think they can get away with. If the manufacturer states that a certain retardant material must be applied in four coats at eight-hour intervals, he normally has a good reason for it. Therefore, it is disheartening to hear a subcontractor say that the manufacturer is only trying to sell more material and that two coats applied at two-hour intervals will do just as well. Let's give the devil his due. The manufacturer is in business for profit and he does want to sell lots of that material, but he wants his material used properly. He usually has his material tested first, and if he feels it takes four coats at eight-hour intervals to do the job, then I'm inclined to go along with him.

What about the subcontractor? By skimping on installation methods he can underbid his more conscientious competitor. It's up to you to choose who is more honest and reliable.

Will Retardant-treated Material Burn?
Yes, fire-retardant-treated material will burn, but only as long as there is an applied flame. If you throw a piece of fire-retardant wood in the fireplace, it will eventually be consumed.

Very few materials are not affected by fire or heat if the fire or heat is hot enough and applied long enough. What we've done is slow down the effects of the combustion. Part of our purpose, after we accept that there is very little that is fireproof, is to keep a structure upright as long as possible. This helps fire fighters and gives the occupants a chance to escape.

Research Recommendations
With so many building materials on the market today you may wonder how the building inspector knows if a product is acceptable. No, he doesn't have it all right off the top of his head. What he does have is the *I.C.B.O. Research Recommendations.*

The International Conference of Building Officials publishes an annual report on all materials approved for construction. All members of the I.C.B.O. receive annual material updates. When a manufacturer presents a material for approval it must be accompanied by a report from an acceptable testing laboratory or agency. The material and report are reviewed by the staff and members of a review committee. If approval is granted, the Research Recommendation is published.

This Recommendation lists the product, the manufacturer's name and address, what the product is and what it does, how it is to be used or applied, and which section of the U.B.C. it pertains to. Some of these are quite brief, while others are quite lengthy. But they do give the inspector the information he needs to make a decision.

To be "acceptable," the product or material must be used or applied *according to the manufacturer's specification as amended by the testing lab.* No other method can be used unless you're prepared to prove to the inspector that your way is superior. The resultant testing and proving may be more expensive than you want to take on.

Adherence To Code Can Save Money

You can save money by following the code. An example is non-bearing partitions. In several occupancy categories, partitions aren't rated ("N" in U.B.C. Table No. 17-A, Figure 4-1). Therefore, you could use plain wood panels in the three-quarter height partitions, since plain wood can be used in all types of construction.

But be careful. What seems to be the most economical way to build something could end up costing more in the long run. What happens is that many builders use wood panels made of thin 3/16-inch material with photo-engraved grain over a shoddy backing. In many cases you can put your fist right through it. I always recommend that it be backed with sheetrock. True, this will add to the cost, but it also adds strength and a certain amount of fire-resistiveness. If you can put your fist through the panels, it's easy to see what a carelessly placed piece of furniture can do to a nicely paneled wall.

In any type of construction, wood veneer can be used over non-combustible surfaces, with certain limitations. Wood trim and unprotected wood doors may be used where unprotected openings are permitted. But what are *unprotected openings?* And how do you know if they're permitted?

Unprotected Openings

Let's go back to U.B.C. Table No. 5-A (Chapter 2, Figure 2-2). On the far right-hand side of that chart is a column that reads, "Openings in Exterior Walls." This explains how close to the property line a building may sit and still have unprotected openings or even any openings. This is to help prevent the spread of fire from one property to another.

What about buildings downtown that are built right to the property line, facing on a street or alley? This requires a little detective work. Let's backtrack to Section 504 (a):

For the purpose of this section the center line of an adjoining street or alley shall be considered an adjacent property line.

Not too much help, is it? That might depend a lot on how wide the streets are in your town. Let's go on to Section 506(a)1:

1. Separation on two sides. Where public space, streets or yards more than 20 feet in width extend along and adjoin two sides of the building . . .

Remember this one? We mentioned it in Chapter Three when discussing area increases. We established that a 20-foot street was the line of demarcation. But Section 1705(d) states:

Regardless of fire-resistive requirements for exterior walls, certain elements of the walls fronting on streets or yards having a width of 40 feet may be constructed as follows . . .

Isn't that curious? The only difference is in our second and third definitions. One states, *"20 feet to the center line"* while the other states *"a street 40 feet wide."* It appears to be the same thing, doesn't it? On this basis, I would have to assume that 20 feet is the magic number.

That takes care of the separation on the street side. Section 506(a)1 covers the doubtful areas. However, U.B.C. Table No. 5-A is much more specific for side lot lines for the various occupancies.

Figure 4-3 A good example of double wall construction. The aluminized sheathing is an insulating board that helps to increase the R factor of the insulation.

Double Walls?

Construction practices are always changing, but I doubt they'll change any more in the next forty years than they have in the last forty. We still don't know for sure how energy conservation will affect the style of our houses or construction techniques. Certainly there will be changes not even contemplated today.

When I learned home building, most sheathing was either shiplap or plain one-inch stock placed horizontally or diagonally on plain studs. A layer of building paper was placed over this and the siding was applied. The framing was nailed together as it lay on the subfloor. Then it was erected and braced. Now, with the advent of plywood sheathing and siding, entire wall sections are constructed on the floor and lifted into place, complete (in some cases) with windows and paint. This diaphragm wall is more air-tight and may even be stronger structurally.

Old-timers wondered why I allowed single-wall construction on homes. Simple—it's permitted by the code. Sections 1707 and 2202 allow you to put siding directly on the studding under certain conditions.

Section 1707 states that building paper must be applied over studs or sheathing of exterior walls. The paper may be omitted when the exterior wall covering consists of weatherproof panels. Exterior plywood of almost any thickness will satisfy this requirement. Section 2202 (by reference to Chapter 25, U.B.C.) states that three-story buildings must have the exterior walls of the first floor covered with solid wood sheathing. This implies that siding will be installed over the sheathing on the first floor of a three-story structure only. Therefore, a house of one or two stories could have bare studs covered with exterior-type plywood and still satisfy the code. But will that satisfy the energy code of your area? It probably would, if you factor in enough R-value for your insulation.

Minimum Plywood Thickness

Section 2516(g)3 covers the minimum thickness of plywood used for exterior wall covering:

3. Plywood. Where plywood is used for covering the exterior of outside walls, it shall be of the Exterior type not less than 3/8 inch thick. Plywood panel siding shall be installed in accordance with Table No. 25-M (See Figure 4-4.) Unless applied over 1-inch wood sheathing or 1/2-inch plywood sheathing, joints shall occur over framing members and shall be protected with a continuous wood batten, approved caulking, flashing, vertical or horizontal shiplaps; or joints shall be lapped horizontally or otherwise made waterproof.

TABLE NO. 25-M—EXPOSED PLYWOOD PANEL SIDING

MINIMUM THICKNESS[1]	MINIMUM NO. OF PLIES	STUD SPACING (INCHES) PLYWOOD SIDING APPLIED DIRECT TO STUDS OR OVER SHEATHING
1. ⅜″	3	16[2]
2. ½″	4	24

[1]Thickness of grooved panels is measured at bottom of grooves.

[2]May be 24 inches if plywood siding applied with face grain perpendicular to studs or over one of the following: (a) 1-inch board sheathing, (b) ½-inch plywood sheathing, (c) ⅜-inch plywood sheathing with face grain of sheathing perpendicular to studs.

From the Uniform Building Code, ©1982, ICBO.

Figure 4-4 Exposed Plywood Panel Siding Requirements

In the opinion of most builders and building officials, 3/8-inch plywood isn't thick enough. But their opinion isn't worth much without the code to back it up. An inspector's opinion is for advice only. But I'd tell you not to settle for less than 1/2 inch of thickness unless it was backed by a sheathing panel.

The 3/8-inch thickness is based on structural engineering practices. Adding a fraction of an inch to achieve the 1/2-inch thickness is just good insurance.

Masonry and Parapet Walls

Wood members aren't allowed for supporting concrete or masonry. All members supporting concrete or masonry in buildings over one story must be fire protected. The underside of lintels, shelf angles, or plates that are not part of the structural frame need not be protected.

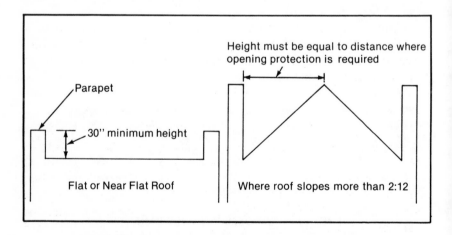

Figure 4-5 Requirements for Parapet Walls

Where required, parapet walls must have the same fire-resistive rating as the walls. Parapets must be at least 30 inches above the point where the roof surface and the wall meet. If the slope of a roof toward a parapet is greater than 2 to 12, the parapet must be as high as any portion of the roof within the distance where protection of wall openings would be required. A parapet can never be less than 30 inches high. Figure 4-5 illustrates these requirements.

General Items of U.B.C. Chapter 17
Eaves, cornices and overhangs may be constructed of unprotected, noncombustible materials, or on Type III buildings, of combustible material protected for one hour.

Folding, portable, or movable partitions are acceptable as long as (1) they don't block required exits or establish exit corridors, (2) they are set in permanent tracks or guides, and (3) the flame spread classification is not less than that for the rest of the room.

Except in residences, rubbish and linen chutes must terminate in rooms separated from the rest of the building by one-hour fire-resistive construction. Openings in the chutes may not open into exit corridors or stairways.

You'll find that code regulations for such shaft enclosures are quite strict and rigidly enforced. That's because these shafts have a way of turning into chimneys in the event of a fire, spreading the flames throughout the building in no time.

Water closet compartments are also closely regulated in most public and semi-public buildings. This includes nearly everything except private dwellings, and is especially critical because many regulations regarding the handicapped are involved.

Bathroom floors must be made of non-absorbent materials, such as cement or ceramic tile. These materials must extend up the walls to a height of 48 inches, 70 inches in shower stalls. Glass or glazing around showers and tubs, even in private residences, must be fully tempered, laminated safety glass or approved plastics.

All weather-exposed surfaces must have a weather-resistive barrier to protect the interior wall covering. Building paper and felt must be free of holes and breaks other than those created by fasteners or attachments. They must be applied weatherboard fashion, lapped at least 2 inches at horizontal joints, and not less than 6 inches at vertical joints. Balconies, landings, exterior stairways, and similar surfaces exposed to the weather and sealed underneath must be waterproofed.

All openings in floors, roofs, balconies or porches that are more than 30 inches above grade must have guardrails at least 42 inches high. The only exceptions are loading docks (none required) and private residences (36-inches is adequate).

The 1982 Edition U.B.C. contains specific provisions in the use of Foam Plastic Insulation. They must have a flame spread rating of not more than 75 and a smoke-developed rating of not more than 450.

The specific requirements in Section 1712(b) cover installation on masonry, attics or crawl spaces, cold storage, metal clad buildings, roofing, doors, and siding backer boards. This was formerly covered in Section 1717. All foam plastics must now be labeled and show ingredients.

Solar energy collectors are now covered as well as atriums.

Helistops
In the last chapter we discussed briefly heliports and helistops. The number of regulations regarding their construction is growing rapidly. Helistops may be erected on buildings or other locations if constructed according to Section 710. Generally, this requires the following:

• If the helicopter weighs less than 3500 pounds, the touchdown area must be at least 20' x 20' and surrounded on all sides by a clear area with a minimum *average* width at roof level of 15 feet. No width can be less than 5 feet.

• The landing area and supports on the roof of a building must be of noncombustible construction. Also, the area must be designed to confine any inflammable liquid spillage and to drain it away from any exit or stairway.

• Exits and stairways must comply with provisions in Chapter 33 of the U.B.C., except that all landing areas on buildings or structures must have two or more exits. If the roof area is less than 60 feet long or less than 200 square feet, the second exit may be a fire escape or a ladder leading to the floor below.

• Approval must be obtained from the Federal Aviation Administration before operating helicopters from any helistop.

Type I Fire-resistive Buildings
The general items just outlined apply to most structures. Now we'll get into specifics, starting with the highest or most fire-resistive building regulations.

The height of Type I buildings is limited only by structural design. The area is limited only in Group A occupancies. But, just because a building is fire-resistive doesn't mean that it's fire-safe. Some of the worst fires in history have been in so-called fireproof buildings. In fact, Type I buildings—the most fire-resistive—have been called "concrete coffins." While the building itself doesn't burn, its contents do.

Building codes can't regulate the amount of combustible goods in a building. A hospital, for example, might be a fire-resistive building but be filled with combustibles. That's why people are seldom burned to death in building fires. Usually, smoke and toxic fumes cause the largest loss of life.

Remember the Chicago school fire a few years ago? One room contained over 30 bodies, yet papers on the desks weren't even singed. A fire-resistive building may give the occupants a better chance of escaping from the building, but *only* if the toxic fumes from burning material inside the building haven't done them in first.

The structural frame of a Type I building must be iron, steel, reinforced concrete, or reinforced masonry and protected for three hours. If members of the structural frame are in the outside wall, they must be protected the same as the outside wall or for four hours.

Type I buildings must have four-hour fire-resistive exterior walls. But non-bearing walls that front streets at least 50 feet wide may be of unprotected, non-combustible construction. In all occupancies except Group H, non-bearing walls may be one-hour where unprotected openings are permitted, and two-hour where protected openings are permitted.

U.B.C. Table No. 17-A (Figure 4-1) illustrates the main requirements for all types of buildings. For miscellaneous items for each type of construction, refer to Chapters 18 through 22 of the U.B.C. Under Type I in Chapter 18 you'll find that a mezzanine floor can't cover more than one third the floor area of a room. Also, you can't have more than two mezzanine floors in any room. Mezzanine floors may be wood or unprotected metal.

Stairs and stair platforms must be reinforced concrete, iron or steel with treads and risers of concrete, iron, or steel.

Group B, Division 2 office buildings and Group R, Division 1 buildings having floors used for human occupancy located more than 75 feet above the lowest level of fire department access must have an approved automatic sprinkler system.

This regulation has been in effect for some time. Some newer provisions cover smoke detection systems, alarm and communication systems, smoke control, emergency power and light systems, and, above all, areas of refuge.

Providing areas of refuge is a fairly recent development. The purpose is to create smoke-free, fire-resistive compartments where people in high-rise buildings can await rescue. Since most elevators are inoperative during emergencies, it would take too long and be too risky to try to evacuate a large high-rise building.

Type II Construction

This category is broken down into three categories (see U.B.C. Table No. 5-C, Figure 3-5 in Chapter Three). These are Type II-FR, Type II 1-hour, Type II-N. Fire-resistive requirements are shown in U.B.C. Table No. 17-A (Figure 4-1). Allowable height and area are shown in U.B.C. Table No. 5-D (Figure 3-6, Chapter Three).

Maximum height depends on the occupancy and varies from two stories for Group H-1 to 12 stories in apartment houses and most business buildings.

There's a fine line between the construction of Type II-FR and 1-hour and N. The first must be of steel, iron, or concrete. In most cases where concrete is listed as a noncombustible building material, it is also taken to include masonry (either brick or concrete block). In the last two types, 1-hour and N, only the structural elements must be noncombustible.

The basic difference is in some of the lesser elements. For instance, Type II-FR requires noncombustible construction throughout. But permanent non-bearing partitions may be made of fire-retardant-treated wood. In Type II 1-hour construction, all elements need only be rated for only one-hour fire resistiveness. In Type II-N there are no fire-resistive ratings on any elements except the structural frame.

The big difference is in area and height allowance. This is pointed out in U.B.C. Tables Nos. 5-C and 5-D. For instance, a Group A-1 occupancy is allowed only in Type II-FR. The area is restricted to 29,900 square feet and limited to four stories. Otherwise, Group A-1 occupancy is not allowed in anything but Type I construction. Type II-FR construction is probably the most common type of commercial and industrial construction where tall or extra large buildings are not needed.

Type II-N Construction

Most people think of Type II-N buildings as stock steel buildings such as service stations, Butler buildings or even the little metal sheds put out by Wards and Sears. Actually, any building that is entirely noncombustible could be a Type II-N building.

A Type II-N building is not required to be protected but must be of noncombustible material. The area and height of a Type II-N building is limited.

I mentioned that stock steel buildings are in this category. Even though the building itself is rated as noncombustible, the skin of the building on the side opposite the fire can get red hot, and will ignite anything touching it. Therefore, allow plenty of setback room for metal buildings, both from the property line and from adjacent buildings.

What can you do to make a Type II-N building into a Type II 1-hour building? Add a layer of 3/4-inch sheetrock to the wall and ceiling surfaces. If the buildings are to be used for miscellaneous storage, install sheetrock on the outside of the frame and attach the skin directly over it. This also reduces the possibility of damage to the sheetrock. When sheetrock is broken, the one-hour fire-resistive rating vanishes.

Type III Construction

Buildings with Type III construction must have four-hour fire-resistive exterior walls. But the other elements need only have a one-hour rating (Type III 1-hour) or no rating (Type III-N). We used to call this construction "masonry walls and wood guts."

One item is of special interest in the Type III category. The height is limited to 65 feet (1-hour) and 55 feet (N). But generally, the number of stories is limited to two in most occupancy groups. Have you ever seen a 65-foot-high, two-story building?

Type IV Construction

Underfloor areas in Type IV buildings must be ventilated. That's because the floors are constructed of wood. The three higher types usually are built on slabs or over basements. Underfloor ventilation requirements will be discussed in detail in Chapter Six.

Type IV-HT (Heavy Timber) is the old "mill-type" construction. This is found in many older industrial buildings, particularly

Figure 4-6   Coast Guard Station Dock—Typical
Type IV-Heavy Timber Construction

on the west coast. Warehouses and shipping docks are usually
Type IV-HT construction, which is characterized by massive
beams and joists.

Columns must be at least 8" x 8" to be classed as heavy timber.
Framed timber trusses or glued-laminated arches that support
floors must be at least 6" x 8". Glued-laminated beams on roofs
must be at least 4" x 6". Beams or girders that support floors must
be at least 6" x 10", but on roofs they need only be 6" x 8". Framed timber trusses for roofs that do not support floors must be 4 inches thick. Roofs must be at least 2 inches thick.

These measurements are nominal lumber sizes. This means that
a 4" x 8" is only about 3½" x 7½", finished on four sides.

Why is something so combustible allowed? Fire safety is not
necessarily a matter of a structure being non-combustible. It's also
how long it will stand after it begins burning. In other words, the
bigger the timber, the longer it will take to burn to the point of
failure or collapse.

Type V Construction

Type V buildings are wood frame or a combination of wood frame
and any other material if the exterior walls are not required to be
noncombustible. In the Type V 1-hour, however, all elements must

be protected for at least one hour. Type V-N buildings are usually single- and multi-family dwellings. Multi-family dwellings are restricted to two stories, while single-family dwellings may be three stories.

Most higher types of construction could easily become Type V by not fulfilling all the requirements of U.B.C. Table No. 17-A.

5

Fire Resistance in Buildings

Many building codes were enacted to promote fire safety in buildings. Chapter Four of this book explained how types of construction are used to provide fire resistance. Some materials such as steel, concrete, glass and most mineral compounds are noncombustible. But are they *nondestructible* as well?

Not on your life! For a long time it was thought that if a material was made of iron or steel it was completely noncombustible. Basically they were right. But they didn't consider what might happen if those materials were heated beyond a certain limit.

Noncombustible is *Not* Nondestructible
Several years ago the Chicago Coliseum caught fire and was a total loss. It was considered noncombustible yet the destruction couldn't have been more complete if the structure had been made of matchsticks and tissue paper.

Two things happened. One, the area was filled with paper, cloth and many other highly combustible materials. Two, the fire gained such great headway in such a short time that fire fighters were unable to control it. What happened to the noncombustible building? Well, it didn't burn. It simply melted into a mass of

Figure 5-1 A good reason for building fire resistance into a building. Fire resistance will not guarantee that a building won't burn, but it does give some assurance of restricting the burning until fire fighters have arrived and all occupants have escaped.

twisted, warped iron and steel girders. Too much faith was placed on the alarm system and not enough effort made in fire prevention.

This is what I try to explain when someone approaches me with a tin building (aluminum buildings are equally bad, sometimes worse) and tells me there's nothing to worry about because it's noncombustible. It's also why steel frame buildings need fire-resistiveness built into them.

Fire Resistiveness—How Do We Get It?
After most major fires everyone looks around and starts thinking about fire safety. Actually, the number of people who die as the

result of burns is remarkably low. And the number of people who die as the result of being trapped and burned to death is even lower.

This doesn't mean we should look the other way when it comes to fire-resistiveness. But it also doesn't mean that after a major fire we should run to our legislators demanding more laws and legislation aimed at eliminating death by fire. What we should do is determine if present laws are being enforced adequately. Often, construction budgets are the problem. Owners and contractors are always trying to find ways to cut costs. Frequently, personal safety is set aside—but only temporarily, or so we say.

Death by fire usually results from one of two things. People are either trapped in the blaze itself and die as a result of burns or they are in an enclosed area and die of asphyxiation from smoke or toxic fumes. Of the two, the latter is more frequent. Building fire-resistiveness into a building doesn't mean that it won't burn or that people won't die from toxic fumes. All it really means is that the rate of combustion will be slowed down enough to give everyone a chance to get out.

One thing this business has taught me is that *nothing is fireproof.* There are materials that are noncombustible and those that are fire-resistive. Noncombustible material may allow or even transmit enough heat to maintain a certain amount of combustion even though the material itself won't burn. Fire-resistive materials may burn when flame is applied, but the degree to which they will maintain combustion when the flame is removed varies from material to material.

Noncombustible Materials

The easiest way to understand *noncombustible* from a building standpoint is to consider its definition in Chapter 4 of the U.B.C.:

Section 415. Noncombustible as applied to building construction material means a material which, in the form in which it is used, is either one of the following:

1. Material of which no part will ignite and burn when subjected to fire. Any material conforming to U.B.C. Standard 4-1 shall be considered noncombustible within the meaning of this section.

2. Material having a structural base of noncombustible material as defined in Item No. 1 above, with a surfacing material not over 1/8 inch thick which has a flame-spread rating of 50 or less.

Noncombustible does not apply to surface finish materials. Material required to be noncombustible for reduced clearances to flues, heating appliances, or other sources of high temperature shall refer to material conforming to Item No. 1. No material shall be classed as noncombustible which is subject to increase in combustibility or flame-spread rating, beyond the limits herein established, through the effects of age, moisture or other atmospheric condition.

Flame-spread rating as used herein refers to rating obtained according to tests conducted as specified in U.B.C. Standard No. 42-1.

Flame-spread

Now that you know what noncombustible means, what about *fire-resistive*? This is a term that will appear again and again throughout this book. But to understand this term you must first understand *flame-spread*.

In addition to the fire resistance required of structural members and the fire-resistive rating of walls and ceilings, finish materials of walls and ceilings must have a flame-spread classification, which is based on occupancy. The flame-spread classification, however, does not apply to the Group M occupancy.

Flame-spread is classified in U.B.C. Table No. 42-A (Figure 5-2) as I, II, or III, although in some codes you may find it listed as Class A, B, or C. U.B.C. Table No. 42-B, also in Figure 5-2, shows the maximum flame-spread classification for the various occupancies. These finish requirements, however, do not apply to doors and windows or their frames and trim. Material which is less than 1/28 inch thick and cemented to the surface of walls and ceilings is also exempt if its flame-spread characteristics are less than paper under the same circumstances. If an automatic fire-extinguishing system is installed, the flame-spread classification may be reduced, but it can't be greater than Class III.

Determining flame-spread: A flame-spread rating is *not* a fire-resistive rating. It's a comparison of the time it takes flame to spread on the surface of a material with the time it takes the same flame to spread on untreated oak. Red oak has an arbitrary rating of ''100,'' and cement asbestos board has a rating of ''0.'' All other material is compared to this and rated accordingly. The flame-spread is not the only item considered in this rating or during the test. The density of the smoke developed and the amount of fuel consumed are also compared, using cement asbestos board and red oak as the basis for comparison.

TABLE NO. 42-A—FLAME-SPREAD CLASSIFICATION

MATERIAL QUALIFIED BY:	
Class	Tunnel Test
I	0- 25
II	26- 75
III	76-200

TABLE NO. 42-B—MAXIMUM FLAME-SPREAD CLASSIFICATIONS[4]

OCCUPANCY GROUP	ENCLOSED VERTICAL EXITWAYS	OTHER EXITWAYS[5]	ROOMS OR AREAS
A	I	II	III
E	I	II	III
I	I	II	II[1]
H	I	II	III[2]
B	I	II	III
R-1	I	II	III
R-3	III	III	III[3]
M	NO RESTRICTIONS		

[1]In rooms in which personal liberties of inmates are forcibly restrained, Class I material only shall be used.
[2]Over two stories shall be of Class II.
[3]Flame-spread provisions are not applicable to kitchens and bathrooms of Group R, Division 3 Occupancies.
[4]Foam plastics shall comply with the requirements specified in Section 1712.
[5]Finish classification is not applicable to interior walls and ceilings of exterior exit balconies.
From the Uniform Building Code, ©1982, ICBO.

Figure 5-2   Flame-spread Classifications

It's easy to see why cement asbestos board is used at "0," but what's so special about red oak? Red oak was chosen because of its uniform density and uniform burning rate, not because of its resistance to flames. Also, the smoke developed by burning red oak is more uniform than that of most woods.

Tunnel test: This is the method of testing material for flame-spread. It was developed by the Underwriter's Laboratory. The code, however, will recognize any independent testing lab equipped to make the same test. At present, to my knowledge, U.L. and one outfit in Texas are the only places equipped with the tunnel testing apparatus.

Building Code Standard 42-1-79 describes the testing equipment to be used and the method of testing for flame-spread. The "fire test chamber" is described as follows:

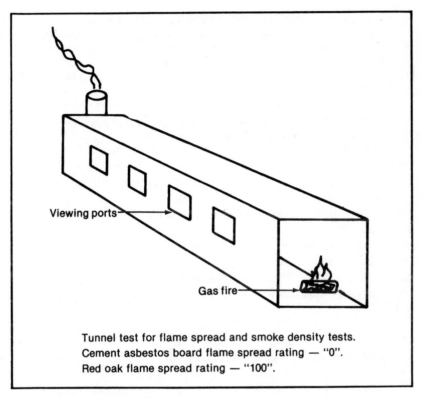

Viewing ports

Gas fire

Tunnel test for flame spread and smoke density tests.
Cement asbestos board flame spread rating — "0".
Red oak flame spread rating — "100".

Figure 5-3 Tunnel Test for Flame-spread and Smoke Density

The fire test chamber supplied with gas fuel of uniform quality shall be employed for this test method.

The fire test chamber is to consist of a horizontal duct having an inside width of 17½ inches plus or minus ½ inch, a depth of 12 inches plus or minus ½ inch measured from the bottom of the test chamber to the ledge of the inner walls on which the specimen is supported, and a length of 25 feet. The sides and base of the duct are to be lined with insulated masonry. One side is to be provided with draft-tight observation windows so that the entire length of the test sample may be observed from outside the fire-test chamber.

The top is to consist of removable noncombustible insulated structure of a size necessary to cover completely the fire test chamber and to accommodate the test samples. The top is to be designed so that it can be sealed against the leakage of air into the fire test chamber during the test, and it is to be designed to permit the attachment of test samples when necessary.

One end of the test chamber, designated as the "fire end," is to be provided with two gas burners delivering flames upward against the surface of the test sample, and 7½ inches plus or minus ½ inch below the under surface of the test sample. The burners are to be positioned transversely approximately 4 inches on each side of the center line of the furnace so that the flame is evenly distributed over the cross section of the furnace. . .

It goes on to establish the type and number of controls, the amount of gas metered in, the air allowed, and other test criteria. The room in which the test is made must have a free inflow of air during the test to ensure that the room is kept at atmospheric pressure during the test. The test chamber is then calibrated so that flame will spread 19'6" in 5½ minutes on red oak flooring. It is also zeroed in with the photoelectric cells for determining the smoke density.

Computing flame-spread: The progress of the flame is observed, and when it has traveled 19½ feet, the time is noted. This is compared to the red oak by one of the following formulas:

• Where the time is 5½ minutes or less, it is 100 times 5½ divided by 19½.

• Where it took more than 5½ minutes, but less than 10 minutes, the formula is 100 times 5½ divided by the time it took the flame to spread 19½ feet plus 1/2 the difference between the result and 100.

• Where the flame did not travel the 19½ feet in 10 minutes, the formula is 100 times the distance in feet that it traveled divided by 19½.

Confusing, isn't it? This is one of those crazy tests which someone developed probably because no other type of equipment or measurement was available at the time. Since then, no one has bothered to make it simpler or more logical. The reasoning is, if it works, why bother?

Figure 5-2 shows U.B.C. Tables Nos. 42-A and 42-B. Table 42-A, *Flame-Spread Classification*, indicates that Class I material has a flame-spread rating of 0 to 25, or about 1/4 that of red oak. Class II material has a flame-spread rating of 26 to 75, or about 3/4 that of red oak. Class III material has a flame-spread rating of 76 to 225. On that basis, red oak at 100 comes under the Class III rating.

U.B.C. Table No. 42-B gives flame-spread requirements for finish material in various occupancies for stairs, corridors and rooms. Generally, you'll find that most wood products fall under the Class III category.

Determining Fire Resistance

Fire resistance of materials and assemblies is established in much the same manner. A sample is placed in a test chamber, fire is applied to one side, and thermocouples measure the temperature on the opposite side. If the temperature doesn't exceed 250 degrees on the exposed side for the time tested, the sample is rated accordingly regardless of its condition. If the sample is a load-bearing member, it is loaded and must support the load for the time required.

When a door or window is tested for a time rating, the entire assembly must be tested including the frame, hardware, and any other items that will be a part of the assembly in actual service. If any part of the assembly fails, the assembly is rated according to the time before failure. A door assembly that failed at 59 minutes would not have a one-hour rating but a 3/4-hour rating.

Wall covering materials such as sheetrock must undergo the fire test and then be subjected to a hose stream test. This test is made on duplicate samples after half the fire exposure time rating. Immediately after the fire is shut off, a hose stream is directed against the sample. The method of applying the stream, the size of the nozzle, the distance from the sample, and the water pressure are spelled out in the test procedures.

These test methods and procedures are found in the Building Code Standards, the book frequently referred to throughout the U.B.C. and in this book. The Standards book is a companion to the U.B.C. The layman, however, will seldom need to consult the Standards.

Openings in Fire Assemblies

So far we've concentrated on fire-resistive assemblies and coverings, but very little has been said about openings in these assemblies. Sooner or later most fire-resistive assemblies will have to be pierced for a variety of reasons—plumbing, wiring, or doors, for example. If you have a room that requires a certain amount of fire-resistiveness, what are you going to do about the doors? What about heat ducts and lighting fixtures? Also, changes are made after a structure is completed. Will the plumber or electrician create any problems when he pierces these assemblies?

Let's lead off with ductwork. Fire dampers must be installed wherever ductwork passes through a wall, ceiling or floor that is part of a fire-resistive assembly. These dampers may be in the duct itself or in a collar fastened to the wall or ceiling. But they must be capable of operating even if the duct is damaged. Dampers must be made to close when the temperature rises 50 degrees above the normal operating temperature. Dampers in ducts must be at least 16-gauge steel in ducts up to 18 inches in diameter, 12-gauge in ducts up to 36 inches in diameter, and 7-gauge in ducts over 36 inches in diameter.

Openings in area-separation walls must be protected according to the time requirements of the separation. In other words, if a four-hour separation is required, any openings would have to be protected for four hours. These assemblies must be operated by a fusible link on each side of the wall. A smoke detection device may be required for the fire assembly. A word of caution: Don't paint over them!

It isn't unusual to find fusible links that have been completely painted over with many coats of paint. Although paint isn't very thick, it can be sufficient to require a few degrees more of heat and a few minutes more of time where time and heat can be critical. As most of you know, the first five minutes of a fire are the most critical.

Structural members such as beams, trusses, floor joists, and rafters may be individually protected or protected by a fire-resistive ceiling of the same rating. Sometimes one method is more practical than another. If one-hour protection is sufficient, steel members may be painted with approved fire-retardant paint, provided they are not exposed to the weather. If the members are protected by a ceiling, the ceiling must be noncombustible and the assembly must be rated.

Allowable Openings

There can be small openings for pipe, duct, and electric boxes of ferrous metal provided there is not more than 100 square inches of opening for any 100 square feet of ceiling. You may have a client who wants to group four 100-inch openings at the center of a 400-square-foot ceiling, claiming there are only 100-square-inches in each 100-square-foot section. Is this a correct interpretation?

The 100 square feet in which those grouped openings are shown doesn't conform to the intent of the code. The code says "100

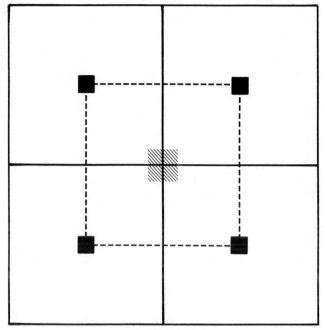

Allowable Openings

Each square with a solid line equals 100 square feet.

Solid squares indicate acceptable openings.

Broken lines indicate 100 square feet in which four groups of openings might erroneously be placed.

Figure 5-4 Allowable Openings

square inches in any 100 square feet." Your client's arrangement is not allowable. (See Figure 5-4.)

You may find yourself in situations where the exact interpretation of this is difficult. It's best to consult the inspector. Explain your problem and see if he has any suggestions.

Fire Rated Assemblies

The U.B.C. defines fire-resistive terminology in the following manner:

Fire Code is the Uniform Fire Code promulgated jointly by the Western Fire Chiefs' Association and the International Conference of Building Officials, as adopted by this jurisdiction.

Fire Resistance or *Fire-Resistive Construction* is construction to resist the spread of fire, details of which are specified in this code.

Fire-retardant Treated Wood is lumber or plywood impregnated with chemicals and which, when tested in accordance with U.B.C. Standard No. 42-1 for a period of 30 minutes, shall have a flame-spread of not over 25 and show no evidence of progressive combustion. Materials which may be exposed to the weather shall maintain this fire-retardant classification when tested in accordance with the rain and weathering tests of U.B.C. Standard No. 32-7.

All materials shall bear identification showing the fire performance rating thereof and, if intended for exterior use, shall be further identified to indicate suitability for exposure to the weather. Such identifications shall be issued by an approved agency having a service for inspection of materials at the factory.

The terms above are found in the definitions section (Chapter 4) of the U.B.C. Section 4306 (b) contains the following definitions:

Fire Assembly is the assembly of a fire door, fire windows, or fire damper, including all required hardware, anchorage, frames and sills. Fire dampers shall be fabricated and installed in accordance with U.B.C. Standard No. 43-7.

How do you achieve fire-resistive construction? Many combinations of materials will provide fire-resistiveness. Chapter 43 in the U.B.C. deals with this topic, U.B.C. Tables Nos. 43-A, 43-B and 43-C being especially helpful.

Fire-Resistive Construction

U.B.C. Table No. 43-A, *Minimum Protection of Structural Parts Based On Time Periods for Various Noncombustible Insulating Materials* applies to the structural frame and the exterior walls. A note of caution about U.B.C. tables: Check all footnotes. They often specify certain conditions that may apply to your project.

How does the inspector use this chart? First he'll check your plans and will note, for instance, that you have a steel 6" x 6" column encased in Grade A concrete (not including sandstone, granite or siliceous gravels). The concrete will be a minimum of 2½ inches thick around all portions of the steel column. Next, he'll consult U.B.C. Table No. 43-A, where he'll find that it just happens to be the first item listed. Reading across he'll note that 2½ inches of concrete provides a maximum 4-hour protection which is good enough for a Type I construction. This means that the 2½ inches of concrete should insulate the column from fire failure for at least four hours.

Will the concrete be up to it? The inspector consults your specs and determines that the concrete complies. Your structural frame qualifies for Type I construction.

Of course, your architect has probably done this already, and his specs should comply with the code. If not, the inspector will note this and probably return your plans for modification. He may downgrade the type of construction in your building. If he does, it may severely restrict the intended use of the building, as explained in Chapter Four.

Fire Resistance for Walls and Partitions

U.B.C. Table No. 43-B, *Rated Fire-Resistive Periods for Various Walls and Partitions,* will do for your walls and partitions what Table 43-A did for the structural frame. The process of determining the fire rating is exactly the same. If you were designing the building, which one would you elect to use? That depends on a number of things.

First, you must determine the fire-resistive rating you need. Then select the combinations of construction that would give you that rating. From there it's a matter of which materials are available and the overall cost of the job. But remember, the code only requires the *minimum* rating. How far you go above the minimum is up to you and your client.

U.B.C. Table No. 43-B gives the fire-resistive rating for different wall assemblies. Any substitution in these assemblies does not carry a rating unless it is shown elsewhere in the table. Each assembly was tested and rated with the construction noted. Only that construction carries that particular rating. In one-hour construction, ceilings may be omitted over unusable space, and floors may be omitted under usable space.

Calculating the rating is the same as for Table 43-A. Select the hour rating you want, then look for the components that will give you that rating.

Fire Resistance for Floors and Roofs

U.B.C. Table No. 43-C, *Minimum Protection for Floor and Roof Systems,* does for floors and roofs exactly what the other two tables did for the structural frame and the walls and ceilings. The table also works in the same manner as the other two.

Penetration must be watched for in this category. Fire-resistive floors must be continuous; all openings for mechanical and electrical equipment must be enclosed as specified in Section 1706. There are two exceptions. One is that some pipes may be installed within or through fire-resistive floors as long as they don't reduce the required fire resistance of the assembly.

The second exception states that the provisions of Section 1706 do not apply when openings comply with results of tests made under provisions of Section 4302(b). The result of these two exceptions, of course, is that you must prove your point to the inspector. It may be faster and cheaper to figure out another solution.

Protective Covering

Now that we've examined the method of determining flame-spread and some of the fire-resistive standards, let's take a look at the little things that can cause trouble.

Let's start with protective covering. The thickness of protective covering can't be less than that set forth in U.B.C. Table No. 43-A, except as modified in Chapter 43. This pertains to all products, from fire-resistive paint to concrete. The figures shown must be the net thickness of the protecting materials and must not include any hollow space in back of the protection.

Where required, metal ties must be embedded in transverse joints of unit masonry to protect steel columns. These ties must meet the requirements of U.B.C. Table No. 43-A. Unit masonry, of course, is brick, block or any combination of the two.

Conduit and pipes cannot be embedded in required fire protection or structural members. If the fire-resistive covering on columns is exposed to possible damage, it must be protected.

Fire Doors

Fire doors must have automatic or self-closing hardware. Automatic closing devices must be equipped with heat-actuated devices on each side of the wall at the top of the opening. If the ceiling is more than three feet above the opening, there must be a fusible link located at the ceiling on each side of the wall.

Glazed openings of 100 square inches are permitted, provided they are wire-glass or heat tempered. Doors of 3/4-hour rating may have 84 square feet of area. That means you could have a delivery door approximately 8' x 10'6''.

Windows required to have a 3/4-hour fire-resistive rating may not be larger than 84 square feet, with neither width nor height exceeding 12 feet. The glass must be not less than 1/4 inch thick and reinforced with wire mesh. Glass must be held in place by steel glazing angles except in casement windows where clips may be used.

One more note about fire doors. If the Fire Marshal inspects your plans, he'll probably insist that all fire doors be marked **Fire Door. . .Do Not Obstruct.**

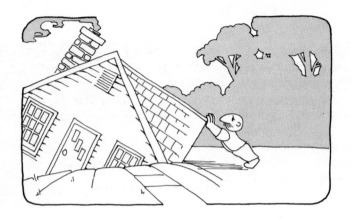

6
Foundations

We've explored occupancies, compared types of construction with occupancies, and discussed fire-resistiveness of materials and how they are rated. Now let's get to the building itself.

One of the most important parts of your new structure is the foundation. Without a firm base on which to place your building, anything that follows is useless. But before we get to the foundation, we must consider the building site.

Site Consideration
At the site, check for the following: Do you have a water problem? (Either too much or too little?) Does the land slope excessively? Will you need to move dirt to place the building on the property? What are you going to do with the cut-banks that remain? What will happen to the excess dirt remaining after the backfill has been completed?

And all you're trying to do is build a house! These things may sound somewhat remote from the building code, yet they are in one way or another part of the code.

Figure 6-1 Site preparation is probably one of the first physical acts of construction. In this case they are working in a new subdivision and streets and walks have already been installed.

Say you have a water problem. How does that come under the building code? Probably the first thing the inspector will want to know is how much water you have and what you plan to do with it. Are you planning on using a sump pump, a drainage system to carry the water to a lower portion of land, or do you have some other method in mind such as dumping it into a sanitary sewer (not usually allowed). Perhaps you were planning to leave it there and waterproof the basement. Maybe the building doesn't have a basement. In that case, will your house sit on piles or on fill? Will you have a post and beam floor or a slab on grade?

These are some of the first questions you should consider. You can bet they're some of the first questions the building inspector is going to ask.

Make sure you know exactly where the property lines are, that the corners are properly staked, and that a surveyor has set the stakes for your house. Yes, this will cost a little more. But I've seen houses that encroached on the legal setback area and several that even went over the property line. One building was even on the wrong lot.

Funny? You bet—unless you're the one caught in the net. It's not only embarrassing but awfully expensive. Using a surveyor can be your cheapest insurance against such trouble.

Excavation and Fill

Chapter 29 of the U.B.C. covers the quality and design of structural materials used in excavations and foundations. This chapter is backed up by Chapter 70 in the Appendix of the U.B.C., which regulates grading on private property. Its purpose is to safeguard life, limb, property and public welfare. It also lists the conditions for permits and permit fees. (See U.B.C. Tables Nos. 70-A and 70-B, Figure 6-2.)

Section 7003 of the U.B.C. states that a permit is required for certain types of excavations and landfills. You do not need a permit, however, for the following:

1. Grading in an isolated, self-contained area if there is no danger apparent to private or public property.

2. An excavation below finished grade for basements and footings of a building, retaining wall or other structure authorized by a valid building permit.

3. Cemetery graves.

4. Refuse disposal sites controlled by other regulations.

5. Excavations for wells, tunnels or utilities.

6. Mining, quarrying, excavating, processing, stockpiling of rock, sand, gravel, aggregate or clay where established and provided for by law, provided such operations do not affect the lateral support or increase the stresses upon any adjacent or contiguous property.

7. Exploratory excavations under the direction of soil engineers or engineering geologists.

8. An excavation which (a) is less than 2 feet in depth, or (b) which does not create a cut slope greater than 5 feet in height or steeper than one and one-half horizontal to one vertical.

9. A fill less than 1 foot in depth and placed on natural terrain with a slope flatter than five horizontal to one vertical, or less than 3 feet in depth, not intended to support structures, which does not exceed 50 cubic yards on any one lot and does not obstruct a drainage course.

So you see, there are many things you can do about digging and filling. In fact, under the code, unless you're working on steep slopes, few operations actually require a permit. So I won't spend a great deal of time on it. One item, however, that does need further mention is backfilling.

Backfilling

Proper backfilling is something few contractors really know much about. This is unfortunate because nothing can spoil a good job like a sloppy backfill slowly settling.

TABLE NO. 70-A—GRADING PLAN REVIEW FEES

50 cubic yards or less	No Fee
51 to 100 cubic yards	$10.00
101 to 1000 cubic yards	15.00
1001 to 10,000 cubic yards	20.00

10,001 to 100,000 cubic yards—$20.00 for the first 10,000 cubic yards, plus $10.00 for each additional 10,000 cubic yards or fraction thereof.

100,001 to 200,000 cubic yards—$110.00 for the first 100,000 cubic yards, plus $6.00 for each additional 10,000 cubic yards or fraction thereof.

200,001 cubic yards or more—$170.00 for the first 200,000 cubic yards, plus $3.00 for each additional 10,000 cubic yards or fraction thereof.

Other Fees:

Additional plan review required by changes, additions or revisions to approved plans .... $15.00 per hour (minimum charge—one-half hour)

TABLE NO. 70-B—GRADING PERMIT FEES

50 cubic yards or less	$10.00
51 to 100 cubic yards	15.00

101 to 1000 cubic yards—$15.00 for the first 100 cubic yards plus $7.00 for each additional 100 cubic yards or fraction thereof.

1001 to 10,000 cubic yards—$78.00 for the first 1000 cubic yards, plus $6.00 for each additional 1000 cubic yards or fraction thereof.

10,001 to 100,000 cubic yards—$132.00 for the first 10,000 cubic yards, plus $27.00 for each additional 10,000 cubic yards or fraction thereof.

100,001 cubic yards or more—$375.00 for the first 100,000 cubic yards, plus $15.00 for each additional 10,000 cubic yards or fraction thereof.

Other Inspections and Fees:

1. Inspections outside of normal business hours .... $15.00 per hour (minimum charge—two hours)
2. Reinspection fee assessed under provisions of Section 305 (g) .... $15.00 each
3. Inspections for which no fee is specifically indicated ... $15.00 per hour (minimum charge—one-half hour)

The fee for a grading permit authorizing additional work to that under a valid permit shall be the difference between the fee paid for the original permit and the fee shown for the entire project.

From the Uniform Building Code, ©1982, ICBO.

Figure 6-2   Plan-checking fees and grading permit fees

You've probably seen homes in your area where the steps have pulled away from the house or where shrubbery around the house has sunk. Usually this is because the area around the basement backfill wasn't properly compacted. If backfilling is done without proper supervision, only a density test can determine if it was done correctly.

Compaction
The U.B.C. calls for 90 percent compaction. But in dry climates this is seldom achieved. Dry soil packs loosely. When a contractor passes over it with a wheeled vehicle—the usual form of compaction—all he does is compact the top several inches. Seldom is the backfill placed into the trench in layers, so there isn't much more than six to ten inches of dirt at the most that receives compaction.

Water settling is a very effective method of compaction. But it takes longer, so few builders even consider it. Eventually, Mother Nature does the job. She compacts the earth by settling. This settling can be gradual or it can happen all at once. Suddenly the home owner finds his shrubbery in a hole that wasn't there before or his steps separated from his house.

For proper compaction, the fill material should be placed in layers (not to exceed 12 inches deep) and then compacted. A little water will help if you are in a dry area. The deeper the excavation, the more difficult it will be and the longer it will take to get proper compaction. Compacting a water line trench three feet deep won't be as difficult as a sewer trench seven feet deep. There are several machines on the market, hand held and powered by small gasoline engines that do this job very well. They're known in the trade as "wacker-tampers."

Excavation Cut Slopes
According to the code, cut slopes for permanent excavation must not be steeper than two horizontal to one vertical. The same applies to slopes for permanent fill. (See Figure 6-3.) Those are units of measure: feet, inches, or yards. Don't place fill or surcharge next to any building or struc-

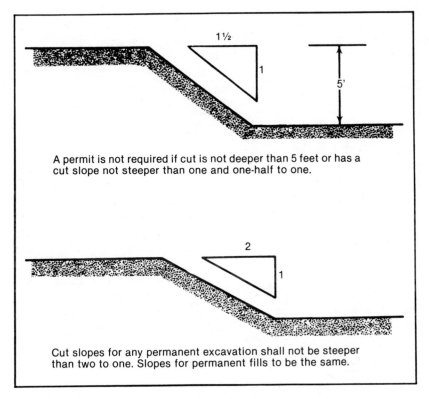

A permit is not required if cut is not deeper than 5 feet or has a cut slope not steeper than one and one-half to one.

Cut slopes for any permanent excavation shall not be steeper than two to one. Slopes for permanent fills to be the same.

Figure 6-3   Cut Slope Dimensions for Excavations

ture unless the building can withstand the additional loads caused by the fill. The usual curing time for concrete in basement walls is about seven days. Only then is it safe to backfill against it.

Cut-Slope Setbacks

In steep, hilly country you may find that your project is subject to setbacks from the top of cuts and toes of fills. Chapter 70, U.B.C., has several illustrations of this, shown here in Figure 6-4. These setbacks are minimums. In some areas the inspector, acting on the recommendations of soils engineers or his own knowledge of the area, will require greater dimensions than those shown in Figure 6-4.

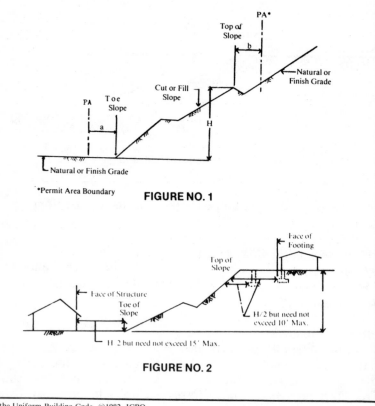

TABLE NO. 70-C
REQUIRED SETBACKS FROM PERMIT AREA BOUNDARY
(IN FEET)

	SETBACKS	
H	a	b¹
Under 5	0	1
5 - 30	H/2	H/5
Over 30	15	6

¹Additional width may be required for interceptor drain.

FIGURE NO. 1

FIGURE NO. 2

From the Uniform Building Code, ©1982, ICBO.

Figure 6-4   Required Setbacks

In some instances retaining walls may be used to shorten some of these distances. But, unless the cut or fill is shallow, you may be required to have your wall engineered.

Fill Must Be Stable

The quality of fills, fill material, and fill compaction is just as critical as that for excavations. The book says that fills used to support the foundation of any building or structure must be placed according to acceptable engineering practice. This means they should be treated like backfill and should be placed by layering. Roller compactors may be used to achieve the proper density.

On large commercial buildings the owner or architect may call for compaction testing of backfills on trenches, foundations, or other excavations. Compaction tests are seldom required for standard residences unless they're built on a large fill in a new area. These tests may be required for subdivisions in hilly areas where a lot of cuts and fills were necessary.

If the fill has been in place for at least a year or two without any problems, it's probably stable.

Few building departments are equipped to make compaction tests. That's one reason why compaction is frequently overlooked by many inspectors. But if the inspector is on his toes and suspects there's a problem, he can order that tests be made, at the expense of the owner. This can be difficult and expensive because many areas don't have adequate testing facilities.

Soils Classification and Geology

Problems are not always caused by fill material or its placement or compaction. Sometimes it's what is under the fill that causes trouble. Here's what Section 2904 of the U.B.C. has to say about soil:

Section 2904 (a) Soil Classification: General. For the purposes of this chapter, the definition and classification of soil materials for use in Table No. 29-B (see Figure 6-5) shall be according to U.B.C. Standard No. 29-1.

TABLE NO. 29-B—ALLOWABLE FOUNDATION AND LATERAL PRESSURE

CLASS OF MATERIALS[2]	ALLOWABLE FOUNDATION PRESSURE LBS. SQ. FT.[3]	LATERAL BEARING LBS./SQ. FT./FT. OF DEPTH BELOW NATURAL GRADE[4]	LATERAL SLIDING[1]	
			COEFFICIENT[5]	RESISTANCE LBS./SQ. FT.[6]
1. Massive Crystalline Bedrock	4000	1200	.79	
2. Sedimentary and Foliated Rock	2000	400	.35	
3. Sandy Gravel and/or Gravel (GW and GP)	2000	200	.35	
4. Sand, Silty Sand, Clayey Sand, Silty Gravel and Clayey Gravel (SW, SP, SM, SC, GM and GC)	1500	150	.25	
5. Clay, Sandy Clay, Silty Clay and Clayey Silt (CL, ML, MH and CH)	1000[7]	100		130

[1]Lateral bearing and lateral sliding resistance may be combined.

[2]For soil classifications OL, OH and PT (i.e., organic clays and peat), a foundation investigation shall be required.

[3]All values of allowable foundation pressure are for footings having a minimum width of 12 inches and a minimum depth of 12 inches into natural grade. Except as in Footnote 7 below, increase of 20 percent allowed for each additional foot of width and/or depth to a maximum value of three times the designated value.

[4]May be increased the amount of the designated value for each additional foot of depth to a maximum of 15 times the designated value. Isolated poles for uses such as flagpoles or signs and poles used to support buildings which are not adversely affected by a ½-inch motion at ground surface due to short-term lateral loads may be designed using lateral bearing values equal to two times the tabulated values.

[5]Coefficient to be multiplied by the dead load.

[6]Lateral sliding resistance value to be multiplied by the contact area. In no case shall the lateral sliding resistance exceed one half the dead load.

[7]No increase for width is allowed.

From the Uniform Building Code, ©1982, ICBO.

Figure 6-5 Allowable Foundation and Lateral Pressure

(b) Expansive Soil. When the expansive characteristics of a soil are to be determined, the procedures shall be in accordance with U.B.C. Standard No. 29-2 and the soil shall be classified according to Table No. 29-C. (See Figure 6-6.) *Foundations for structures resting on soils with an expansion index greater than 20, as determined by U.B.C. Standard No. 29-2, shall require special design consideration. In the event the soil expansion index varies with depth, the weighted index shall be determined according to Table No. 29-D.* (See Figure 6-6.)

The only way you're going to get this information (if the inspector requires you to have it) is by employing a soils geologist. He'll get his figures through core samples, ag-

TABLE NO. 29-C—CLASSIFICATION OF EXPANSIVE SOIL

EXPANSION INDEX	POTENTIAL EXPANSION
0-20	Very low
21-50	Low
51-90	Medium
91-130	High
Above 130	Very high

TABLE NO. 29-D—WEIGHTED EXPANSION INDEX[1]

DEPTH INTERVAL[2]	WEIGHT FACTOR
0-1	0.4
1-2	0.3
2-3	0.2
3-4	0.1
Below 4	0

[1]The weighted expansion index for nonuniform soils is determined by multiplying the expansion index for each depth interval by the weight factor for that interval and summing the products.

[2]Depth in feet below the ground surface.

From the Uniform Building Code, ©1982, ICBO.

Figure 6-6 Expansive Soil Classification and Weighted Expansion Index

gregate testing, and so forth. It may be expensive but is seldom required except on large jobs or where the soil may be questionable.

Soil under pressure can do some pretty strange things. I recall a highway that was placed across an area of thick, black peat soil that extended downward several hundred feet in some places. This land was subject to high moisture content because it was in a river bottom. The fill was made from material selected by the highway department. Even before the fill was completed, there was trouble with uneven settling. About the same time, several farmers noted huge "land boils" rising in their fields. It was found that when the roadway settled, the displaced material caused lateral forces to push up the adjacent fields. Corrective action was both costly and time consuming.

TABLE NO. 29-A—FOUNDATIONS FOR STUD BEARING WALLS—MINIMUM REQUIREMENTS[1] [2]

NUMBER OF FLOORS SUPPORTED BY THE FOUNDATION[3]	THICKNESS OF FOUNDATION WALL (Inches)		WIDTH OF FOOTING (Inches)	THICKNESS OF FOOTING (Inches)	DEPTH BELOW UNDISTURBED GROUND SURFACE (Inches)
	CONCRETE	UNIT MASONRY			
1	6	6	12	6	12
2	8	8	15	7	18
3	10	10	18	8	24

[1]Where unusual conditions or frost conditions are found, footings and foundations shall be as required in Section 2907 (a).

[2]The ground under the floor may be excavated to the elevation of the top of the footing.

[3]Foundations may support a roof in addition to the stipulated number of floors. Foundations supporting roofs only shall be as required for supporting one floor.

From the Uniform Building Code, ©1982, ICBO.

Figure 6-7   Foundations for Stud Bearing Walls

Foundations and Frost Line

Now let's take a look at the foundation itself. Requirements for foundations vary considerably around the country. The code requires footings, or footers, to be placed below frost grade or as shown in U.B.C. Table No. 29-A (Figure 6-7).

Frost grade varies from city to city. There may even be variances within the counties. Here in Kennewick, Washington, the frost depth is figured for building purposes at 24 inches. All footings and water lines must be at least that deep. But, for practical reasons the city elected to install all water lines at 36 inches. This allows the water lines to be brought in below the foundation, except for basements.

It isn't always necessary to excavate for your footings. If your lot is in a low area and you plan to fill after the house is constructed, you may place the footings on the surface, excavating only enough so that the footing will be level. However, when the house is completed and the fill material brought in, the footings must be at or below the frost line. This, of course, is the bottom of the footing pad—not the bottom of the footing wall. Figure 6-8 shows this measurement and other footing and foundation requirements. Typical footings and foundation walls are shown in Figure 6-9.

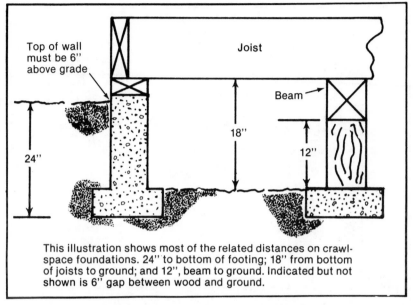

Top of wall must be 6'' above grade

Joist

Beam

18''

24''

12''

This illustration shows most of the related distances on crawl-space foundations. 24'' to bottom of footing; 18'' from bottom of joists to ground; and 12'', beam to ground. Indicated but not shown is 6'' gap between wood and ground.

Figure 6-8 Foundation Requirements

In preparing your site for the foundation, bear in mind that all stumps and roots must be removed from the soil to a depth of at least 12 inches below the surface of the ground under your structure. Also, when you're finished with the building there shouldn't be any form material or work scraps under the house or buried in the backfill. This reduces the possibility of termites.

If you had to dig down to put in your footings to the frost line, make sure that your crawl space is at least 18 inches below any joists. This is shown in Figure 6-8.

If you're going to install an underfloor furnace, you'll need to furnish some additional space, plus a crawl hole large enough to allow the heating plant to be removed or serviced without dismantling. Pipes and ducts must not interfere with access to or within any crawl space.

All accessible underfloor space must have an access hole at least 18'' x 24''. Note the word "accessible." That's just what it means. It can't be hidden in a closet or under a rug, and 18 x 24 is the *minimum* size.

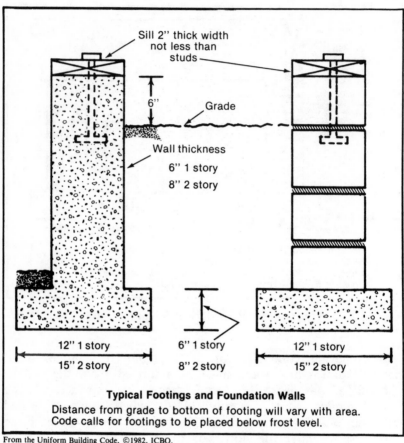

Typical Footings and Foundation Walls

Distance from grade to bottom of footing will vary with area.
Code calls for footings to be placed below frost level.

From the Uniform Building Code, ©1982, ICBO.

Figure 6-9 Residential Foundations

Underfloor Ventilation

Whenever you have an underfloor area created by a crawl space but which is not a basement or a usable space, or a space that is not used for habitation, you must provide adequate ventilation. This may be done by cutting vent holes in the foundation walls or by mechanical means such as a fan. Vent holes must have a net area of 1½ square feet for each 25 linear feet of exterior foundation wall. To reduce dry rot in the foundation, arrange the vents to give cross ventilation to all areas of the unused space.

Figure 6-10 Prefabricated Wall Vent Cast in Wall at Time of Pouring

Figure 6-11 Corrugated Sheet Metal Window Well Fixture Surrounding Crawl Space Access

Vent holes must be covered with corrosion-resistant wire mesh not less than 1/4 inch or more than 1/2 inch in any dimension. This keeps your crawl space from becoming a maternity ward for cats.

Prefabricated vents, like those shown in Figures 6-10 and 6-11, are now available. They're made of plastic or galvanized metal, complete with screen, louvered cover, and a hinged flap. Many people feel that to have warm floors in winter, they must cover their vents. This isn't necessarily so, but hinged flaps are available and it is permissible to use them. The only drawback is that the vents are often left covered in the spring, which can lead to dry rot and other problems.

Foundation Plates

On the top of the foundation wall is a wooden member called a *plate*. This is required whether the foundation wall surrounds a crawl space or a basement. It is *not* required, however, if the rest of the structure is masonry. The plate is normally a 2 x 6 laid flat and fastened to the foundation wall with bolts that were placed in the concrete when the foundation slab was laid.

I mentioned that the plate is usually a 2 x 6 laid flat. That's what is normally used in my area, but the code merely states that the plate will be used. Section 2517(c)3 states that all plates, sills, and sleepers must be treated wood or Foundation-grade redwood or cedar. This reduces the hazard of termites. If you don't have a termite problem, you can use any wood approved by the inspector.

Proper installation of anchor bolts and plates is shown in Figures 6-12 and 6-13 and in the sketch in Figure 6-9.

Bolting the plate to the foundation wall requires 1/2-inch steel bolts placed to a depth of 10 inches in concrete or 15 inches in masonry foundations. These bolts are placed at intervals not to exceed 6 feet. There must be at least two bolts in each piece of plate material and neither may be more than 12 inches from the end. That means that an 8-foot plate would need two anchor bolts, but a 9-foot piece would require three.

A big problem is that these bolts are often placed incorrectly—as though there's a continuous 26-foot piece of plate material. When the framers come along to splice the plate, several anchor bolts won't conform. Some builders keep extra plate material on hand for the foundation subcontractors. But this isn't always possible and it doesn't always work, anyway.

Figure 6-12 Foundation Bolts Cast in Place in Foundation Wall

Figure 6-13 Foundation Plates Installed. Bolts are properly placed within 12 inches of the end of the plate.

You'll find information about foundation plates and sills in Sections 2905(d) and 2517(b). U.B.C. Table No. 29-A (Figure 6-7) lists the size of the footing and foundation wall for one-, two- and three-story buildings. In the right-hand column note *Depth of Foundation Below Natural Surface of Ground and Finish Grade.* Previously I mentioned that the foundation must go to the frost line, but if you're in a frost-free area this would be the depth of the footing according to the code.

Anchor bolts are supposed to keep the house anchored to the foundation, but I have some misgivings about their effectiveness. I have several photos of homes in earth-quake and tornado zones. In these photos the anchor bolts and the plates are still in place—it's the structure that's missing. But at the moment there's no viable alternative to anchor bolts.

Post and Beam Foundation

Many houses were built on the post and beam principle, without solid concrete or masonry foundations. The code doesn't prohibit this. It simply ignores it. What it does say is set forth in Section 2907(b):

Bearing walls. Bearing walls shall be supported on masonry or concrete foundations or piles or other approved foundation system which shall be of sufficient size to support all loads. Where a design is not provided, the minimum foundation requirements for stud bearing walls shall be as set forth in Table 29-A. (See Figure 6-7.)

Exceptions: 1. A one-story wood or metal frame building not used for human occupancy and not over 400 square feet in floor area may be constructed with walls supported on a wood foundation plate when approved by the building official.

2. The support of buildings by posts embedded in earth shall be designed as specified in Section 2907(f). Wood posts or poles embedded in earth shall be pressure treated with an approved preservative. Steel posts or poles shall be protected as specified in Section 2908(h).

Confusing, isn't it? If you want to use a "post and beam" foundation, the building inspector will have to approve your plans. This means that if the inspector is inexperienced, is not an engineer, or just doesn't like post and beam con-

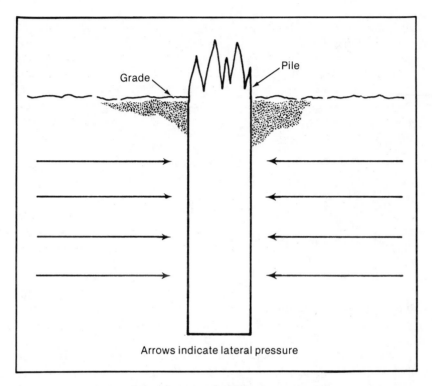
Arrows indicate lateral pressure

Figure 6-14   Direction of Lateral Pressure

struction, you may run into difficulty. Therefore, it's best to know what you're doing so you can convince him.

Pole Buildings
These are generally agricultural or light industrial buildings. They're referred to in the second exception to Section 2907(b) mentioned above.

Section 2907(f) describes how to calculate the depth of embedment to get the required lateral constraint to support your load. This lateral force is illustrated in Figure 6-14.

To calculate these pressures you must know what the loading will be on your building. We'll discuss loads and loading in the next chapter. But I suggest you employ a structural engineer to give you the load values. If you are constructing an engineered building, however, these values should be part of your building plans and specifications.

Different Types of Foundations

There are many foundations designed for large multi-story buildings, unusual soil types, extreme climatic conditions or any combination of these. The following are typical foundation piles:

- Round wood piles.
- Uncased cast-in-place concrete piles.
- Metal-cased concrete piles.
- Pre-cast concrete piles.
- Pre-cast, pre-stressed concrete piles.
- Structural steel piles.
- Concrete-filled steel pipe piles.

These piles are usually driven or placed in the ground and covered by slabs. The size of the pile, its depth in the ground, and the number required are determined by complex formulas which I won't go into. I will point out, however, that the type of pile used depends on lateral pressures in different types and conditions of soils as well as on the loads to be carried. This information is listed in U.B.C. Table 29-B, *Foundation and Allowable Lateral Pressure;* Table 29-C, *Classification of Expansive Soil;* and Table 29-D, *Weighted Expansion Index.* (See Figures 6-5 and 6-6.)

Footing and Foundation Summary

Most small contractors never have to deal with the more sophisticated foundations. If you do, have a structural engineer design them. This prevents problems and can really help when you approach the building inspector for approval of your plans.

In calculating your concrete foundation wall, be sure to make the wall high enough to be at least 6 inches above grade. Here's what I mean. If the footing must go 24 inches below grade, the distance between the top of the wall and the bottom of the footing must be at least 30 inches. The difference of 6 inches is to keep any wooden members at least that far above any normal amount of rain or other moisture.

You may use a stepped footing if the ground slopes too much. Section 2907(c) states that the foundation must be level if your ground slopes more than one foot in ten, or it may be stepped so that both the top and bottom of the foundation are level. This means that if your lot slopes too much, you can step-down your foundation and use framing material to finish the walls up to the plate line of the first floor.

Remember to protect adjoining property from work you're doing on your lot. If, for instance, by leveling your lot the finish grade will be higher than that of adjoining property, you must protect that property from your fill material. This can be done by a slope setback, as shown in Figure 6-3, or by building a retaining wall, or both. If, on the other hand, you wish to excavate to level your lot, you must protect the adjoining property by the same type of cut bank or a retaining wall. If the hillside is steep, the procedure shown in Figure 6-4 may be necessary.

Retaining Walls

There isn't too much in the code about retaining walls. Section 2308(b) covers them very briefly:

Retaining Walls. Retaining walls shall be designed to resist the lateral pressure of the retained material in accordance with accepted engineering practice. Walls retaining drained earth may be designed for pressure equivalent to that exerted by a fluid weighing not less than 30 pounds per cubic foot and having a depth equal to that of the retained earth. Any surcharge shall be in addition to the equivalent fluid pressure.

Most inspectors require the footing of a retaining wall to go at least to the frost line, the same as any footing. They're not really as concerned about the danger of frost heaving as they are about the wall tipping if the load behind it becomes too great. As for thickness, my rule of thumb is that a retaining wall up to 6 feet high should be at least 8 inches thick. Walls higher than 6 feet should be engineered to determine the thickness or the amount of reinforcing steel that might be needed.

This is only for the part of the wall subject to lateral pressure from the soil behind it. Any part of the wall above the dirt line could be reduced in thickness to suit the builder's purposes. If the wall is engineered, there should be adequate reinforcing steel to make up for any lack of thickness.

This method might not be accurate, but it worked for me. Otherwise, check Section 2907, find the formula, then go to Chapter 27 and compute the amount of steel needed.

7
Engineering and Design Requirements

Sooner or later you'll come to the engineering and design sections of the code. Sometimes these can be pretty confusing.

Engineering is first mentioned in the U.B.C. in Chapter 23:

Section 2301 Scope.   This chapter prescribes general design requirements applicable to all structures regulated by this code.

It's not an easy subject to cover because it involves complicated formulas that few people other than engineers really understand. Therefore, we'll cover only those formulas which you'll need to get a basic understanding of engineering regulations.

Loads and Loading
Section 2302 jumps right to the heart of the matter: *Loads* and *Loading*. This comprises three items which we'll take in the order they're defined in the U.B.C.:

Dead Load *is the vertical load due to the weight of all permanent structural and nonstructural components of a building, such as walls, floors, roofs, and fixed service equipment.*

Live Load is the load superimposed by the use and occupancy of the building not including the wind load, earthquake load, or dead load.

Load Duration is the period of continuous application of a given load, or the aggregate of periods of intermittent application of the same load.

Another load implied by the definition of live load is the *Unit Live Load.* This is "the load superimposed by the use and occupancy of the building." Loads for various uses and occupancies are shown in U.B.C. Tables Nos. 23-A and 23-B. (See Figures 7-1 and 7-2.)

Unit Live Loads

The unit live loads shown in U.B.C. Table 23-A are used to design floors and foundations for both uniform and concentrated loads. If you're designing a factory or shop building, use the column under "Uniform Load" to design the floor. But if isolated machinery is involved, or machinery that is different from the rest of the equipment in the building, the area around the machinery should be designed according to the column headed "Concentrated Load." Table 23-B covers special situations that have to be treated individually. Here's an example. Say the floor of your building is a concrete slab 4 inches thick with wire mat reinforcing. If heavy machinery is involved, you may have to beef up the area under your machine by increasing the floor thickness to 6 inches and adding 1/2-inch rebar reinforcing.

Another example is a private garage where the load is imposed on four points—one under each wheel of a car. Because cars must drive into and out of a garage, these four points become paths and should be designed to support 2000 pounds without uniform live loads. According to Section 2304(c), each load-bearing area must be 40 percent of the gross weight of the heaviest vehicle stored. The standard four-inch-thick slab will support most autos, but if you're planning to store a motor home, take another look at the thickness of the slab. This applies to your driveway as well.

Roof Loads and Design

Most people are more concerned with the loading inside of a building than with the *roof load.* They're probably more interested in knowing that their floor won't collapse under the weight of a piano than if their roof will support two feet of snow. Floors,

TABLE NO. 23-A—UNIFORM AND CONCENTRATED LOADS

USE OR OCCUPANCY		UNIFORM LOAD[1]	CONCEN-TRATED LOAD
CATEGORY	DESCRIPTION		
1. Armories		150	0
2. Assembly areas[4] and auditoriums and balconies therewith	Fixed seating areas	50	0
	Movable seating and other areas	100	0
	Stage areas and enclosed platforms	125	0
3. Cornices, marquees and residential balconies		60	0
4. Exit facilities[5]		100	0[8]
5. Garages	General storage and/or repair	100	[3]
	Private pleasure car storage	50	[3]
6. Hospitals	Wards and rooms	40	1000[2]
7. Libraries	Reading rooms	60	1000[2]
	Stack rooms	125	1500[2]
8. Manufacturing	Light	75	2000[2]
	Heavy	125	3000[2]
9. Offices		50	2000[2]
10. Printing plants	Press rooms	150	2500[2]
	Composing and linotype rooms	100	2000[2]
11. Residential[6]		40	0[8]
12. Rest rooms[7]			
13. Reviewing stands, grandstands and bleachers		100	0
14. Roof deck	Same as area served or for the type of occupancy accommodated		
15. Schools	Classrooms	40	1000[2]
16. Sidewalks and driveways	Public access	250	[3]
17. Storage	Light	125	
	Heavy	250	
18. Stores	Retail	75	2000[2]
	Wholesale	100	3000[2]

[1]See Section 2306 for live load reductions.
[2]See Section 2304 (c), first paragraph, for area of load application.

From the Uniform Building Code, ©1982, ICBO.　　*(Continued on next page)*

Figure 7-1　Uniform and Concentrated Loads

[3]See Section 2304 (c), second paragraph, for concentrated loads.

[4]Assembly areas include such occupancies as dance halls, drill rooms, gymnasiums, playgrounds, plazas, terraces and similar occupancies which are generally accessible to the public.

[5]Exit facilities shall include such uses as corridors serving an occupant load of 10 or more persons, exterior exit balconies, stairways, fire escapes and similar uses.

[6]Residential occupancies include private dwellings, apartments and hotel guest rooms.

[7]Rest room loads shall be not less than the load for the occupancy with which they are associated, but need not exceed 50 pounds per square foot.

[8]Individual stair treads shall be designed to support a 300-pound concentrated load placed in a position which would cause maximum stress. Stair stringers may be designed for the uniform load set forth in the table.

Figure 7-1 (continued)   Uniform and Concentrated Loads

however, are subjected to known loading whereas roofs are subjected to loads that are often temporary and totally unpredictable.

Wind Loads

There are two other important loads that affect buildings: *wind loads* and *snow loads*. The U.B.C. gets pretty technical on this issue and for a very good reason—these two loads can vary from zero to very substantial forces. Builders in Los Angeles couldn't care less about a snow load, but the Santa Ana winds common to Southern California can give them serious problems.

Because snow and wind loads can vary so greatly, you'll probably want to get good advice from an engineer when the issue comes up. Your local building official can explain the local practice to you. Of course, Chapter 23 in the U.B.C. explains the requirements. But you need a background in engineering to understand some of the formulas. Here's some plain English from the code:

Section 2311(a) General. Every building or structure and every portion thereof shall be designed and constructed to resist the wind effects determined in accordance with the requirements of this section. Wind shall be assumed to come from any horizontal direction. No reduction in wind pressure shall be taken for the shielding effect of adjacent structures.

It then goes on to describe particular types of buildings. These sections apply to large buildings and will be of interest primarily to engineers and designers. The 1982 U.B.C. refers you to ANSI 58.1. That's a standard published by the American National Stan-

TABLE NO. 23-B—SPECIAL LOADS[1]

USE		VERTICAL LOAD	LATERAL LOAD
CATEGORY	DESCRIPTION	(Pounds per Square Foot Unless Otherwise Noted)	
1. Construction, public access at site (live load)	Walkway See Sec. 4406	150	
	Canopy See Sec. 4407	150	
2. Grandstands, reviewing stands and bleachers (live load)	Seats and foot-boards	120[2]	See Footnote 3
3. Stage accessories, see Sec. 3902 (live load)	Gridirons and fly galleries	75	
	Loft block wells[4]	250	250
	Head block wells and sheave beams[4]	250	250
4. Ceiling framing (live load)	Over stages	20	
	All uses except over stages	10[5]	
5. Partitions and interior walls, see Sec. 2309 (live load)			5
6. Elevators and dumbwaiters (dead and live load)		2 x Total loads[6]	
7. Mechanical and electrical equipment (dead load)		Total loads	
8. Cranes (dead and live load)[7]	Total load including impact increase	1.25 x Total load[7]	0.10 x Total load[8]
9. Balcony railings, guard rails and handrails	Exit facilities serving an occupant load greater than 50		50[9]
	Other		20[9]
10. Storage racks	Over 8 feet high	Total loads[10]	See Table No. 23-J

[1]The tabulated loads are minimum loads. Where other vertical loads required by this code or required by the design would cause greater stresses they shall be used.

[2]Pounds per lineal foot.

[3]Lateral sway bracing loads of 24 pounds per foot parallel and 10 pounds per foot perpendicular to seat and footboards.

(Continued on next page)

Figure 7-2 Special Loads

⁴All loads are in pounds per lineal foot. Head block wells and sheave beams shall be designed for all loft block well loads tributary thereto. Sheave blocks shall be designed with a factor of safety of five.

⁵Does not apply to ceilings which have sufficient total access from below, such that access is not required within the space above the ceiling. Does not apply to ceilings if the attic areas above the ceiling are not provided with access. This live load need not be considered acting simultaneously with other live loads imposed upon the ceiling framing or its supporting structure.

⁶Where Appendix Chapter 51 has been adopted, see reference standard cited therein for additional design requirements.

⁷The impact factors included are for cranes with steel wheels riding on steel rails. They may be modified if substantiating technical data acceptable to the building official is submitted. Live loads on crane support girders and their connections shall be taken as the maximum crane wheel loads. For pendant-operated traveling crane support girders and their connections, the impact factors shall be 1.10.

⁸This applies in the direction parallel to the runway rails (longitudinal). The factor for forces perpendicular to the rail is 0.20 × the transverse traveling loads (trolley, cab, hooks and lifted loads). Forces shall be applied at top of rail and may be distributed among rails of multiple rail cranes and shall be distributed with due regard for lateral stiffness of the structures supporting these rails.

⁹A load per lineal foot to be applied horizontally at right angles to the top rail.

¹⁰Vertical members of storage racks shall be protected from impact forces of operating equipment or racks shall be designed so that failure of one vertical member will not cause collapse of more than the bay or bays directly supported by that member.

From the Uniform Building Code, ©1982, ICBO.

Figure 7-2 (continued)   Special Loads

dards Institute. Other standards were used in previous U.B.C. editions. The ANSI reference makes it a bit difficult for the small designer or builder. You'll have to discuss this with your building official unless you happen to have a copy of the ANSI Standards.

Generally, wind and snow loads are not a problem for residences and small commercial structures. Normal frame or masonry construction has the strength to withstand whatever nature can be expected to send your way.

But in some areas special precautions are needed. You probably know if you live in an area that has unusually high snow or wind loads. Sometimes homes adjacent to natural land features have wind patterns worse than other homes nearby.

Figure 4 in the 1982 edition of the U.B.C. (Figure 7-3 in this manual) is a wind speed map of the U.S. This map, as explained in

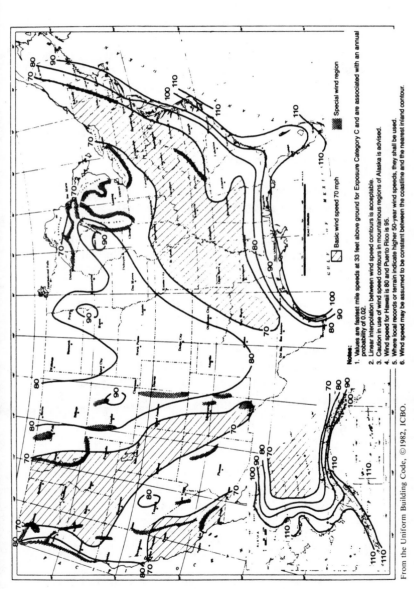

Figure 7-3 Basic Wind Speeds in Miles Per Hour

From the Uniform Building Code, ©1982, ICBO.

the footnotes, represents the fastest wind speeds at 33 feet above the ground for Exposure Category C. It also indicates an annual probability of 0.02, which means you might get these winds only 7.3 days per year.

Even if most mathematical formulas throw you into a panic, you can handle this one. The wind load, or *design wind pressure*, is calculated in the following formula:

$$p = C_e \, C_q \, q_s \, I \text{ where}$$

p = Design wind pressure

C_e = Combined height, exposure and gust factor coefficient as given in Table 23-G (see Figure 7-4)

C_q = Pressure coefficient for the structure or portion of structure under consideration as given in Table 23-H (see Figure 7-5)

q_s = Wind stagnation pressure at the standard height of 30 feet as set forth in Table 23-F (see Figure 7-6)

I = Importance factor as set forth in Section 2311(h). This pertains to a factor of 1.5 if you are building a hospital, fire or police station, disaster operations or communications center, or a similar structure of an emergency station. On all other buildings a factor of 1.0 is adequate.

With that in mind let's see what the *design wind pressure* would be for a residential roof with a 4 in 12 pitch in Kennewick, Washington. The wind speed map shows this area to be in the 70 miles per hour speed zone which still gives us a "q-s" factor of 13. Notice in U.B.C. Table 23-H (Figure 7-5) that a roof element on an enclosed structure with a 4 in 12 pitch would have a factor of 1.1.

Now go to U.B.C. Table 23-G (Figure 7-4). You should see the problem right away: Will our structure have Exposure B or Exposure C? A structure under 20 feet above the average adjoining

TABLE NO. 23-G—COMBINED HEIGHT, EXPOSURE AND GUST FACTOR COEFFICIENT (C_e)

HEIGHT ABOVE AVERAGE LEVEL OF ADJOINING GROUND, IN FEET	EXPOSURE C	EXPOSURE B
0- 20	1.2	0.7
20- 40	1.3	0.8
40- 60	1.5	1.0
60-100	1.6	1.1
100-150	1.8	1.3
150-200	1.9	1.4
200-300	2.1	1.6
300-400	2.2	1.8

From the Uniform Building Code, ©1982, ICBO.

Figure 7-4   Combined Height, Exposure and Gust Factor Coefficient

ground carries a factor of 1.2 in Exposure C. But it's only 0.7 in Exposure B. Which is right in our case?

Section 2311(c) tells us that Exposure C represents the most severe exposure—the terrain is flat and generally open, extending one-half mile or more from the site. Exposure B has terrain with buildings, forest or surface irregularities 20 feet or more in height covering at least 20 percent of the area extending one mile or more from the site. That makes sense. You'll get the full force of the wind if your building is the only obstruction around.

In this case we're in a city and can use the factor for Exposure B. Now our formula, converted to numbers, looks like this:

Multiply 0.7 times 1.1 times 13 times 1 to get the design wind pressure of 10.01 pounds per square foot.

But don't stop here. This isn't the end. Suppose that our Exposure Coefficient comes under Exposure C and that we're building on a knoll which extends considerably above the surrounding terrain. Do you think it would be wise to use the minimum height of 20 feet for a residential structure? I wouldn't recommend it. Instead, add the height of the knoll to the height of your building.

For example, your house will be in Exposure C (flat terrain, generally open for a half mile) but you have chosen to place it on a knoll fifty feet above the height of the surrounding countryside. This puts the roof height in the 60 to 100 bracket in Table 23-G.

TABLE NO. 23-H—PRESSURE COEFFICIENTS (C_q)

STRUCTURE OR PART THEREOF	DESCRIPTION	C_q FACTOR
Primary frames and systems	**Method 1** (Normal Force Method)	
	Windward wall	0.8 inward
	Leeward wall	0.5 outward
	Leeward roof or flat roof	0.7 outward
	Windward roof	
	Slope<9:12	0.7 outward
	Slope 9:12 to 12:12	0.4 inward
	Slope>12:12	0.7 inward
	Wind parallel to ridge	
	Enclosed structures	0.7 outward
	Open structures[1]	1.2 outward
	Method 2 (Projected Area Method)	
	On vertical projected area	
	Structures 40 feet or less in height	1.3 horizontal any direction
	Structures over 40 feet in height	1.4 horizontal any direction
	On horizontal projected area	
	Enclosed structure	0.7 upward
	Open structure[1]	1.2 upward
Elements and components	Wall elements	
	All structures	1.2 inward
	Enclosed structures	1.1 outward
	Open structures	1.6 outward
	Parapets	1.3 inward or outward
	Roof elements	
	Enclosed structures	
	Slope<9:12	1.1 outward
	Slope 9:12 to 12:12	1.1 outward or 0.8 inward
	Slope>12:12	1.1 outward or inward
	Open structures[1]	
	Slope<9:12	1.6 outward
	Slope 9:12 to 12:12	1.6 outward or 0.8 inward
	Slope>12:12	1.6 outward or 1.1 inward
Local areas at discontinuities[2]	Wall corners	2.0 outward
	Canopies or overhangs at eaves or rakes	2.8 upward
	Roof ridges at ends of buildings or eaves and roof edges at building corners	3.0 upward

Figure 7-5   Pressure Coefficient

TABLE NO. 23-H—PRESSURE COEFFICIENTS (C_q)—(Continued)

STRUCTURE OR PART THEREOF	DESCRIPTION	C_q FACTOR
	Eaves or rakes without overhangs away from building corners and ridges away from ends of building	2.0 upward
	Cladding connections Add 0.5 to outward or upward C_q for appropriate location	
Chimneys, tanks and solid towers	Square or rectangular	1.4 any direction
	Hexagonal or octagonal	1.1 any direction
	Round or elliptical	0.8 any direction
Open-frame towers[3] [4]		2.0 any direction
Signs, flagpoles, lightpoles, minor structures		1.4 any direction

[1]A structure with more than 30 percent of any one side open shall be considered an open structure. Nonimpact-resistant glazing shall be considered as an opening.

[2]Local pressures shall apply over a distance from the discontinuity of 10 feet or 0.1 times the least width of the structure, whichever is smaller.

[3]The area to which the design pressure shall be applied shall be the projected area of all elements other than those in planes parallel to the direction of application.

[4]For radio and transmission towers, the area shall be the projected area of the members on one face multiplied by 2.0 for rectangular towers and 1.8 for triangular towers.

From the Uniform Building Code, ©1982, ICBO.

Figure 7-5 (continued) Pressure Coefficient

TABLE NO. 23-F—WIND STAGNATION PRESSURE (q_s) AT STANDARD HEIGHT OF 30 FEET

Basic wind speed (mph)[1]	70	80	90	100	110	120	130
Pressure q_s (psf)	13	17	21	26	31	37	44

[1]Wind speed from Section 2311 (b).

From the Uniform Building Code, ©1982, ICBO.

Figure 7-6 Wind Stagnation Pressure

(The house is 20 feet high; the knoll is 50 feet high). Now our formula will look like this:

Multiply 1.6 times 1.1 times 13 times 1 to get the design wind pressure of 22.88 pounds per square foot.

Not much of a difference but it might have some effect on the type of roof you choose and the method of installing it.

Just a minute, though. This is only a recommendation, *not* a requirement. It's not in the book and it's not based on engineering data. It's based on pure and simple common sense. Normally, a little added strength in your calculation won't be that expensive, especially in a home.

That's all there is to wind loads. But don't try to build that roof for a 10.01 pounds per square foot load. It turns out that the expected wind loads are less than the expected live loads. U.B.C. Table 23-C (Figure 7-7 in this book) gives the minimum roof live loads. These are the *minimum* figures you can use, regardless of the wind load calculations.

Don't stop reading the U.B.C. when you *think* you have the answer. Read the next paragraph.

Snow Loads
According to Section 2305(d) of the U.B.C.:

Snow loads, full or unbalanced, shall be considered in place of loads set forth in U.B.C. Table 23-C (Figure 7-7), where such loading will result in larger members or connections.

It seems that snow can create some unusual conditions on a roof. For instance, the shady part of a roof is the last part to thaw, and when it does it will react strangely. The snow melts a little and then freezes, melts a little and then freezes, causing the snow and ice to pile up on the roof. While the shady side is thawing and freezing, the exposed side may be completely bare after a few days. This creates what is known as an unbalanced load.

Even though it's temporary, somewhat like the wind load, snow load still must be calculated into the overall roof load. This is referred to in Section 2305(d):

Potential accumulation of snow at valleys, parapets, roof structures and offsets in roofs of uneven configuration shall be considered. Where snow loads occur, the snow loads shall be determined by the building official.

The pitch of a roof influences snow load. U.B.C. Table No. 23-C (Figure 7-7) shows this under Method 1, indicating a gradual reduction in load as the roof pitch increases. This works well—until you get to the third column where the "Tributary Loaded

TABLE NO. 23-C—MINIMUM ROOF LIVE LOADS[1]

ROOF SLOPE	METHOD 1			METHOD 2		
	TRIBUTARY LOADED AREA IN SQUARE FEET FOR ANY STRUCTURAL MEMBER			UNIFORM LOAD[2]	RATE OF REDUC-TION r (Percent)	MAXIMUM REDUC-TION R (Percent)
	0 to 200	201 to 600	Over 600			
1. Flat or rise less than 4 inches per foot. Arch or dome with rise less than one-eighth of span	20	16	12	20	.08	40
2. Rise 4 inches per foot to less than 12 inches per foot. Arch or dome with rise one-eighth of span to less than three-eighths of span	16	14	12	16	.06	25
3. Rise 12 inches per foot and greater. Arch or dome with rise three-eighths of span or greater	12	12	12	12	No Reductions Permitted	
4. Awnings except cloth covered[3]	5	5	5	5		
5. Greenhouses, lath houses and agricultural buildings[4]	10	10	10	10		

[1]Where snow loads occur, the roof structure shall be designed for such loads as determined by the building official. See Section 2305 (d). For special purpose roofs, see Section 2305 (e).

[2]See Section 2306 for live load reductions. The rate of reduction r in Section 2306 Formula (6-1) shall be as indicated in the table. The maximum reduction R shall not exceed the value indicated in the table.

[3]As defined in Section 4506.

[4]See Section 2305 (e) for concentrated load requirements for greenhouse roof members.

From the Uniform Building Code, ©1982, ICBO.

Figure 7-7 Minimum Roof Live Loads

Area'' exceeds 600 square feet. If you don't want to use this chart, you can calculate your reduction by the following formula:

$$R_2 = \frac{S}{40} - \frac{1}{2}$$

Where: R_2 = Snowload reduction in pounds per square foot per degree of pitch over 20°.

S = Total snow load in pounds per square inch.

Varying Snow Loads

Do you know what the snow loading in your community is? If you have a lot of snow you may. But if you're a contractor working in a large county, you may find that snow loading varies considerably from one community to another.

In Washington State some counties vary in elevation from sea level to 8,000 feet or more. At sea level the snowfall may be only a few inches and may last just a few hours or a few days, often with little or no freezing. In the mountain areas, however, it can be 15 feet or more and stay on the ground from October to June. Is the entire county considered a snow area? It sure is, but the problem is, how do you determine the snow loads for the different areas? Where do you draw the line? At what point do you have a 30-pound load, a 40-pound load or a 50-pound load? You can't always depend on elevation because snowfall varies, even at the same elevation. So, too, will freezing and thawing conditions.

I once asked the Snohomish County building official about this. Here's what he told me:

"In Snohomish County it only snows back of the section line. On one side of the section line you get one rating, on the other side it's something completely different."

This was based on years of experience and observation in his county. Often, lacking professional assistance and reference data, that's the only route an inspector can take. He has to make a decision, and if he bases it on his best judgement, he's probably trying to be fair. If not, then it's up to you to prove that your standards are better.

Uplift Loads

Ever heard of *uplift load*? If you haven't, don't worry. It's seldom used as a loading factor in construction. I guess that's because nearly everyone thinks of a load as *bearing down* and not *bearing up*. Roofs suffer most from this.

Winds can have a strange effect on roofs. A roof with a parapet wall is especially vulnerable because winds may produce vortexes which create a vacuum (negative pressure) on the roof. Large sections of roofing have been literally sucked off by this force. High-rise buildings with large areas of glass can be extremely dangerous under these conditions. About the only defense is to design a building to resist wind loads.

Gable roofs are affected also. Winds blowing over the roof create negative pressure on the lee side (side away from the wind) of the roof and can send shingles flying. If your chimney is too short or improperly placed, the same force can cause draft problems.

Although much is known about the effects of wind, conditions vary considerably from place to place. The problem is compounded by the proximity of trees and other buildings. Try to be aware of any conditions that may create uplift loads on your building.

Roofs of unenclosed buildings, roof overhangs, architectural projections, eaves, canopies, cornices, marquees or similar structures unenclosed on one or more sides also have to be designed and built to withstand upward pressures.

In other words, when the inspector tells you to bolt your patio or carport cover to the concrete pad or at least to the footings, he's worried about uplift load. He doesn't want the patio cover to go sailing across the neighbor's yard.

Earthquake Loads

Earthquakes come under the same category as fire. In most cases they are totally unpredictable.

There are about six pages of formulas in the U.B.C. to help you protect against damage from earthquakes. There's also an Earthquake Probability Map (see Figure 7-8). This map divides the country into Seismic Zones 0 through 4. Zone 0 is where earthquakes are least likely; Zone 4 is where they are most probable.

When you hear that an area is practically earthquake-free, just remember that there have been disastrous earthquakes in areas where none had occurred before. In the 16th century, the city of Lisbon, in Portugal, had a severe earthquake that almost leveled the area. Loss of life was enormous. But the surprising thing is that

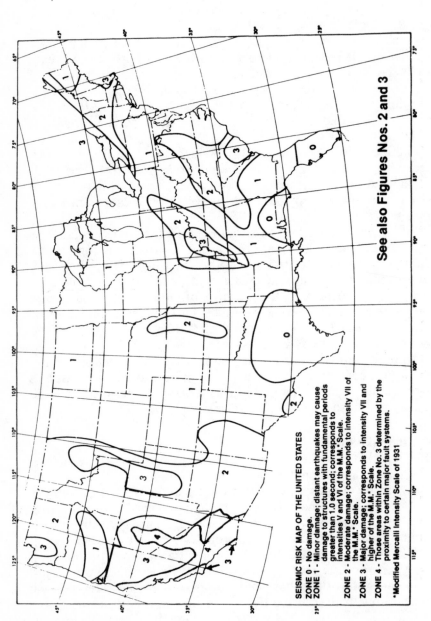

SEISMIC RISK MAP OF THE UNITED STATES

ZONE 0 - No damage.
ZONE 1 - Minor damage; distant earthquakes may cause
         damage to structures with fundamental periods
         greater than 1.0 second; corresponds to
         intensities V and VI of the M.M.* Scale.
ZONE 2 - Moderate damage; corresponds to intensity VII of
         the M.M.* Scale.
ZONE 3 - Major damage; corresponds to intensity VII and
         higher of the M.M.* Scale.
ZONE 4 - Those areas within Zone No. 3 determined by the
         proximity to certain major fault systems.
*Modified Mercalli Intensity Scale of 1931

See also Figures Nos. 2 and 3

Figure 7-8 Earthquake Probability Map

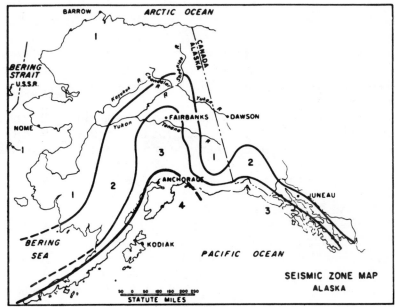

FIGURE NO. 2

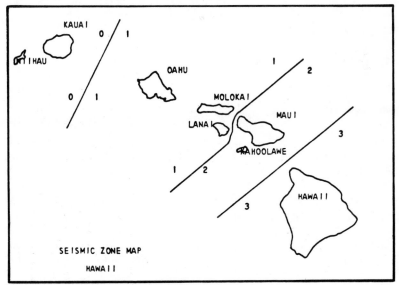

FIGURE NO. 3

From the Uniform Building Code, ©1982, ICBO.

Figure 7-8 (continued) Earthquake Probability Map of Alaska and Hawaii

this is the only major earthquake ever to hit western Europe. Portugal hasn't had a serious one since. Reelfoot Lake in Tennessee was formed in the early 19th century when an earthquake caused land to settle in a large depression that eventually filled with water. There had never been an earthquake in the area before, nor has there been one since.

It's a good idea to use the Earthquake Probability Map when designing a building. Many of the structural requirements in the U.B.C. are based on the seismic zone in which the construction is to take place.

Design and Build for the Ultimate?
There are many forces that work on a building. But it's just too expensive to build for every possible situation. Besides, if you're near a known fault area, it's impossible to build an earthquake-proof building, regardless of how much money you spend.

You must remember that the code offers *minimum* standards for *average* conditions. If the code should ever be designed for the ultimate in catastrophe, the construction industry will be brought to a screeching halt because no one could afford to build anything.

Reductions In Live Loads
The code allows for certain reductions in live loads other than those I've mentioned. There are formulas that show how and when these reductions apply, but I'll spare you those. Engineers and architects usually work them out, anyway. If you're working on a large building, have the designer check his original figures. The same applies to deflection allowed in structural members. Section 2307 spells it out this way:

The deflection of any structural member shall not exceed the values set forth in U.B.C. Table No. 23-D (Figure 7-9), based upon the factors set forth in U.B.C. Table No. 23-E (Figure 7-10). The deflection criteria representing the most restrictive condition shall apply. Deflection criteria for materials not specified shall be developed in a manner consistent with the provisions of this section. See Section 2305(f) for camber requirements. Span tables for light wood frame construction as specified in Sections 2518(d) and 2518(h)2, shall conform to the design criteria contained therein, except that where the dead load exceeds 50 percent of the live load, U.B.C. Table No. 23-D shall govern. (For aluminum, see Section 2803.)

TABLE NO. 23-D—MAXIMUM ALLOWABLE DEFLECTION FOR STRUCTURAL MEMBERS [1]

TYPE OF MEMBER	MEMBER LOADED WITH LIVE LOAD ONLY (L.L.)	MEMBER LOADED WITH LIVE LOAD PLUS DEAD LOAD (L.L. + K D.L.)
Roof Member Supporting Plaster or Floor Member	$L/360$	$L/240$

[1]Sufficient slope or camber shall be provided for flat roofs in accordance with Section 2305 (f).

$L.L.$ = Live load
$D.L.$ = Dead load
K = Factor as determined by Table No. 23-E
L = Length of member in same units as deflection

From the Uniform Building Code, ©1982, ICBO.

Figure 7-9 Maximum Allowable Deflection for Structural Members

TABLE NO. 23-E—VALUE OF "K"

WOOD		REINFORCED CONCRETE [2]	STEEL
Unseasoned	Seasoned [1]		
1.0	0.5	$[2 - 1.2\,(A'_s/A_s)] \geqq 0.6$	0

[1]Seasoned lumber is lumber having a moisture content of less than 16 percent at time of installation and used under dry conditions of use such as in covered structures.

[2]See also Section 2609.
A'_s = Area of compression reinforcement.
A_s = Area of nonprestressed tension reinforcement.

From the Uniform Building Code, ©1982, ICBO.

Figure 7-10 Value of "K"

Special Purpose Loads

The following are special loads which are usually grouped under the title of "miscellaneous":

• Greenhouse roof bars, purlins, and rafters must be designed to support a 100-pound minimum concentrated load in addition to the live load.

• Roofs must have enough slope or camber to ensure adequate drainage even if the roof sags. Or, you must design the roof to support maximum loads including possible ponding of water caused by deflection.

• Properly anchor the roof to walls and columns, and the walls and columns to the foundation to resist overturning, uplift, and sliding.

• Fences less than 12 feet high, greenhouses, lath houses, and all agricultural buildings must be designed according to the horizontal wind pressures in U.B.C. Table No. 23-H (see Figure 7-5). If the height of the structure is 20 feet or less, only 2/3 of the first line of listed values need be used. The structures must be designed to withstand an uplift wind pressure equal to 3/4 the horizontal pressure.

• To determine stresses, consider all vertical design loads except the roof live-load and crane loads as acting simultaneously with the wind pressure. An exception is where snow loading is a problem. At least 50 percent of the snow load must be considered as acting with the wind load. The building official may require that a greater percentage of snow load be considered, depending on local conditions.

8
Masonry Walls

The foundation is now down on our structure. I've shown you
how to calculate loading. The next step is to put up the walls.

Block or Frame?
The most common walls for small structures are frame and
masonry. In the next chapter we'll cover the requirements for
frame walls. But for now let's focus on masonry.

By masonry I'm referring almost exclusively to concrete block.
Today, very few structures are built entirely of brick. The brick
homes you see today are nearly all brick veneer and don't have to
follow the same rules. In both the frame and masonry structures
there are a number of variations, even combinations of the two, so
you'll never be very far away from one or the other.

With concrete block you won't need the wooden plate we used
to top our foundation wall in Chapter Six. You may even omit the
concrete foundation wall and build right up from the footing with
concrete block. In this case you probably would have put iron reinforcing dowels in the footing when it was poured. These dowels
should be spaced four feet apart. (See Figure 8-1.) When the
blocks are in place, the cells in which the dowels are placed must be
filled with concrete grout.

Figure 8-1   Rebar Dowels in Place in Masonry Wall Construction

It's not necessary to use dowels that are as high as the wall you're building. And there's a practical reason for that, too. Masons don't like dropping blocks over 14 or 15 feet of rebar. It's cumbersome and results in a lot of broken blocks. The code doesn't state that the rebar must be continuous, only that its *strength* be continuous. This can be done by splicing (wiring) or welding shorter pieces together, as shown in Figure 8-2.

This is one of those areas that most inspectors watch very closely. Few block layers weld their steel. Many don't even wire it. They merely jam the rebar into the grout in the cell. About the only way to prevent this is to have an inspector on the site at all times.

Splicing and Placing Rebar
When splicing reinforcing steel, make splices only at such points and in a manner that won't reduce the structural strength of the member. Lapped splices must have enough lap to transfer the stress of the reinforcing by bond and shear, but the lap can never

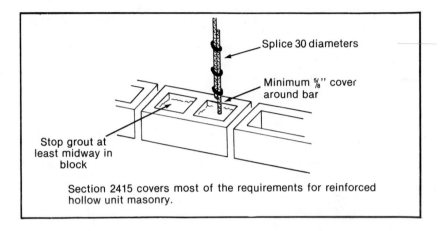

Splice 30 diameters

Minimum ⅝" cover around bar

Stop grout at least midway in block

Section 2415 covers most of the requirements for reinforced hollow unit masonry.

Figure 8-2 Properly Spliced Rebar in Hollow Unit Masonry

be less than 30-bar diameters. (See Figure 8-2.) In other words, if you are using 1/2-inch bar, the lap must be 15 inches. If you are using 5/8-inch bar, lap 18¾ inches; and for 3/4-inch bar, go to 22½ inches.

What about the location of the bar in the cell? Do you just stick it anyplace? Hardly, although on some jobs it may look that way. Joint reinforcement must have at least 5/8-inch mortar coverage from the exposed face. All other reinforcement must have a minimum coverage of one bar diameter over all bars not less than 3/4 inches. If the bars are exposed to the weather or soil, the minimum coverage is 2 inches.

Let's say you're building a block basement and you want to put electrical outlets in the exterior wall. There's no problem as long as you don't reduce the structural stability of the wall itself. If the outlet has been detailed in the plans, there shouldn't be any structural problems. You can run pipe or conduit through the masonry, using a sleeve large enough to pass any hub or coupling on the pipeline. That's for areas where the block must be core-filled or where there may be rebar installed. Pipe or conduit placed in the unfilled cores of hollow unit masonry is not considered embedding. Figure 8-3 shows the minimum coverage required for reinforcing steel under different conditions.

A. Concrete cast against and
    permanently exposed to earth   3

B. Concrete exposed to earth or weather:
        No. 6 through No. 18 bar   2
        No. 5 bar, W31 or D31 wire, and smaller 1½

C. Concrete not exposed to weather or
    in contact with ground:
        Slabs, walls, joists:
           No. 14 and No. 18 bar 1½
           No. 11 bar and smaller . . . .   ¾

        Beams, columns:
           Primary reinforcement, ties, stirrups, spirals   1½

        Shells, folded plate members:
           No. 6 bar and larger . . . .   ¾
           No. 5 bar, W31 or D31 wire, and smaller . . .   ½

2. Precast concrete (manufactured under plant control conditions). The
following minimum concrete cover shall be provided for reinforcement:

MINIMUM COVER, INCHES

A. Concrete exposed to earth or weather:
    Wall panels:
        No. 14 and No. 18 bar 1½
        No. 11 bar and smaller . . . .   ¾

    Other members:
        No. 14 and No. 18 bar   2
        No. 6 through No. 11 bar 1½
        No. 5 bar, W31 or D31 wire, and smaller . . .   1¼

B. Concrete not exposed to weather or in contact
    with ground:
    Slabs, walls, joists:
        No. 14 and No. 18 bar 1¼
        No. 11 bar and smaller . . . .   ⅝

    Beams, columns:
        Primary reinforcement . . . . d_b but not less than ⅝
                                                and need not exceed
                                                1½

        Ties, stirrups, spirals . . . .   ⅜

    Shells, folded plate members:
        No. 6 bar and larger . . . .   ⅝
        No. 5 bar, W31 or D31 wire, and smaller . . .   ⅜

Figure 8-3   Requirements for Minimum Cover of
Reinforcing Steel

3. **Prestressed concrete.** A. The following minimum concrete cover shall be provided for prestressed and nonprestressed reinforcement, ducts and end fittings, except as provided in Section 2607 (h) 3 B and C:

	MINIMUM COVER, INCHES
(i) Concrete cast against and permanently exposed to earth.............................	3
(ii) Concrete exposed to earth or weather:	
Wall panels, slabs, joists..................	1
Other members	1½
(iii) Concrete not exposed to weather or in contact with ground:	
Slabs, walls, joists......................	¾
Beams, columns:	
Primary reinforcement	1½
Ties, stirrups, spirals..................	1

From the Uniform Building Code, ©1982, ICBO.

Figure 8-3 (continued) Requirements for Minimum Cover of Reinforcing Steel

General Masonry Requirements

The first bed joint must be at least 1/4 inch and not more than 1 inch thick. All subsequent bed joints will have the same minimum thickness but will be not more than 5/8 inch thick. Generally, you'll find that most masonry is put up in *lifts* not more than 4 feet high. The code doesn't say this directly; it's just a rule of thumb. But if your wall is much higher than four feet, the mortar will be squeezed out of the bed joints.

Use lifts when you're grouting, especially around rebar. Raise a lift, then stop and grout. Remember, though, that the grout should not be level with the top of the block except on the last course. It should stop at least 1 inch below the top of the block. This means that the grout and bed joint will not occur simultaneously in a horizontal joint.

Make sure that chases and recesses in masonry walls are designed and constructed so that they don't reduce the strength or fire resistance of the wall.

Occasionally you'll run across a *stack* bond. This is where the blocks are placed directly over each other without the lapped joint used on most masonry work. If you use stack bond you must include horizontal reinforcing. This reinforcing must be at least two

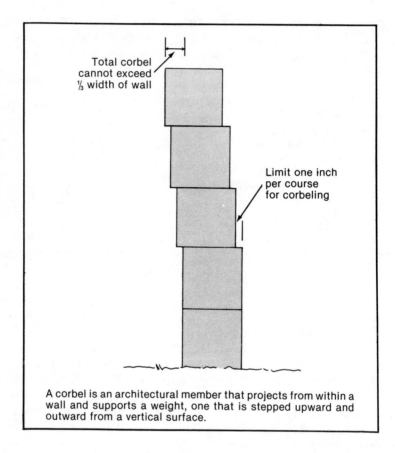

Figure 8-4   Corbeling in Masonry Construction

continuous wires, with a minimum cross-sectional area of 0.017 square inch. These wires must be installed horizontally between courses that are not greater than 16 inches apart.

Corbeling

To work with masonry you'll need to know about *corbeling*. Webster's dictionary says that a corbel is an architectural member that projects from within a wall and supports a weight, one that is stepped upward and outward from a vertical surface. Figure 8-4 illustrates corbeling in masonry construction.

A corbel may be built only into solid masonry walls 12 inches or more in thickness. The projection of each course cannot exceed 1 inch. Maximum projections can't be more than 1/3 the total thickness of the wall when used to support a chimney built into the wall. The top course of all corbels must be a header course.

Be careful when building corbels in earthquake zones. The inspector may have some strict regulations regarding their construction. Many areas require the removal of corbels and cornices because of the danger they present to passersby in the event of an earthquake.

Laying Block in Cold Weather

Can you lay concrete blocks or any type of masonry units in any kind of weather? Not in my book, unless you go a couple of steps further. Check Section 2415(a) of the U.B.C.:

No masonry shall be laid when the temperature of the outside air is below 40 degrees F, unless approved methods are used during construction to prevent damage to the masonry.

That means either covering the work or applying heat to it. If the temperature isn't too low, the simple act of covering the work area may be sufficient. This really isn't too hard when done with large sheets of polyethylene film or other plastics.

Perhaps some of you have seen parts of buildings surrounded by giant plastic cocoons. These cocoons are heated by large electric or gas heaters and often are not supported by any framework. The heated gases keep them inflated, preventing the plastic from clinging to the masonry. This heat must be kept on for 24 hours when using Type III portland cement and 48 hours if Type I portland cement is used.

Even though you may have provisions for heat, make sure your material is free from ice or snow before being laid up.

Thickness-to-Height Ratio

Does thickness of walls have any bearing on height? It sure does, but the height of the wall also depends on the type of masonry used. This is shown in U.B.C. Table No. 24-I (Figure 8-5).

TABLE NO. 24-I—MINIMUM THICKNESS OF MASONRY WALLS

TYPE OF MASONRY	MAXIMUM RATIO UNSUPPORTED HEIGHT OR LENGTH TO THICKNESS	NOMINAL MINIMUM THICKNESS (Inches)
BEARING WALLS:		
1. Unburned Clay Masonry	10	16
2. Stone Masonry	14	16
3. Cavity Wall Masonry	18	8
4. Hollow Unit Masonry	18	8
5. Solid Masonry	20	8
6. Grouted Masonry	20	6
7. Reinforced Grouted Masonry	25	6
8. Reinforced Hollow Unit Masonry	25	4[1]
NONBEARING WALLS:		
9. Exterior Unreinforced Walls	20	2
10. Exterior Reinforced Walls	30	2
11. Interior Partitions Unreinforced	36	2
12. Interior Partitions Reinforced	48	2

[1]Nominal 4-inch-thick load-bearing reinforced hollow clay unit masonry walls with a maximum unsupported height or length to thickness of 27 may be permitted, provided net area unit strength exceeds 8000 psi, units are laid in running bond, bar sizes do not exceed ½ inch with no more than two bars or one splice in a cell, and joints are flush cut, concave or a protruding V section. Minimum bar coverage where exposed to weather may be 1½ inches.

From the Uniform Building Code, ©1982, ICBO.

Figure 8-5 Minimum Thickness of Masonry Walls

You can build a hollow unit masonry wall higher than 18 feet without using reinforcing steel. But have the wall engineered. That's the best way to avoid problems.

With pilasters, for instance, the floor or roof is supported by the pilasters and not by the wall. The block curtain between the pilasters is little more than a non-bearing wall. With non-bearing walls, as you can see from U.B.C. Table No. 24-I, you can build much higher.

A word about reinforcing. Generally, when people in construction hear that word, they think of long lengths of rebar. If you were to say "bracing," they would get a different picture. Yet, reinforcing is a form of bracing, and bracing is a form of reinforcing. What we should really say is that the wall gets additional support or strengthening.

Types of Masonry

Below is a list of masonry materials. These can't necessarily be used as substitutes for each other. In many cases they are made by different methods and have different qualities. A better product could be substituted for a lesser one in most cases, but not vice versa.

Because its use usually determines the masonry's aggregate strength, I'll just list the various masonry types starting with the strongest. This list is based primarily on compressive strength.

1. Brick made with sand-lime.
2. Brick made of clay or shale.
3. Concrete building blocks.
4. Structural clay floor tile.
5. Solid load-bearing concrete masonry units.
6. Unburned clay.

(The code book doesn't describe unburned clay thoroughly, but I suspect it's little more than what we would call *adobe*.)

Thickness Versus Height

Perhaps the best way to show how the method of laying up masonry can increase its strength is to look at U.B.C. Table No. 24-I (Figure 8-5). This table, *Minimum Thickness of Masonry Walls*, is based on a ratio of height to length or thickness. This means that for unburned clay masonry, for example, the height can only be 10 times the thickness of the walls. In this case it would be 160 inches, or 13'4" high. To build a higher unreinforced wall, you would have to increase the thickness of the wall. This is for either height or length, whichever is less.

So, back to U.B.C. Table No. 24-I. Unburned clay, the weakest material based on compressive strength, starts the list with a ratio of 10 times the thickness of the wall. The list goes on up through the various building materials to 25 times the thickness of a 6-inch wall for reinforced hollow unit masonry. As the width of the wall increases, the height may also be increased.

I've told you that the code book is sneaky. Unburned clay masonry walls 16 inches thick will give you a maximum height of 13'4". Solid masonry walls 8 inches thick will also give you a maximum height of 13'4". Reinforced grouted masonry will give you a maximum height of 12'6". How can you build higher? What would you do if you wanted a wall 16 feet high, especially when you look at the table and find that most of these walls figure out to around 13 feet?

It's best to have higher walls designed by a good engineer. For me to give you all the engineering data would take too many pages. To get it done right, get it engineered. Block companies often have people on their staff who can give you this information. Usually they'll be glad to because it will probably lead to an order.

Bond Beams

A *bond beam* is a block cast with three sides and no ends. It is laid into a course with the open side up and filled with concrete. Another form of this is the *lintel block*, which is used to build lintels over doors, windows, and other openings. These are built in various dimensions, and reinforcing is placed in the cavity depending on the strength required. The hole is then filled with concrete. Several types of concrete block and an application of lintel block reinforcing are shown in Figure 8-6.

Lintel blocks for window and door openings are much easier to use. And, in my opinion, they are nicer looking than the usual cast-in-place concrete lintel.

Use of Mass

The use of mass should not be overlooked as a way of gaining additional height by adding strength to a building. By making a wall thicker you can make it higher. Builders have done this for years.

In reviewing earlier building codes on this topic, I discovered that the rule of thumb, stated more directly in New York's old building code, required that such a wall had to be 12 inches thick for the first floor of the building, and for each additional floor another 4 inches of wall thickness had to be added. In this case, the practical limit was usually ten stories, which required a wall on the ground floor to be 4-foot thick.

Masonry Grades

The grade of masonry units is also very important. Building bricks made of clay or shale and those made of sand-lime come in three grades: SW, MW, NW. For bricks made of clay or shale, these symbols indicate the following:

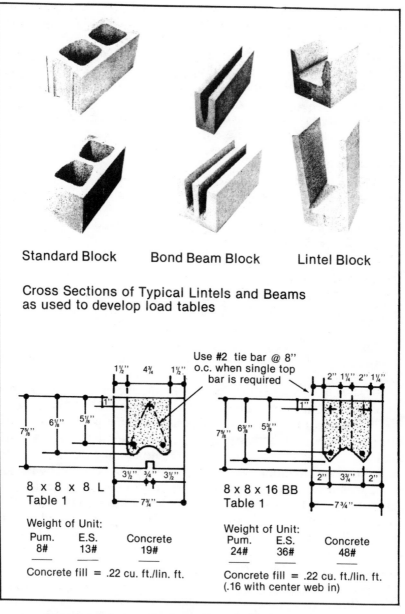

Standard Block   Bond Beam Block   Lintel Block

Cross Sections of Typical Lintels and Beams
as used to develop load tables

Use #2 tie bar @ 8"
o.c. when single top
bar is required

8 x 8 x 8 L
Table 1

Weight of Unit:
Pum.	E.S.	Concrete
8#	13#	19#

Concrete fill = .22 cu. ft./lin. ft.

8 x 8 x 16 BB
Table 1

Weight of Unit:
Pum.	E.S.	Concrete
24#	36#	48#

Concrete fill = .22 cu. ft./lin. ft.
(.16 with center web in)

Figure 8-6 Concrete Blocks and Lintel Block
Reinforcing

SW—Bricks intended for use where high resistance to frost is desired and the exposure is such that the brick may freeze when wet.

MW—Bricks intended for use where exposed to temperatures below freezing but not exposed to water, or where a moderate and somewhat non-uniform degree of resistance to frost action is permissible.

NW—The last of the three grades would be used as backup or interior masonry or, if exposed, for use where no frost action occurs; or, if frost action occurs, where the annual precipitation is less than 20 inches.

SW brick are frequently used in foundation courses and retaining walls in areas subject to frost. MW grade is often used in the face of a wall above ground not exposed to water. The use of NW grade brick is explained in the text above. The three grades for the sand-lime are similar.

Face Bricks and Veneer Anchorage
The building bricks most builders use are face bricks. These bricks are used as veneer on frame buildings and are frequently used with stone in veneer on concrete block buildings as well. These are building bricks, *not* concrete blocks. The difference is important, even though many people interchange the terms easily and frequently.

Most masons use mortar with a high concrete ratio to anchor face bricks to a concrete block wall. This produces a tight, secure bond. Clips are recommended just as on frame walls. These clips are little strips of corrugated sheet metal used to attach brick veneer to the block wall. On a frame building they are nailed to the exterior sheathing and bent outward to lay between the courses.

Most houses with brick veneer have clips. But the clips are not always installed properly. Often, not enough are used, and those that are used are placed at random. Unless you or the inspector is keeping a close eye on the job, you can be sure that some clips will be installed improperly. A good mason, however, will insist on them and will use them regularly and correctly.

Mortaring
Applying mortar is probably the most critical step in the construction of a masonry wall. All bricks must be laid with a full head and

**TABLE NO. 24-A—MORTAR PROPORTIONS BY VOLUME
FOR UNIT MASONRY**

MORTAR TYPE	PARTS BY VOLUME OF PORTLAND CEMENT	PARTS BY VOLUME OF MASONRY CEMENT	PARTS BY VOLUME OF HYDRATED LIME OR LIME PUTTY[1]	AGGREGATE MEASURED IN A DAMP, LOOSE CONDITION
M	1 1	1 —	¼	Not less than 2¼ and not more than 3 times the sum of the volumes of the cements and lime used
S	½ 1	1 —	— over ¼ to ½	
N	— 1	1 —	— over ½ to 1¼	
O	— 1	1 —	— over 1¼ to 2½	

[1] When plastic or waterproof cement is used as specified in Section 2403 (p), hydrated lime or putty may be added but not in excess of one-tenth the volume of cement.

From the Uniform Building Code, ©1982, ICBO.

Figure 8-7   Mortar Proportions for Unit Masonry

bed joints; all interior joints designed to be mortared should be filled. The average thickness of head and bed joints may not exceed 1/2 inch.

Mixing the mortar is also critical. Four types of mortar are used in masonry construction: Types M, S, N, and O. Mix proportions are described in U.B.C. Table No. 24-A (Figure 8-7). U.B.C. Table No. 24-B (Figure 8-8) gives allowable working stresses for unreinforced unit masonry. These tables will help you choose the right mortar and the proper mix for most masonry work.

Most mortar is mixed at the job, so it's easy to control the quality of the mix. The inspector, if he's on his toes, is going to be watching. He may even call for certain tests to be made.

Additional Tables
The three U.B.C. tables shown in Figure 8-9 give allowable shear on bolts for three types of masonry. As usual, be sure to read the footnotes when using these tables.

TABLE NO. 24-B—ALLOWABLE WORKING STRESSES IN UNREINFORCED UNIT MASONRY

MATERIAL	TYPE M Compression[1]	TYPE S Compression[1]	TYPE M OR TYPE S MORTAR Shear or Tension in Flexure[2][3]		Tension in Flexure[4]		TYPE N Compression[1]	TYPE N Shear or Tension in Flexure[2][3]	
1. Special inspection required	No	No	Yes	No	Yes	No	No	Yes	No
2. Solid brick masonry									
4500 plus psi	250	225	20	10	40	20	200	15	7.5
2500-4500 psi	175	160	20	10	40	20	140	15	7.5
1500-2500 psi	125	115	20	10	40	20	100	15	7.5
3. Solid concrete unit masonry									
Grade N	175	160	12	6	24	12	140	12	6
Grade S	125	115	12	6	24	12	100	12	6
4. Grouted masonry									
4500 plus psi	350	275	25	12.5	50	25			
2500-4500 psi	275	215	25	12.5	50	25			
1500-2500 psi	225	175	25	12.5	50	25			
5. Hollow unit masonry[5]	170	150	12	6	24	12	140	10	5
6. Cavity wall masonry solid units[5] Grade N or									
2500 psi plus	140	130	12	6	30	15	110	10	5
Grade S or									
1500-2500 psi	100	90	12	6	30	15	80	10	5
Hollow units[5]	70	60	12	6	30	15	50	10	5
7. Stone masonry									
Cast stone	400	360	8	4	—	—	320	8	4
Natural stone	140	120	8	4	—	—	100	8	4
8. Unburned clay masonry	30	30	8	4	—	—	—	—	—

[1]Allowable axial or flexural compressive stresses in pounds per square inch gross cross-sectional area (except as noted). The allowable working stresses in bearing directly under concentrated loads may be 50 percent greater than these values.

[2]This value of tension is based on tension across a bed joint, i.e., vertically in the normal masonry work.

[3]No tension allowed in stack bond across head joints.

[4]The values shown here are for tension in masonry in the direction of running bond, i.e., horizontally between supports.

[5]Net area in contact with mortar or net cross-sectional area.

From the Uniform Building Code, ©1982, ICBO.

Figure 8-8　Allowable Stresses for Unreinforced Unit Masonry

TABLE NO. 24-C—ALLOWABLE SHEAR ON BOLTS
Masonry of Unburned Clay Units

DIAMETER OF BOLTS (Inches)	EMBEDMENTS (Inches)	SHEAR (Pounds)
$\frac{1}{2}$	—	——
$\frac{5}{8}$	12	200
$\frac{3}{4}$	15	300
$\frac{7}{8}$	18	400
1	21	500
$1\frac{1}{8}$	24	600

TABLE NO. 24-F—SHEAR ON ANCHOR BOLTS AND DOWELS—REINFORCED GYPSUM CONCRETE [1]

BOLT OR DOWEL SIZE (Inches)	EMBEDMENT (Inches)	SHEAR [2] (Pounds)
$\frac{3}{8}$ Bolt	4	325
$\frac{1}{2}$ Bolt	5	450
$\frac{5}{8}$ Bolt	5	650
$\frac{3}{8}$ Deformed Dowel	6	325
$\frac{1}{2}$ Deformed Dowel	6	450

[1]The bolts or dowels shall be spaced not closer than 6 inches on center.
[2]The tabulated values may be increased one third for bolts or dowels resisting wind or seismic forces.

TABLE NO. 24-G—ALLOWABLE SHEAR ON BOLTS FOR ALL MASONRY EXCEPT UNBURNED CLAY UNITS

DIAMETER OF BOLT (Inches)	EMBEDMENT [1] (Inches)	SOLID MASONRY (Shear in Pounds)	GROUTED MASONRY (Shear in Pounds)
$\frac{1}{2}$	4	350	550
$\frac{5}{8}$	4	500	750
$\frac{3}{4}$	5	750	1100
$\frac{7}{8}$	6	1000	1500
1	7	1250	1850 [2]
$1\frac{1}{8}$	8	1500	2250 [2]

[1]An additional 2 inches of embedment shall be provided for anchor bolts located in the top of columns for buildings located in Seismic Zones Nos. 2, 3 and 4.
[2]Permitted only with not less than 2500 pounds per square inch units.

From the Uniform Building Code, ©1982, ICBO.

Figure 8-9 Allowable Shear on Bolts

9
Frame Walls

Chapter 25 of the U.B.C. covers wood framing. The goal here is the same as in the chapter on masonry: we want a secure building that is warm and dry. We'll start with the first section of the chapter:

Section 2501(a) Quality and Design. The quality and design of wood members and their fastenings shall conform to the provisions of this chapter, and to the applicable standards listed in Chapter 60.

This covers just about everything involving wood and wood products. Subsection (b) governs "workmanship":

(b) Workmanship. All members shall be framed, anchored, tied and braced so as to develop the strength and rigidity necessary for the purposes for which they are used.

I interpret this to mean that all portions of the building will be assembled as provided for in this chapter or any other chapter where the assembly of two or more portions is discussed. Perhaps Subsection (c) will help explain this:

(c) Fabrication. Preparation, fabrication and installation of wood members and their fastenings shall conform to accepted engineering practices and to the requirements of this code.

Many pieces of lumber are misgraded. The code recognizes this by allowing a certain amount of overlap in the grading. Unfortunately, there seems to be more junk lumber on the market simply because a grade stamp may not honestly reflect the quality of the material. Subsection (d) covers rejection of framing material:

(d) Rejection. The building official may deny permission for the use of a wood member where permissible grade characteristics or defects are present in such combination that they affect the serviceability of the member.

Do You Accept All Lumber?

Why should you? You wouldn't buy a car with a flat tire, would you? Just because a piece of wood has a grade mark doesn't mean that it conforms to that grade or will do the job you want it to do. If it's poor quality lumber, reject it. If the dealer won't take it back, find another dealer to do business with. However, if you bought the lumber from a stack of bargain material, you may not be able to return faulty planks.

Grade marks must be clearly visible on all framing members for inspection. (See Figure 9-1.) As you can see in Section 2501(d), the building inspector can reject flawed lumber if he finds it on your job. He can make you replace it even if it's already installed. And that might be expensive.

Just because a board has a grade mark doesn't necessarily mean that it's a good piece of lumber. In the first place, the code works in favor of the lumber suppliers because it allows a certain amount of leeway in grading standards. Most lumber—even in this day of computerization—is still graded by eye, and the human eye cannot always see all the defects. Therefore, it's your responsibility to reject any material you think is not up to par. That doesn't mean you have to return it, however. There may be other places you can use it where strength or appearance is not as critical. In many cases the original grading might have been borderline; it was the way that particular piece was used that caused the problem.

Suppose you have a joist with a knot of the maximum size allowable for the dimensions of this particular joist. Then your plumber comes along and makes a notch near enough to this knot

Figure 9-1   Grade Marks Must Be Clearly Visible
on All Framing Members

to weaken the entire member. This will catch the inspector's eye, and he usually has four options available: (1) he can order it replaced, (2) he can order it cut back and headered in, or (3) he can order you to brace it, either with a post or by scabbing another piece to it. If you don't want to do any of these, the inspector has his fourth option: shut down your job and order you to employ a testing agency. At your considerable expense, they will sandbag the floor, test it for deflections, and then certify to the inspector that the assembly has the strength required by the code. Well, that's what he can do, but I doubt if you'll push him that far. In fact, you may have already caught the problem and solved it by (3) above.

Notching Beams and Joists
Section 2517(d)3 of the U.B.C. states, in part:

Notches on the ends of joists shall not exceed one-fourth the joist depth. Holes bored in joists shall not be within 2 inches of the top or bottom of the joist, and the diameter of any such hole shall not exceed one-third the depth of the joist. Notches in the top or bottom of joists shall not exceed one-sixth the depth and shall not be located in the middle third of the span. (See Figure 9-2.)

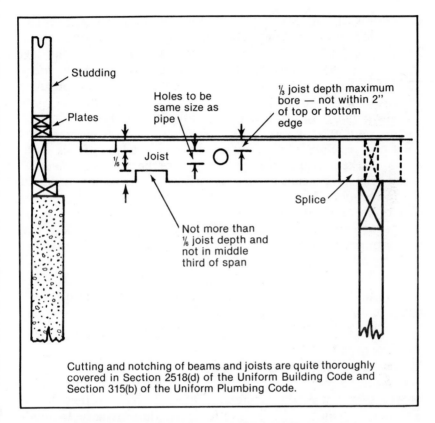

Studding

Plates

Holes to be
same size as
pipe

⅓ joist depth maximum
bore — not within 2"
of top or bottom
edge

⅙ Joist

Splice

Not more than
⅙ joist depth and
not in middle
third of span

Cutting and notching of beams and joists are quite thoroughly
covered in Section 2518(d) of the Uniform Building Code and
Section 315(b) of the Uniform Plumbing Code.

Figure 9-2   Proper Cutting and Notching of Joists
and Beams

Section 315(b) of the Uniform Plumbing Code states:

*All piping in connection with a plumbing system shall be so installed that piping
or connections will not be subject to undue strain or stresses, and provisions shall
be made for expansion and structural settlement in concrete or masonry walls or
footings. No structural member shall be seriously weakened or impaired by cutting, notching or otherwise, and unless impractical due to structural conditions,
all wood beams, girders, joists, studs and similar construction shall be bored with
holes approximately the same diameter as the pipes passing through them.*

It seems that quite a few plumbers were cutting the framing
members to fit their needs. This was especially true around

bathrooms. A plumber would find himself in the position of having to place a water closet bend where a joist would have to run. Instead, he'd get out his saw and make a few alterations. The next thing the general contractor knew, I'd be knocking on his door and informing him that this little problem would have to be taken care of by headering. By this time the pipes were already in place and the plumber was off on another job. Placing a header in such a spot is not an easy job.

Of course, a good framer would have been aware of this situation and taken the proper steps long before the plumber arrived. It might only have meant laying out the joists from the other side of the foundation. However, the big problem in too many cases is lack of supervision. If you feel that the framer might not be experienced enough, lay out the job in greater detail. Show him where pipe chases and cut-outs should be, how to header them, and any other important details.

In many trades an individual is not expected to look out for problems that are not his responsibility. The ultimate authority lies with the owner, and is passed down from him through the general contractor to the other crafts and subs involved in the work.

What Should Be Done About Holes?

We've talked about cutting holes in joists for pipe, conduit, wires or whatever, but we didn't mention what to do about these holes. Technically, you shouldn't have to do anything because the code clearly states that holes should be the size of the pipe or conduit going through them. However, the holes are often much larger for the convenience of the wire-puller or the person installing the pipe. The code covers this in Section 2516(d), where it states that fire stops must be provided: "In openings around vents, pipes, ducts, chimneys, fireplaces, and similar places which could afford a passage for fire at ceilings and floor levels, with non-combustible materials."

This is one of our main concerns: the passage of fire. Another concern is the strength of the member. Let's take a look at 2517(g)6:

6. *Pipes in Walls. Stud partitions containing plumbing, heating, or other pipes shall be so framed and the joists underneath so spaced as to give proper clearance for the piping. Where a partition containing such piping runs parallel to the floor*

Figure 9-3 Pipes Through Stud Blocking. Note the approximate ⅝ inch space from the edge of the block to the edge of the hole, and the galvanized plates on the edge of the blocking.

joists, the joists underneath such partitions shall be doubled and spaced to permit the passage of such pipes and shall be bridged. Where plumbing, heating or other pipes are placed in or partly in a partition, necessitating the cutting of the soles or plates, a metal tie not less than 1/8 inch thick and 1½ inches wide shall be fastened to the plate across and to each side of the opening with not less than four 16d nails.

There is still more on pipes in the walls; Figure 9-3 shows some of the concerns. Section 2517(g)9 approaches it this way:

9. Bored Holes. A hole not greater in diameter than 40 percent of the wood stud width may be bored in any wood stud. Bored holes not greater than 60 percent of the width of the stud are permitted in nonbearing partitions or in any wall where each bored stud is doubled, provided not more than two such successive doubled studs are so bored.

In no case shall the edge of the bored hole be nearer than 5/8 inch to the edge of the stud. Bored holes shall not be located at the same section of stud as a cut or notch.

What the code is talking about is preventative construction. "6" mentions fastening a 1/8-inch plate across the area of the hole. "9" states that the edge of hole can't be nearer than 5/8 inch from the edge of the member. These two items serve a single purpose—to prevent sheetrock nails from puncturing water lines. This can be critical. Unfortunately, if the tip of the nail does puncture the line, it may not show up immediately. The normal vibrations and shrinkages in a new structure will either gradually work the nail loose or enlarge the hole and, presto! a leak appears. It may take a week or it may take a couple of months, but it will be expensive to repair when it shows up.

Determining Wood Strength
Basically, this involves methods and formulas which determine the strength of wood, wood joints, and other wood assemblies. Since most of these methods and formulas are used for large structures where stress, strength and such are needed from a design standpoint, let's leave them for the engineers and designers. The average contractor will find nearly all of the information he needs in U.B.C. Tables Nos. 25-A-1, 25-T-J-1, 25-T-J-6, and 25-T-R-1, 2, 7, 8, 10, 11, 13, and 14.

U.B.C. Table No. 25-A-1, *Allowable Unit Stresses—Structural Lumber*, breaks down the usual structural lumber by name and grade and shows the various allowable unit stresses in pounds per square inch. The other tables cover the allowable spans for floor joists, ceiling joists and high and low slope rafters.

This is a complex subject, but I'll do my best to keep it as brief and simple as possible. What I'd like to stress is that by following these tables, you can avoid having to work with difficult formulas, symbols and figures.

Modulus of Elasticity
This is what I call the "first line of defense." By knowing the *modulus of elasticity* (E factor), you can find most of the other information you'll need to determine wood strength. But you'll need to know more. To use U.B.C. Table No. 25-A-1, you need to know the type or name of the material used. In my area most framing material is Douglas Fir (North). You'll note when you look at this table that Douglas Fir follows Coast Sitka Spruce. Because we're hoping to use 2" x 8" Douglas Fir joists, 16" on

Figure 9-4 Joists in Place

center (o.c.) we'll start here. We'll need a grade, however, so let's use "Construction" since it's one of the most commonly used types.

But can we use it? Go to the next column, "Size Classification." This column shows that construction grade is only used in timbers 2 to 4 inches thick, 4 inches wide. Our 2 x 8 joists won't fit. Through experience I have found that a "Modulus of Elasticity" should be about 1,500,000.

Okay, so what grade of lumber can we use? Dropping down the page we come to this dimension, "2" to 4" thick, 5" and wider." Here we find that "No. 3 and Stud" has the same Modulus of Elasticity as Construction grade above. (Modulus of Elasticity is found in the second column from the right.) However, before we make a firm decision let's go to the column, "Extreme Fiber in Bending." Now, in comparing these two grades we find that, although the "E" factor is the same, the "Fb" factor is not. Is this the one we should use?

Let's put those figures aside for a moment.

Allowable Spans for Joists and Rafters
Beams are often used as single members, but joists seldom are.
Usually they're ganged in groups of four or more. That's what the
code calls "Repetitive Member Uses," the second column under
the "Extreme Fiber in Bending" column. In this column the F_b
factor for "No. 3 and Stud" is 850, compared to 1200 for Construction grade. Are we still in trouble?

Let's go to U.B.C. Table No. 25-T-J-1, *Allowable Spans for
Floor Joists, 40 lbs. per sq. ft., Live Load*, to find the joists we
should use. This table might look tricky, but it's really quite simple.

Look at the column "Joist/Size Spacing." It lists the common
joist dimensions for light frame buildings and the common spacing: 12-, 16- and 24-inch. The columns to the right give the E factors, beginning at 800,000 psi and ranging up to 2.2 million psi.
So, taking the first column and the first line, which would be 2 x 6
joists, 12 inches on center, E factor of 0.8 psi., we find a set of
numbers that looks like this: 8-6/720. Translated, that means that
a 2 x 6 joist, 12 inches o.c. with a F_b (Extreme Fiber in Bending)
factor of 720 will span 8'6".

The hyphenated number is the span in feet and inches for a 2 x 6
joist with a F_b factor of 720 (the bottom number) when it is placed
12 inches o.c. If we were to use that same timber 16 inches o.c., the
span would be reduced to 7'9", but the F_b factor would be increased to 790.

So what about our problem? Let's say that the house we're
building is 25 feet wide with a beam down the middle of the floor.
Therefore, my span will be 12'6". We were figuring for 2 x 8, 16
inches o.c. Finding that on U.B.C. Table No. 25-T-J-1, we go to
the right until we come to the figure closest to our span. That is
12'7" which requires an F_b of 1200. That is 400 over our 800
figure derived from U.B.C.Table No. 25-A-1, and we can't use it.
So let's take a look at laying them 12" o.c. When that line is run
out we find that the F_b factor is 850, which gives us a span of between 12'1" and 12'6". Actually, the latter is getting close. Should
we use that?

It might depend on how strict the inspector is. I think it would
do the job, but it might give you some pretty springy floors. My
recommendation is to go to a larger timber, a 2 x 10, 16 inches o.c.

This would be more expensive, but would provide a better job. The difference might be worth it.

You may be able to push the lighter material past the inspector, but remember that he'll be looking at the same charts we've just been reviewing.

If you are using an engineered plan, the drawings will probably indicate not only the size of the joists but the spacing and the direction of run. They should also include the name of the species and the grade.

Diaphragms and Framing

A wood diaphragm is an assembly of lumber and plywood designed to resist horizontal and vertical pressures and loads. Certain deflections are allowed. The permissible deflection is that point up to which the diaphragm and any attached distributing or resisting elements will not maintain their structural integrity under the assumed load conditions. In other words, they will continue to support the assumed loads without danger to the structure or its occupants.

A roof, floor, or wall can be a diaphragm. U.B.C. Table No. 25-J (Figure 9-5) gives *Allowable Shear in Pounds per Foot for Horizontal Plywood Diaphragms with Framing of Douglas Fir-Larch or Southern Pine* and provides some examples of typical diaphragms.

Miscellaneous Requirements

I mentioned that in addition to the crawl space required under a house you must also have a crawl hole big enough to allow replacement or removal of such items as an underfloor furnace. What if you don't have an underfloor furnace? A crawl hole is still required. It must be at least 18" x 24". Even if you have a partial basement, you still must have a crawl hole or access to the unexcavated portion. (See Figure 9-6.)

Often you'll find that beams are to be set in pockets constructed in the foundation wall. Just remember to leave at least 1/2 inch of space on tops, sides and ends of the beams unless an approved wood of natural resistance to decay or a treated wood is used. The only woods available that I know of with a natural resistance to decay are redwood and cypress.

TABLE NO. 25-J—ALLOWABLE SHEAR IN POUNDS PER FOOT FOR HORIZONTAL PLYWOOD DIAPHRAGMS WITH FRAMING OF DOUGLAS FIR-LARCH OR SOUTHERN PINE[1]

PLYWOOD GRADE	Common Nail Size	Minimum Nominal Penetration in Framing (in inches)	Minimum Nominal Plywood Thickness (in inches)	Minimum Nominal Width of Framing Member (in inches)	BLOCKED DIAPHRAGMS — Nail spacing at diaphragm boundaries (all cases), at continuous panel edges parallel to load (Cases 3 and 4) and at all panel edges (Cases 5 and 6)				UNBLOCKED DIAPHRAGM — Nails spaced 6" max. at supported end	
					6	4	2½²	2²	Load perpendicular to unblocked edges and continuous panel joints (Case 1)	Other configurations (Cases 2, 3 & 4)
					Nail spacing at other plywood panel edges 6	6	4	3		
STRUCTURAL I	6d	1¼	5/16	2 / 3	185 / 210	250 / 280	375 / 420	420 / 475	165 / 185	125 / 140
	8d	1½	3/8	2 / 3	270 / 300	360 / 400	530 / 600	600 / 675	240 / 265	180 / 200
	10d	1⅝	1/2	2 / 3²	320 / 360	425 / 480	640² / 720	730² / 820	285 / 320	215 / 240
C-D, C-C, STRUCTURAL II and other grades covered in U.B.C. Standard No. 25-9	6d	1¼	5/16	2 / 3	170 / 190	225 / 250	335 / 380	380 / 430	150 / 170	110 / 125
			3/8	2 / 3	185 / 210	250 / 280	375 / 420	420 / 475	165 / 185	125 / 140
	8d	1½	3/8	2 / 3	240 / 270	320 / 360	480 / 540	545 / 610	215 / 240	160 / 180
			1/2	2 / 3	270 / 300	360 / 400	530 / 600	600 / 675	240 / 265	180 / 200
	10d	1⅝	1/2	2 / 3²	290 / 325	385 / 430	575² / 650	655² / 735	255 / 290	190 / 215
			5/8	2 / 3²	320 / 360	425 / 480	640² / 720	730² / 820	285 / 320	215 / 240

Figure 9-5 Allowable Shear for Horizontal Plywood Diaphragms

[1] These values are for short-time loads due to wind or earthquake and must be reduced 25 percent for normal loading. Space nails 10 inches on center for floors and 12 inches on center for roofs along intermediate framing members.

Allowable shear values for nails in framing members of other species set forth in Table No. 25-17-J of U.B.C. Standards shall be calculated for all grades by multiplying the values for nails in STRUCTURAL I by the following factors: Group III, 0.82 and Group IV, 0.65.

[2] Framing shall be 3-inch nominal or wider and nails shall be staggered where nails are spaced 2 inches or 2½ inches on center, and where 10d nails having penetration into framing of more than 1⅝ inches are spaced 3 inches on center.

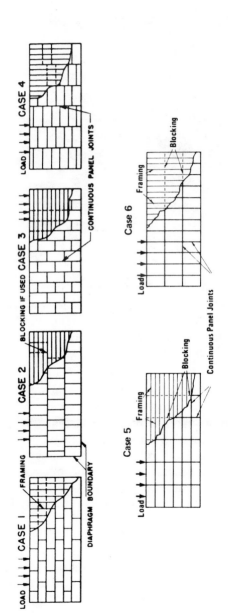

NOTE: Framing may be located in either direction for blocked diaphragms.

Figure 9-5 (continued) Allowable Shear for Horizontal Plywood Diaphragms

From the Uniform Building Code, © 1982, ICBO.

Figure 9-6 Foundation and Underfloor Access Hole with Galvanized Steel Window Well. The code does not specify which type of window well is acceptable—concrete or steel. Be sure that there is space enough for an adult to enter the access hole.

We've already discussed foundation ventilation and how the wood or framing material must be at least six inches from any earth unless separated by at least three inches of concrete. But what about the planter boxes installed adjacent to wood framing, those huge masonry affairs placed on the ground, often adjacent to the entry. These must have at least two inches of space and the adjacent wall must have flashing where the space is less than six inches.

Firestops
Actually, the average dwelling has little need for any firestopping that isn't already built into the house. There are a few areas, however, that may require additional firestops.

Firestopping is installed to cut off all concealed draft openings and to form an effective barrier between floors. According to Section 2516(f), firestopping should be used in the following places:

Figure 9-7 Fireblocking Along a Stair Run. This is not a conforming blocking since only the points of the 2" x 4" touch the adjoining stud. The blocking should be cut at an angle to give a minimum of one inch of wood at point of contact.

A. In concealed spaces of stud walls and partitions, including furred spaces, at the ceiling and flooring levels and at 10-foot intervals along the length of the wall. **Exception:** *Firestops may be omitted at floor and ceiling levels when approved smoke-actuated fire dampers are installed at these levels.*

B. At all interconnections between concealed vertical and horizontal spaces such as occur at soffits, drop ceilings and cove ceilings.

C. In concealed spaces between stair stringers at the top and bottom of the run and between studs along and in line with the run of the stairs if the walls under the stairs are unfinished.

D. In openings around vents, pipes, ducts, chimneys, fireplaces and similar openings which afford a passage for fire at ceiling and floor levels, with noncombustible materials.

Firestops must be nominal 2-inch-thick wood, gypsum board, cement asbestos board, mineral wool, or other approved noncombustible materials securely fastened in place. (See Figure 9-7.)

Figure 9-8 Plywood Siding Being Installed Over Aluminized Sheathing

Siding

Siding should be at least 3/8 inch thick unless placed over sheathing permitted by the code. This thickness is based on a maximum stud spacing of 16 inches on center. There is a movement afoot to get the maximum spacing increased to 24 inches for studding in the exterior walls. In that case you would have to use thicker plywood or use sheathing underneath the siding.

All weatherboarding or siding must be nailed securely to each stud. Use at least one nail every 6 inches on the edges and every 12 inches on the field. If conventional siding is used, there should be at least one nail per stud. If conventional siding is installed over 1-inch nominal sheathing or 1/2-inch plywood sheathing, it must be fastened with a line of nails spaced not more than 24 inches on center in each piece of weatherboarding or siding.

Unless you have applied the siding over sheathing, joints must be over the framing members and be covered with a continuous wood batt, or be lapped horizontally or otherwise made waterproof to the satisfaction of the inspector. This may be done with caulking or flashing.

Shingles or shakes, whether of wood, asbestos cement or other approved materials, bring up some different rules. They may be applied over furring strips, wood sheathing or approved fiberboard shingle backer. But they must be placed over building paper

**TABLE NO. 25-L—WOOD SHINGLE AND
SHAKE SIDEWALL EXPOSURES**

SHINGLE OR SHAKE	MAXIMUM WEATHER EXPOSURES			
	Single-Coursing		Double-Coursing	
Length and Type	No. 1	No. 2	No. 1	No. 2
1. 16-inch Shingles	7½ "	7½ "	12"	10"
2. 18-inch Shingles	8½ "	8½ "	14"	11"
3. 24-inch Shingles	11½ "	11½ "	16"	14"
4. 18-inch Resawn Shakes	8½ "	—	14"	—
5. 18-inch Straight-Split Shakes	8½ "	—	16"	—
6. 24-inch Resawn Shakes	11½ "	—	20"	—

From the Uniform Building Code, ©1982, ICBO.

Figure 9-9   Wood Shingle and Shake Sidewall Exposures

unless they are applied over solid sheathing. If fiberboard backing is used, they must be attached with corrosion-resistant annular grooved nails.

The weather exposure of wood shingles or shake siding must not exceed the maximums set forth in U.B.C. Table No. 25-L (see Figure 9-9).

Nails
U.B.C. Table No. 25-Q, (Figure 9-10), gives nailing requirements for almost all carpentry joints used in residential construction. U.B.C. Table No. 25-G (Figure 9-11) lists *Safe Lateral Strength and Required Penetration of Box and Common Wire Nails Driven Perpendicular to Grain of Wood*. This table also lists the comparative length of all standard nails. Spacing and penetration of nails and other fasteners are very important. Nails and spikes, for which the wire gauge or length is not specified in this table, have a required penetration of at least 11 diameters; allowable loads may be interpolated.

The code also spells out the spacing for nailing. For wood-to-wood joints the spacing center-to-center must be not less than the required penetration. Edge and distances may be not less than one-

TABLE NO. 25-Q—NAILING SCHEDULE

CONNECTION	NAILING[1]
1. Joist to sill or girder, toenail	3-8d
2. Bridging to joist, toenail each end	2-8d
3. 1″ x 6″ subfloor or less to each joist, face nail	2-8d
4. Wider than 1″ x 6″ subfloor to each joist, face nail	3-8d
5. 2″ subfloor to joist or girder, blind and face nail	2-16d
6. Sole plate to joist or blocking, face nail	16d at 16″ o.c.
7. Top plate to stud, end nail	2-16d
8. Stud to sole plate	4-8, toenail or 2-16d, end nail
9. Double studs, face nail	16d at 24″ o.c.
10. Doubled top plates, face nail	16d at 16″ o.c.
11. Top plates, laps and intersections, face nail	2-16d
12. Continuous header, two pieces	16d at 16″ o.c. along each edge
13. Ceiling joists to plate, toenail	3-8d
14. Continuous header to stud, toenail	4-8d
15. Ceiling joists, laps over partitions, face nail	3-16d
16. Ceiling joists to parallel rafters, face nail	3-16d
17. Rafter to plate, toenail	3-8d
18. 1″ brace to each stud and plate, face nail	2-8d
19. 1″ x 8″ sheathing or less to each bearing, face nail	2-8d
20. Wider than 1″ x 8″ sheathing to each bearing, face nail	3-8d
21. Built-up corner studs	16d at 24″ o.c.
22. Built-up girder and beams	20d at 32″ o.c. at top and bottom and staggered 2-20d at ends and at each splice

[1]Common or box nails may be used except where otherwise stated.
[2]Common or deformed shank.
[3]Common.
[4]Deformed shank.
[5]Nails spaced at 6 inches on center at edges, 12 inches at intermediate supports (10 inches at intermediate supports for floors), except 6 inches at all supports where spans are 48 inches or more. For nailing of plywood diaphragms and shear walls, refer to Section 2513 (c). Nails for wall sheathing may be common, box or casing.
[6]Corrosion-resistant siding or casing nails conforming to the requirements of Section 2516 (j) 1.

Figure 9-10   Nailing Schedule

CONNECTION	NAILING[1]
23. 2" planks	2-16d at each bearing

24. **Particleboard:**[5]
   Wall Sheathing (to framing):
      ⅜"-½"
	6d[3]

⅝"-¾"	8d[3]

25. **Plywood:**[5]
   Subfloor, roof and wall sheathing (to framing):
      ½" and less
	6d[2]

⅝"-¾"	8d[3] or 6d[4]
⅞"-1"	8d[2]
1⅛"-1¼"	10d[3] or 8d[4]
Combination Subfloor-underlayment (to framing): ¾" and less	6d[4]
⅞"-1"	8d[4]
1⅛"-1¼"	10d[3] or 8d[4]
26. **Panel Siding (to framing):** ½" or less	6d[6]
⅝"	8d[6]
27. **Fiberboard Sheathing:**[7] ½"	No. 11 ga.[8] 6d[3] No. 16 ga.[9]
25⁄32"	No. 11 ga.[8] 8d[3] No. 16 ga.[9]

[7]Fasteners spaced 3 inches on center at exterior edges and 6 inches on center at intermediate supports.

[8]Corrosion-resistant roofing nails with 7⁄16-inch-diameter head and 1½-inch length for ½-inch sheathing and 1¾-inch length for 25⁄32-inch sheathing conforming to the requirements of Section 2516 (j) 1.

[9]Corrosion-resistant staples with nominal 7⁄16-inch crown and 1⅛-inch length for ½-inch sheathing and 1½-inch length for 25⁄32-inch sheathing conforming to the requirements of Section 2516 (j) 1.

From the Uniform Building Code, ©1982, ICBO.

Figure 9-10 (continued)   Nailing Schedule

half the required penetration. Holes for nails, when they are necessary to prevent splitting, should be bored to a diameter less than that of the nails.

Staples
Not all buildings are put together with nails. Today, staples are widely used by most building trades.

**TABLE NO. 25-G—SAFE LATERAL STRENGTH AND REQUIRED
PENETRATION OF BOX AND COMMON WIRE NAILS DRIVEN
PERPENDICULAR TO GRAIN OF WOOD**

SIZE OF NAIL	STANDARD LENGTH (Inches)	WIRE GAUGE	PENETRATION REQUIRED (Inches)	LOADS (Pounds)[1,2]	
				Douglas Fir Larch or Southern Pine	Other Species
BOX NAILS					
6d	2	12½	1⅛	51	See U.B.C. Standard No. 25-17
8d	2½	11½	1¼	63	
10d	3	10½	1½	76	
12d	3¼	10½	1½	76	
16d	3½	10	1½	82	
20d	4	9	1⅝	94	
30d	4½	9	1⅝	94	
40d	5	8	1¾	108	
COMMON NAILS					
6d	2	11½	1¼	63	See U.B.C. Standard No. 25-17
8d	2½	10¼	1½	78	
10d	3	9	1⅝	94	
12d	3¼	9	1⅝	94	
16d	3½	8	1¾	108	
20d	4	6	2⅛	139	
30d	4½	5	2¼	155	
40d	5	4	2½	176	
50d	5½	3	2¾	199	
60d	6	2	2⅞	223	

[1]The safe lateral strength values may be increased 25 percent where metal side plates are used.
[2]For wood diaphragm calculations these values may be increased 30 percent. (See U.B.C. Standard No. 25-17.)

From the Uniform Building Code, ©1982, ICBO.

Figure 9-11　Nail Specifications

Staples and staplers can be very effective. The problem (as with most tools and appliances) is the operator. Regardless of how hard someone works to make a tool almost perfect or a material the finest thing since mother's milk, there's always someone who can foul it up.

Staples are an acceptable replacement for nails in most cases, but only if the right staple is used for the particular job at hand. You wouldn't staple down a roof with an ordinary office stapler. Well, using the wrong staple can have the same effect. And, once the job is finished and the paint is on, who can tell the difference?

Trusses
Staples aren't the only alternative to nails or screws. Manufactured roof trusses, a fairly recent development, are frequently used. They are factory assembled, their components attached with metal connectors or gussets. These connectors are, in effect, a form of "gang-nail." These pieces of galvanized metal are engineered for a particular application with definite loadings and are pressure installed. The strength of the truss is determined by the size and grade of the timber as well as by the size of the connector and the number of "spikes" it has.

One problem with these trusses is that certain manufacturers don't follow the engineered design. Sometimes they cheat on the material grades or on the size of the metal connectors. It's a good idea to get your hands on the engineer's specs and make sure the manufacturer is following them. If he isn't, return the trusses. This may delay your job, but if you don't use the proper materials, the inspector may find out. If he does find out, it may cost you a lot more than just a short delay.

Ideally, each job would require a different type of truss, and it would be impractical to list them all. I suggest you use the *Research Recommendations* your inspector has on his bookshelf to check various types and manufacturers.

Joists and Joist Problems
We've already discussed problems of determining joist sizes and loading. But there's more involved than just laying them out on top of the foundation plate. Joists must be supported laterally at the ends and at the support by solid blocking, except where the ends of the joists are nailed to a header, band, rim joist, or to an adjoining stud, or by other approved means. Solid blocking must be at least two inches thick and the full depth of the joist. That information comes from Chapter 25 of the U.B.C. Cross-bridging or blocking *between the ends* of the joists is not required except as noted below. Notice that I wrote, "between the ends" of joists;

the ends themselves must still be solid blocked. Here's what Section 2506(g) says about blocking:

(g) Lateral Support. Solid-sawn rectangular lumber beams, rafters and joists shall be supported laterally to prevent rotation or lateral displacement in accordance with the following:
If the ratio of depth to thickness, based on nominal dimension, is:
  1. Two to 1, no lateral support is required. (Note: 2 x 4, 3 x 6 or 4 x 8.)
  2. Three to 1 or 4 to 1, the ends shall be held in position, as by full-depth solid blocking, bridging, nailing or bolting to other framing members, approved hangers or other acceptable means. (Note: 2 x 6, 2 x 8, etc.)
  3. Five to 1, one edge shall be held in line for its entire length. (Note: Floor or roof sheathing should suffice for this on 2 x 10's.)
  4. Six to 1, bridging, full-depth solid blocking or cross bracing shall be installed at intervals not exceeding 8 feet unless both edges are held in line.
  5. Seven to 1, both edges shall be held in line for their entire length.

Joists joining from opposite sides of a beam, girder, or partition should be lapped by at least four inches on the opposing joists or fastened together in an approved manner. Joists running parallel under bearing partitions must be doubled.

Trimmer and header joists must be doubled or made of lumber or equivalent cross section when the span of the header exceeds four feet. The ends of header joists more than six feet long must be supported by framing anchors or joist hangers unless they are bearing on a beam. This means that if your opening is less than four feet, a single header will do. In any case it must be as wide as the joist it supports.

Floors
On the subject of floors and floor construction, let's first look at subflooring. This is where the trouble usually begins. Very often squeaky, noisy floors can be traced to the subfloor.

I once owned a house with a squeaking floor in the hall and bathroom. Tiles kept popping up. Finally I tore up the floor to see what the trouble was. The subfloor was nothing but scrap lumber laid (not nailed) on the joists. It was not even laid tight but appeared to have been thrown on and the underlayment placed on top. This meant replacing the entire floor from the joists up in both the bath and the hallway.

Laying Subfloor

Joints in subflooring should be over the supports unless end-matched lumber is used. End-matched means the ends of the lumber are tongue and grooved. When properly installed they act as one continuous piece of lumber. Each piece must rest on at least two joists. If you are using plywood for subflooring, as nearly everyone does now, you will have to meet the requirements shown in Table No. 25-S-1 (Figure 9-12).

TABLE NO. 25-S-1—ALLOWABLE SPANS FOR PLYWOOD SUBFLOOR AND ROOF SHEATHING CONTINUOUS OVER TWO OR MORE SPANS AND FACE GRAIN PERPENDICULAR TO SUPPORTS[1, 9]

| PANEL IDENTIFICATION INDEX[3] | PLYWOOD THICKNESS (Inch) | ROOF[2] | | | | FLOOR MAXIMUM SPAN[4] (In Inches) |
| | | Maximum Span (In Inches) | | Load (In Pounds per Square Foot) | | |
		Edges Blocked	Edges Unblocked	Total Load	Live Load	
1. 12/0	5/16	12		155	150	0
2. 16/0	5/16, 3/8	16		95	75	0
3. 20/0	5/16, 3/8	20		75	65	0
4. 24/0	3/8	24	16	65	50	0
5. 24/0	1/2	24	24	65	50	0
6. 30/12	5/8	30	26	70	50	12[5]
7. 32/16	1/2, 5/8	32	28	55	40	16[7]
8. 36/16	3/4	36	30	55	50	16[7]
9. 42/20	5/8, 3/4, 7/8	42	32	40[6]	35[6]	20[7, 8]
10. 48/24	3/4, 7/8	48	36	40[6]	35[6]	24

[1]These values apply for C-C, C-D, Structural I and II grades only. Spans shall be limited to values shown because of possible effect of concentrated loads.

[2]Uniform load deflection limitations: $\frac{1}{180}$ of the span under live load plus dead load, $\frac{1}{240}$ under live load only. Edges may be blocked with lumber or other approved type of edge support.

[3]Identification index appears on all panels in the construction grades listed in Footnote No. 1.

[4]Plywood edges shall have approved tongue-and-groove joints or shall be supported with blocking unless 1/4-inch minimum thickness underlayment, or 1 1/2 inches of approved cellular or lightweight concrete is placed over the subfloor, or finish floor is 25/32-inch wood strip. Allowable uniform load based on deflection of $\frac{1}{360}$ of span is 165 pounds per square foot.

(Continued on next page)

Figure 9-12 Allowable Spans for Plywood Subfloor and Roof Sheathing

[5]May be 16 inches if $^{25}/_{32}$-inch wood strip flooring is installed at right angles to joists.

[6]For roof live load of 40 pounds per square foot or total load of 55 pounds per square foot, decrease spans by 13 percent or use panel with next greater identification index.

[7]May be 24 inches if $^{25}/_{32}$-inch wood strip flooring is installed at right angles to joists.

[8]May be 24 inches where a minimum of 1½ inches of approved cellular or lightweight concrete is placed over the subfloor and the plywood sheathing is manufactured with exterior glue.

[9]Floor or roof sheathing conforming with this table shall be deemed to meet the design criteria of Section 2516.

TABLE NO. 25-S-2—ALLOWABLE LOADS FOR PLYWOOD ROOF SHEATHING CONTINUOUS OVER TWO OR MORE SPANS AND FACE GRAIN PARALLEL TO SUPPORTS[1] [2]

	THICKNESS	NO. OF PLIES	SPAN	TOTAL LOAD	LIVE LOAD
STRUCTURAL I	½	4	24	35	25
	½	5	24	55	40
Other grades covered in U.B.C. Standard No. 25-9	½	5	24	30	25
	⅝	4	24	40	30
	⅝	5	24	60	45

[1]Uniform load deflection limitations: $^1/_{180}$ of span under live load plus dead load, $^1/_{240}$ under live load only. Edges shall be blocked with lumber or other approved type of edge supports.

[2]Roof sheathing conforming with this table shall be deemed to meet the design criteria of Section 2516.

From the Uniform Building Code, ©1982, ICBO.

Figure 9-12 (continued) Allowable Spans for Plywood Subfloor and Roof Sheathing

Figure 9-13 gives *Allowable Spans for Lumber Floor and Roof Sheathing*. Note the second table in Figure 9-13, U.B.C. Table No. 25-Q. This one lists the types and grades of lumber to be used in floor or roof sheathing. The Standard's numbers following each category merely list the spot in the U.B.C. Standards where these grades are defined. Actually, all you should need to do is check the grade markings on the timber.

A companion table that goes with U.B.C. Table No. 25-R-1 is U.B.C. Table No. 25-T (Figure 9-14). This one has a sneaky little number in it that might surprise you. See the column called "Species Groups"? Here you must refer to Table No. 25-9-A from the U.B.C. Standards (Figure 9-15) to find out what the groups are.

TABLE NO. 25-Q—ALLOWABLE SPANS FOR LUMBER FLOOR AND ROOF SHEATHING[3]

SPAN (Inches)	MINIMUM NET THICKNESS (Inches) OF LUMBER PLACED			
	PERPENDICULAR TO SUPPORTS		DIAGONALLY TO SUPPORTS	
	Surfaced Dry[2]	Surfaced Unseasoned	Surfaced Dry[2]	Surfaced Unseasoned
FLOORS				
24	$\frac{3}{4}$	$\frac{25}{32}$	$\frac{3}{4}$	$\frac{25}{32}$
16	$\frac{5}{8}$	$\frac{11}{16}$	$\frac{5}{8}$	$\frac{11}{16}$
ROOFS				
24	$\frac{5}{8}$	$\frac{11}{16}$	$\frac{3}{4}$	$\frac{25}{32}$

[1]Installation details shall conform to Sections 2518 (e) 1 and 2518 (h) 7 for floor and roof sheathing, respectively.

[2]Maximum 19 percent moisture content.

[3]Floor or roof sheathing conforming with this table shall be deemed to meet the design criteria of Section 2517.

SHEATHING LUMBER SHALL MEET THE FOLLOWING MINIMUM GRADE REQUIREMENTS: BOARD GRADE

SOLID FLOOR OR ROOF SHEATHING	SPACED ROOF SHEATHING	U.B.C. STANDARD NUMBER
1. Utility	Standard	25-2, 25-3 or 25-4
2. 4 Common, or Utility	3 Common, or Standard	25-2, 25-3, 25-4 25-5 or 25-8
3. No. 3	No. 2	25-6
4. Merchantable	Construction Common	25-7

From the Uniform Building Code, ©1982, ICBO.

Figure 9-13 Allowable Spans for Lumber Floor and Roof Sheathing

Post and Beam—Plank and Beam

The two names are often used interchangeably although they are not the same in a true sense. Figure 9-16 shows a post and beam floor system.

The same general requirements hold true for post and beam floor systems as for other types. However, where you were using 2-inch-thick joists on edge and 5/8-inch or 3/4-inch subflooring, now you would be using 2-inch-thick planks or decking, then heavier beams and greater spans. The same requirements hold true, however, for end-matched lumber. The joints do not have to

**TABLE NO. 25-T—ALLOWABLE SPAN FOR PLYWOOD
COMBINATION SUBFLOOR-UNDERLAYMENT[1]**
Plywood Continuous over Two or More Spans and
Face Grain Perpendicular to Supports

SPECIES GROUPS[2]	MAXIMUM SPACING OF JOISTS		
	16″	20″	24″
1	½″	5⁄8″	¾″
2, 3	5⁄8″	¾″	7⁄8″
4	¾″	7⁄8″	1″

[1]Applicable to Underlayment grade, C-C (plugged) and all grades of sanded exterior-type plywood. Spans limited to values shown because of possible effect of concentrated loads. Allowable uniform load based on deflection of 1⁄360 of span is 125 pounds per square foot. Plywood edges shall have approved tongue-and-groove joints or shall be supported with blocking, unless ¼-inch minimum thickness underlayment is installed, or finish floor is 25⁄32-inch wood strip. If wood strips are perpendicular to supports, thicknesses shown for 16- and 20-inch spans may be used on 24-inch span. Except for ½ inch, Underlayment grade and C-C (plugged) panels may be of nominal thicknesses 1⁄32 inch thinner than the nominal thicknesses shown when marked with the reduced thickness.

[2]See U.B.C. Standard No. 25-9 for plywood species groups.

From the Uniform Building Code, ©1982, ICBO.

Figure 9-14   Allowable Span for Plywood Combination Subfloor—Underlayment

be on the joists as they would if plain unmatched planks were used. If you are using the usual "5-quarter" or "4-for-1" plywood, the requirements of U.B.C. Table No. 25-S-1 would apply.

"5-quarter" or "4-for-1" plywood panels should be able to span 48 inches when laid perpendicular to the joists and when the code allows it. However, most builders have found that this has a tendency to give a slightly springy or spongy floor when heavy loads—water beds, pianos, etc.—are applied. Most builders now use 32-inch spacing in their floor beams. The additional cost is not that great.

Scantling

After the subfloor is down, the next step is to get the studding up. According to my references, all studs are made from *scantlings*. When I was a young builder, all 2 x 4's were called scantlings. Here's how Webster's defines the terms: "The breadth and thickness of timber and stone used in buildings; a small piece of lumber (as an upright in house framing)."

TABLE NO. 25-9-A—CLASSIFICATION OF SPECIES

Group 1	Group 2	Group 3	Group 4
Aptiong[a][b]	Cedar, Port Orford	Alder, Red	Aspen
Beech, American	Cypress	Birch, Paper	Bigtooth
Birch	Douglas Fir 2[c]	Cedar, Alaska	Quaking
Sweet	Fir	Fir, Subalpine	Cativo
Yellow	California Red	Hemlock, Eastern	Cedar
Douglas Fir[c]	Grand	Maple, Bigleaf	Incense
Kapur[a]	Noble	Pine	Western Red
Keruing[a][b]	Pacific Silver	Jack	Cottonwood
Larch, Western	White	Lodgepole	Eastern
Maple, Sugar	Hemlock, Western	Ponderosa	Black (Western Poplar)
Pine	Lauan	Spruce	Pine
Caribbean	Almon	Redwood	Eastern White
Ocote	Bagtikan	Spruce	Sugar
Pine, Southern	Mayapis	Black	
Loblolly	Red Lauan	Englemann	
Longleaf	Tangile	White	
Shortleaf	White Lauan		
Slash	Maple, Black		
Tanoak	Mengkulang[a]		
	Meranti, Red[a][d]		
	Mersawa[a]		
	Pine		
	Pond		
	Red		
	Virginia		
	Western White		
	Spruce		
	Red		
	Sitka		
	Sweetgum		
	Tamarack		
	Yellow-poplar		

(a) Each of these names represents a trade group of woods consisting of a number of closely related species.

(b) Species from the genus Dipterocarpus are marketed collectively: Apitong if originating in the Philippines; Keruing if originating in Malaysia or Indonesia.

(c) Douglas fir from trees grown in the states of Washington, Oregon, California, Idaho, Montana, Wyoming, and the Canadian Provinces of Alberta and British Columbia shall be classed as Douglas fir No. 1. Douglas fir from trees grown in the states of Nevada, Utah, Colorado, Arizona and New Mexico shall be classed as Douglas fir No. 2.

(d) Red Meranti shall be limited to species having a specific gravity of 0.41 or more based on green volume and oven dry weight.

From the Uniform Building Code, ©1982, ICBO.

Figure 9-15   Classification of Species

Figure 9-16   Post and Beam Floor System. These
beams are spaced 32'' o.c. and all the underfloor
facilities have already been installed.

Apparently it comes to us from the Middle English "scantilon"
and the Old North French "escantilon." These were the terms
stone cutters used to refer to a member twice as wide as it was
thick, hence the reference to 2 x 4's. I haven't heard the term for
many years. It has probably disappeared with the old timers with
whom I apprenticed.

Studding are the slender sticks that form the walls of a structure
and on which the siding and wallboard are hung (see Figure 9-17).
They are also what the second floor, if you have one, or the roof
will rest on. Whether you call them studding or scantling they are
an important component in most buildings.

Stud Spacing
Studs supporting floors must be placed not more than 16 inches
o.c., but 2 x 4 studs supporting only a ceiling and a roof may be
spaced up to 24 inches o.c. This also applies to non-bearing in-

Figure 9-17 Studding in Place. Note the double plate along the top of the bearing partition at the right.

terior walls. If 24-inch spacing is used, the roof trusses must be centered directly over the studding. This transfers the vertical roof load directly through the studding to the foundation; the studding then acts as a column. Studding sizes and heights are given in Figure 9-18.

When placing the studding, be sure that the wide dimension of the timber is perpendicular to the wall and that at least three studs are used at every corner of an exterior wall. Lately it's been the practice to use a single plate on all interior non-bearing partitions, and the code does provide for it. However, now that studs are purchased in bundles pre-cut to measured lengths, most contractors are going back to double plates rather than having to carry two different sizes of studs to the job.

Joints in the double top plates must be offset at least 48 inches. Joining partitions must be overlapped on the top plate. Studs

Timber Size	Number of Stories	Maximum Height
2 x 3	1 story	10 feet
2 x 4	2 stories	14 feet
3 x 4	3 stories	14 feet
2 x 6	*3 stories	20 feet

*2 x 6 and/or 3 x 4 studs must be used for the bottom of the second floor joists and 2 x 4 studs may be used for the upper two floors

Figure 9-18   Studding Sizing

should bear on a plate or sill not less than 2 inches thick; the bottom plate must be at least as wide as the wall stud.

I once inspected a job where I doubted if there was any uniformity in the spacing of the studding. It varied from 10 to 16 inches o.c. in the exterior walls. On the interior walls I noted the same practice, but this time the spacing varied up to 24 inches o.c. I'd never seen anything like it. But checking my code book I found that stud spacing on exterior walls could not *exceed* 16 inches o.c. and on interior walls could not *exceed* 24 inches o.c. The only person who could get mad in this case was the poor sheetrocker; he had a nightmare on his hands.

Corner Bracing

Exterior walls must be braced. The most common method is placing plywood panels at each corner. Another method uses a 1" x 4" brace inset at an angle into the studs. This is usually referred to as an angle brace, which runs from the floor to the upper plate at an angle not to exceed 60 degrees.

There are certain manufactured wallboards of "structural" quality. These may be used instead of either angle bracing or plywood. Before you buy, check with the inspector and consult his Research Recommendations to make sure your brand has been approved and to determine how it must be installed. Yes, even to the number of nails required to attach it. If you refer to Figure 9-8, you'll see plywood siding being attached over aluminized sheathing. This particular brand has qualified as "structural" grade.

All Openings Must Be Headered

Section 2517 of the U.B.C. contains an interesting note about the framing of headers. Headers and lintels over openings four feet wide or less can be of double 2 x 4's on edge. The common rule of thumb is, *for each two feet of opening over four feet, increase the lumber size two inches.* In other words, a four-foot opening would require double 2 x 4's on edge: six-foot openings would need 2 x 6's; eight-foot, 2 x 8's, and so on. It need not be doubled two-inch stock. Solid or 4-inch-thick material will do as well. There's no reason why a 4 x 6 wouldn't substitute for two 2 x 6's.

All headers and lintels must have at least 2-inch solid bearing at each end to the floor or bottom plate, unless other approved framing methods or joint devices are used. There are a number of sizes and shapes of these brackets on the market now. Some are made of plastic but most are galvanized steel.

Some contractors prefer to use solid headers over window and door openings rather than the narrower size, which requires a certain amount of blocking between them and the top plate. Some will even extend this header to each side of the window opening instead of using curtain blocking. However, the latter is not required.

Cripples and Cripple Walls

Of course, there are many more details involved in framing a house than those we've discussed. For instance, in framing a window opening it's customary to put cripples under the lower side of the opening. A *cripple* is a short piece of stud material. They double up the stud at the point where the lower framing cross member touches the studs forming the opening sides. This gives additional support to that member. Although not required by the code, I recommend using a cripple because it increases the strength of the wall.

A *cripple wall*, is referred to in Section 2517(g)4 of the code where it states that foundation walls must be framed of studs at least the size of the studding above with a minimum length of 14 inches. If the cripple wall exceeds 4 feet in height then the studs must be the size required for an additional story.

There are many other items like this. Some are code items and some are not. But all are good building practice, and good craftsmen use them.

10
Entrances and Exits

At this point let's consider just how you're going to get into or out of the place. Sometimes we just assume that every building and every room will have a door.

I once plan-checked a building in which one room did not have *any* door. You might think this is silly, but having drawn a few plans myself, I know what can happen when you begin to make revisions. Someone had decided that the original door was not in a good location. The draftsman had removed the door, closed up the space, and then was probably interrupted before he could draw in the new location. He never got back to it, and the reviewer never caught it. I did.

Therefore, as long as we need a way in and out, let's take a closer look at exiting. You'll recall that we discussed this briefly in Chapter Three under occupancy requirements. Chapter 33 in the U.B.C. describes what we're looking for.

The next item on the agenda is the definition of "exit." Many of us think of an exit as merely a door. The code goes further in its definition, however. Included are such things as exit court, exit passageway, and horizontal exit:

Exit is a continuous and unobstructed means of egress to a public way and shall include intervening aisle, doors, doorways, corridors, exterior exit balconies, ramps, stairways, smokeproof enclosures, horizontal exits, exit passageways, exit courts and yards.

Exit court is a yard or court providing access to a public way for one or more required exits.

Exit passageway is an enclosed exit connecting a required exit or exit court with a public way.

Horizontal Exit is an exit from one building into another building on approximately the same level or through or around a wall constructed as required for a two-hour occupancy separation and which completely divides a floor into two or more separate areas so as to establish an area of refuge affording safety from fire or smoke coming from the area from which escape is made.

In other words, an exit is all the ways out of a building. But there's more to it than that. The inspector needs to know how many people can get out quickest from any given point. The fire marshal needs to know this, too. And there's more to that access business than meets the eye. For example: You could have a door forty feet wide, as in a hangar, but if one person could not easily get out of the building during a catastrophe, then you don't have adequate exits.

Public Way

The implication in the above definitions is that, eventually, all exits lead outdoors and to safety. To be more precise, when you leave a building through an exit, it will eventually lead to a "public way." What does a public way look like? What is a public way? The code book defines it this way:

Public Way is any street, alley or similar parcel of land essentially unobstructed from the ground to the sky which is deeded, dedicated or otherwise permanently appropriated to the public for public use and having a clear width of not less than 10 feet.

To determine the size and number of exits for a building, you must determine how many people will normally be occupying a given space. In Chapter Three we discussed how to determine the occupant load. For this you must use U.B.C. Table No. 33-A, *Minimum Egress and Access Requirements*, (Figure 3-1 in Chapter Three).

Many arguments over the building code are about occupant load. The owner of a store or shop may try to bargain with the inspector, saying, "You know I probably won't have that many customers in my store on opening day. Why can't we figure it on what I *think* I'll have?"

Most inspectors don't have a good answer to such a question. They'll usually come back with the typical reply, "Because it says so in The Book!"

A Standard Must Be Set

The codes are set up to establish building standards. Of course, there'll always be those who question these standards. Usually they'll complain that the standards are too strict. But often the regulations are too generous. Most were designed to set minimum standards, leaving the inspector a certain amount of freedom for interpretation. Such is the case with occupant loads.

The occupant load permitted in any building or portion thereof is determined by dividing the floor area by the square feet per occupant as set forth in U.B.C. Table No. 33-A. When the square feet per occupant is not given for a particular occupancy it will be determined by the building official, based on the area given for the occupancy it most nearly resembles.

Naturally, there are several exceptions. One is that the occupant load may be increased above that specified if the necessary exits are provided. However, most inspectors are skeptics, and an approved aisle or seating diagram may be required to prove your point.

Determining Occupant Load for Exits

In determining the occupant load, all areas of a building are presumed to be occupied at the same time. Does that mean that the whole building will be rated the same as the most restrictive or the least restrictive?

It means neither. What it does mean is that if you have a building of mixed occupancy, with most of the occupants using the same exit or exits, the building must be calculated as though each occupancy was being used to the maximum all the time. What it does *not* mean is that the most restrictive provisions apply to the entire building. Each separate occupancy is rated on its own merit or usage, but all areas are considered as being used simultaneously.

In Chapter Three we discussed a lodge building that contained a dance floor, dining room, reading room, bar and kitchen. We used

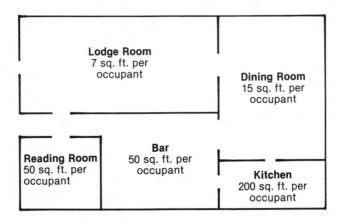

Figure 10-1   Sketch of Lodge

the figure of 7 square feet per occupant for the dance floor, 15 square feet per occupant for the dining room and the bar, the reading room came to 50 square feet per occupant and the kitchen came to 200 square feet per occupant. To better understand how exit requirements are determined, let's take another look at that lodge building. You'll find it in Figure 10-1.

In Chapter Three we found that the lodge building could be 9,000 square feet and accommodate 664 people because each major area had its own loading requirements. Now, suppose the lodge met only once a week, the restaurant or dining room was open only from 3 p.m. to midnight, the reading room was open only from 10 a.m. until 5 p.m., and a dance was held in the lodge hall once a week. Would they need an exit way designed to handle the whole crowd of 664 or would they only need an exit way to handle the crowd at the time the various functions took place?

Unfortunately, the exits would have to be designed to handle the entire group of 664 people.

Also, consider the overflow that would occur in the bar if there were an intermission during the dance. Although this is a hypothetical case, provisions could be made to handle this overflow. If the owner hadn't thought of it, the builder should suggest it.

Overloading an Occupancy

Section 3302(c) warns that the number of occupants of any building or portion thereof may not exceed the permitted or posted capacity. The owner or manager of the facility must enforce this rule. If he doesn't, the fire marshal has the authority to shut them down until the crowd is thinned out. Subsection (c) also says that any room with fixed seats having an occupant load of more than 50 must have the capacity clearly posted. This becomes an enforcement problem when the building is occupied. If you think this situation might develop, get together with the fire marshal and see if something could be worked out to get a better ratio between the bar and the dance floor. Fortunately, this is not a big problem because most dance floors are located in or next to the bar.

Determining Size of Exits

The first point to make here is that every building or usable portion of it must have at least one exit.

U.B.C. Table No. 33-A has one column that reads "Minimum of Two Exits Required Where Number of Occupants is Over . . ." Suppose the dance floor you need is 900 square feet. Table 33-A shows that we must allow 7 square feet per occupant, and by dividing 900 by 7 we get an occupant load of 128 plus. The table also shows that we need at least two exits. But we still haven't established how big they'll be.

Exit width is discussed in Section 3303(f) of the U.B.C:

The total width of exits in feet shall not be less than the total occupant load served divided by 50. Such width of exits shall be divided approximately equally among the separate exits.

Looks easy, doesn't it? Seems like you'll need only three feet of exit width. But the book says you must have two exits. What happens now? Do you put in two 18-inch doors?

Normally it would only be necessary to install two 3-foot doors. This is also reinforced by the code. Section 3303(e) states that every required exit doorway must be large enough to allow the installation of a door at least three feet wide. In other words, what you thought was going to be three feet of exit has now become six feet.

Position of Exits

So, you'll need two 3-foot doors where you originally thought that
three feet of total doorway area would be enough. Just put in a
double door and everything will be rosy. But if you do, you'll have
the inspector breathing down your neck. The code states that if
two or more doors are required they must be positioned apart
from each other. Section 3303(c) says this:

*(c) Arrangement of Exits. If only two exits are required they shall be placed a
distance apart equal to not less than one-half of the length of the maximum
overall diagonal dimension of the building or area to be served measured in a
straight line between exits . . .*

*Where three or more exits are required, they shall be arranged a reasonable
distance apart so that if one becomes blocked the others will be available.*

Let's look at a sketch of a dance floor. This floor (Figure 10-2)
is 900 square feet (30 feet wide by 30 feet long). The longest
diagonal measurement of this square dance floor will be about 42
feet. This was determined by figuring the square of the length of
the two sides, adding them up, and then taking the square root of
the total.

So, if the diagonal measurement is about 42 feet and we need
half of that figure, our doors would have to be at least 21 feet
apart, as shown on the sketch. Wouldn't it be better to have a door
at the front and one at the rear? Yes—if you have access to a
public way. In fact, I highly recommend it, but check the code
first. Is this allowed? I think so, because it states that exits:

*. . .shall be placed a distance apart equal to not less than one-half of the length of
the maximum overall diagonal dimension . . .*

All it specifies is distance. Therefore, one door at the front and
one at the rear would conform to the code because they would be
at least 30 feet apart and our minimum figure was 21 feet. The problem is that sometimes the back is not available for a suitable exit.

What If The Building Isn't Square?

Up till now we've been talking about a square building of 900
square feet (30 by 30). Suppose your building was 20 feet wide by
45 feet long, still 900 square feet, as shown in Figure 10-3. Could
you put two doors directly opposite each other on the long sides?

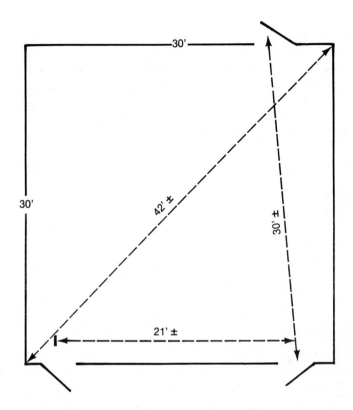

Section 3302(c) indicates the location of the exits is not dictated, only the distance between them.

Figure 10-2 Exits on Dance Floor

Off the top of my head I would say "No," even though we're allowed a 21-foot minimum separation between exits. Though the same square footage is involved, the arrangement is now quite different. There's a new set of dimensions. We will have to recalculate our longest dimension.

Take the new length and width and do some squaring. Twenty squared would be 400; 45 squared would be 2025, and together they add up to 2425. The square root of 2425 would be almost 50 feet. This would be the maximum diagonal dimension of our building—50 feet. Remember, we can't be less than one half that

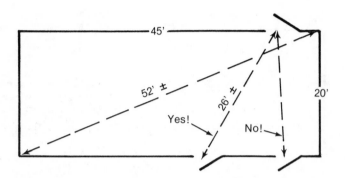

What if your building isn't square? Exits may be on the sides of
the building provided the minimum distance between them is
equal to one-half the maximum diagonal distance across the
building.

Figure 10-3   Exits on Long, Narrow Building

figure as a minimum distance between exits when only two exits
are used. Therefore, our two exits would have to be at least 25 feet
apart, and we wouldn't have that by putting them directly opposite
in a 20-foot-wide building. You could put them at each end, but
not opposite each other on the sides.

What About Three Exits?

If you were to put three exits in that type of a building, you could
have two exits directly opposite or even on the same wall at opposite corners. If three or more exits are required they must be a
reasonable distance apart, so that if one becomes blocked, others
will be available. If the building is unsprinklered, no part of it may
be more than 150 feet from an exterior exit door, a horizontal exit,
an exit passageway, or an enclosed stairway. This distance has to
be measured along the line of travel. If you have to go around ob-
jects such as desks, files, machinery, or any permanent or semi-
permanent fixtures, the 150 feet will have to take into account that
you must go around them.

On the other hand, if your building is sprinklered (and I hope it
is) this distance may be increased to 200 feet.

Exits may be made into adjoining or intervening rooms or areas
if those rooms or areas are easily accessible and provide a direct

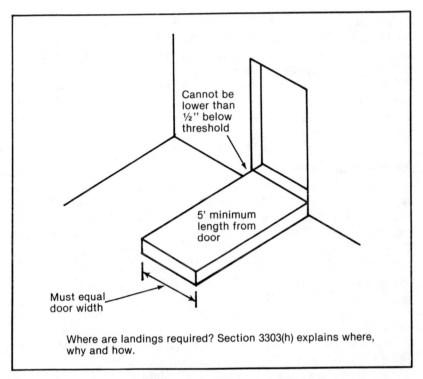

Cannot be lower than ½" below threshold

5' minimum length from door

Must equal door width

Where are landings required? Section 3303(h) explains where, why and how.

Figure 10-4 Approved Landings

route to an outside exit. Exits *cannot* pass through kitchens, storerooms, rest rooms, closets, or spaces used for similar purposes.

Landings Required
Most exit requirements are based on an occupancy of more than 10, but there are two exceptions. Section 3304(h) covers these. But notice the difference between occupancy and occupant load. Landings are required, regardless of occupant load. But several occupancies are excepted.

(h) Change in Floor Level at Doors. Regardless of the occupant load, there shall be a floor or landing on each side of a door. The floor or landing shall be not more than 1/2 inch lower than the threshold of the doorway. Where doors open over landings, the landing shall have a length of not less than five feet. (See Figure 10-4.)

Although four exceptions are listed, only two subjects are covered. If the door opens into a smokeproof enclosure, the landing may be less than five feet. The other three exceptions cover private residences and are fairly simple. A stair opening is excepted if it doesn't open over the top step or a landing and the first step or landing is not more than 7½ inches below floor level. Other landings in homes need not be wider than the door. Screen or storm doors do not require a landing.

Requirement for Exterior Exit Doors

The code has some rigid requirements for exit doors. The book says revolving, sliding and overhead doors must not be used as a required exit, even though they're all over town. You've probably seen pneumatically-operated doors, overhead doors and various forms of sliding doors. But take a good look at those sliding and pneumatically-operated doors. You'll find a little note, probably in one of the upper corners, that says something like: "In case of emergency, push on door panel."

That means that in an emergency such as a power outage or equipment failure, the door panel will either push out or swivel out so that people inside can get out. Occasionally you'll run across some of the older models that don't operate this way. They were designed and installed according to regulations then in force and were grandfathered in when the code changed. If they are ever replaced or changed, the newer style must be used—the ones with the warnings and the armor plate glass.

Rolling Overhead Doors

You may have a modern shopping mall in your area where the shops are secured at night by either overhead rolling doors or doors that slide into enclosures somewhere along the sides or top of the opening. In spite of the code, these are legal. It is one of those areas where you have to understand the intent of the code to get the answer.

Normally, these huge doors are not used during the day when the business is open. When the store closes at the end of the day, these doors are closed for security reasons. Therefore, since they're required to be open during regular business hours, they are considered legal exits. Figure 10-5 shows a rolling overhead door typically found in shopping malls.

Figure 10-5 Rolling Overhead Door in a Modern
Shopping Mall. These doors are locked in an open
position during business hours and are closed only
for security reasons during other times.

Doors and Corridors

Not only is there a minimum size for a door, there is also a maximum size. No leaf of an exit door may be more than four feet
wide. In other words, if you have a double door, the width of the
opening would have to be at least six feet and not more than eight
feet. Here's another way to look at it: If you need five feet of exit
width, you'll have to install two 3-foot doors, because no door
may be five feet wide.

All exit doors must be clearly marked. We don't want strangers
in the building winding up in a broom closet in an emergency. And
the hardware for these doors must be designed so that it does not
require any unusual skill or strength to open the door.

Now for corridors. A corridor in a public building must be at
least 44 inches wide and must be unobstructed. In private
residences, 36 inches is the minimum width. There are a few special

conditions, but they normally are limited to trim, handrails, and some forms of hardware.

Doors opening into corridors may not reduce the required width of the corridor by more than seven inches when fully opened. Doors in any position may not obstruct more than half of the corridor. That means that if you have a three-foot-wide door and a 44-inch-wide hallway, you will either have to reverse the swing of your door or the doorway itself will have to be inset into the room.

If you decide to reverse the swing of your door, check your occupant load. Remember? Occupant loads over fifty require that the door swing in the direction of exit travel.

One final word about corridors: A dead-end corridor may not be more than 20 feet long.

Stairways

The rise of each step must not be more than 7½ inches; the tread cannot be less than 10 inches deep. There are, of course, exceptions. Stairs or ladders used only for equipment are exempt. Stairs in private residences have a whole new set of rules—the maximum rise is 8 inches and the minimum tread only 9 inches.

Stairs, generally, may not rise more than twelve feet without a landing at least as wide as the stairs. But the run of the landing doesn't have to be more than 4 feet. Further, there must be a minimum of 6'6'' of headroom between a line drawn over the nose of the treads and any ceiling or projection in the ceiling above. This is shown in Figure 10-6.

Private stairways may be as small as 30 inches wide. Public stairways serving an occupant load of up to 50 must be at least 36 inches wide. If the occupant load is greater than 50, you must go to a 44-inch stairway.

Spiral and Circular Stairs

The basic differences between a spiral and a circular stairway are the radius, and where they may be used. A circular stairway may be used as a public stairway if the minimum width of run is not less than 10 inches and the smallest radius is not less than twice the width of the stair. For example, if you had a 5-foot-wide circular stairway in a commercial building, it couldn't curve any faster

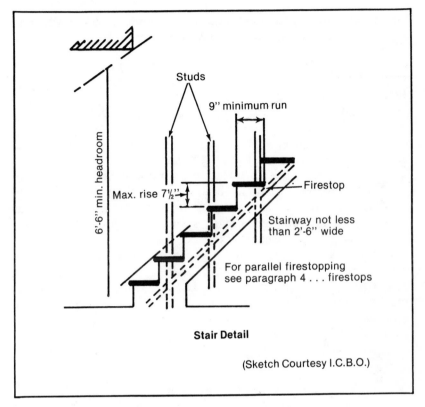

Studs

9" minimum run

6'-6" min. headroom

Max. rise 7½"

Firestop

Stairway not less
than 2'-6" wide

For parallel firestopping
see paragraph 4 . . . firestops

Stair Detail

(Sketch Courtesy I.C.B.O.)

Figure 10-6   ICBO's Stair Detail

than it would take to circle a 10-foot column or circular space.

The spiral stairway, on the other hand, may only be used in Group R-3 occupancies. Here, the required width of run of 7½ inches must be provided at a point not more than 12 inches from the side of the stairs where the tread is narrowest. The rise must provide 6'6" between the stair and the ceiling, but it must not exceed 9½ inches.

Spiral stairs are used in many homes and for access to mechanical rooms (rooms where heating and air conditioning equipment are located). However, they cannot be used for public exit.

These are the stair requirements in a nutshell, with the exception that on public stairs the floor number, the terminus of the top and bottom levels, and the identification of the stairs must appear at each floor in buildings over four stories high.

Understair Space

If the stairs in your building go down to the basement or an area below grade level, there must be an approved barrier at grade level to prevent anyone from accidentally continuing into the basement during an emergency. Also, any usable space under stairways in an exit enclosure must be left open and unused.

Now the question is sure to come up about private residences with closets under the stairs. These closets are usually used to store clothes, Christmas decorations, or hot water tanks. Here, I must remind you of a comment I made a long time ago—generally, exit requirements are based on an occupancy of ten, and most households are less than that. Also, most single-family residences are exempt.

Get to know Chapter 33 of the U.B.C. Many of the items I've discussed are exempt in Group R and M occupancies. So go ahead and put your hot water tank and Christmas ornaments under the stairs at home—but don't do it in your office!

Ramps

A ramp must be used for any change in elevation in a corridor if the change is less than 10 inches vertically. The same general conditions regarding width and clearances for corridors also apply to ramps. There is one glaring exception, set forth in U.B.C. Table No. 33-A:

Access by means of a ramp or an elevator must be provided for the physically handicapped as indicated.

Figure 10-7 shows a typical ramp. Whenever Table 33-A calls for a ramp or elevator, the slope of the ramp must not exceed one vertical inch to ten horizontal inches. All ramps other than those specified for the handicapped, must have slopes no greater than one vertical to eight horizontal inches, a slightly steeper slope.

If your ramp exceeds one vertical to fifteen horizontal, you must install a handrail. Also, the surface must be roughened or made of a non-slip material.

Figure 10-7 Ramp Providing Access for the Handicapped. Making facilities accessible is now required by the code, particularly in public buildings.

My feelings on ramps mirror those of my professor when I was studying architecture. He had a favorite expression: "Two steps or no steps." He was saying that a single step was a stumbling block, particularly for people wearing bifocal glasses. According to the professor, if you couldn't put in at least two risers, then you should build a ramp.

Exit Enclosures
The question here is when should an exit be enclosed? The code states that every interior stairway, ramp, or escalator must be enclosed as specified. But there is an exception. If you have a stairway, ramp, or escalator serving only one adjacent floor and not connected with corridors or stairways serving other floors, you don't need an enclosure.

Exit enclosures usually means emergency exits. Though they may never be needed for an emergency, they must be ready. That's the reason for the strict requirements. Consequently, you can't have any openings into exit enclosures except at exit doorways and at landings and parts of floors connecting stairway flights. Also there must be a corridor on the ground floor leading outside from the stairway. All exits must be fire assemblies with self-closing or automatic closing devices.

Smokeproof Enclosures

If a floor is more than 75 feet above the highest grade, one of the required exits must be a smokeproof enclosure. This must have a vestibule at least 44 inches by 72 inches. Both the vestibule and the continuous stairway must be enclosed by walls of at least two-hour fire-resistive construction. The ceiling of the vestibule serves as a smoke and heat trap.

The smokeproof enclosure must have mechanical ventilation unless the building is completely air-conditioned. Emergency lights are also required.

Exit Width, Multi-Story or Exit Court

If your exit doesn't have access to a public way, it may open onto an exit court. The size of the exit court depends on the number of occupancies it must serve. This is determined by Section 3303 and is based on the number of occupants. The exit court adheres to the same width requirements as though it served a single, multi-story building. Section 3303(b) says, in part:

> . . . *The total exit width required from any story of a building shall be determined by using the occupant load of that story plus the percentages of the occupant loads of floors which exit through the level under consideration, as follows:*
>
> *1. Fifty percent of the occupant load in the first adjacent story above and the first adjacent story below, when a story below exits through the level under consideration.*
>
> *2. Twenty-five percent of the occupant load in the story immediately beyond the first adjacent story.*
>
> *The maximum exit width required from any story of a building shall be maintained.*

How would this affect our exit court? Let's assume that we have three buildings that form a central court. Each of the three buildings has an occupant load of 300. Section 3303(b) also says,

The total width of exits in feet shall be not less than the total occupant load divided by 50.

Therefore, with 300 people in three different buildings, a total of 900 people, presumably, want out. Nine hundred divided by 50 equals an exit 18 feet wide. This can be a single exit or a total of 18 feet spread among several exits.

That's assuming that all the occupants will be coming out at once and reaching the exit at the same time. We know they can't all move like that even if they were waiting for the signal to go. However, this was assuming a single-story building. Let's see what's required for a three-story building.

We'll assume that the occupants are divided equally throughout the buildings, 100 to each floor. In that case, your figures might look something like this, according to Section 3303(b):

First floor: Full count — 100 people

Second floor: 50% of count — 50 people

Third floor: 25% of count — 25 people

This is the estimated number of people who would be passing through the exit within a very short time. That totals 175 people; divide that by 50 and you get 3.75 feet of exit width. Thus, you must have a door at least 4 feet wide.

Now we come to the $64,000 question. If one building only needs 4 feet of exit, why do three buildings need 18 feet of exit? (Remember, these figures are mine; different inspectors might figure them differently.) I'm figuring that the occupants from the three buildings are going to arrive at the exits simultaneously. That might not seem fair, but I have to follow the code to the letter. Remember, if the buildings were single story we would have to assume all the occupants would exit at once. However, by converting those figures to three-story buildings, we've altered our exit figures. Now, you might look at these figures and say, knowing that only a few could get to the gate in time, "Well, I'll figure the exit count from the sum of the required exit widths."

If you do that, you'll find that three single-story buildings opening onto an exit court with a total occupant load of 900 people require an exit width of 18 feet. However, with multi-story buildings you would only need the sum of the three required exits; that would mean an exit width of 12 feet.

Light the Exit

Any time the building is occupied, the exits must be illuminated with light having an intensity of at least one foot candle at floor level. This doesn't apply to standard residences because the code excludes Group R-3 occupancies. The light must have separate circuits or separate power sources; however, they are not necessarily separate signs.

Exit Signs

Exit signs are required at each doorway and other required locations. The lettering on exit signs must be at least 5 inches high. Groups A-1 through A-4, Group I and Group R-1 (motels and apartments) with an occupant load of 50 or more, must have signs. All other occupancies with occupant load of more than 100 also are required to have signs. Most of the occupancies of 100 or more must have illuminated signs. If your occupancy calls for an illuminated sign, it must be lighted with at least two 15-watt lamps.

Why two lamps? This is purely a safety precaution. You never know when these lamps are going to burn out. Providing two lamps reduces the odds of both lamps burning out at the same time.

What Color?

There used to be a lot of arguing about whether exit signs should be red or green. Some said that red would be easy to spot. Others pointed out that in a dark, smoke-filled room fire fighters had occasionally wasted time and water on a red glow that turned out to be an exit sign. Both sides must have compromised because the code doesn't specify which color to use. It can be either red or green.

Certain high-density occupancies are required to have two separate power sources for the exit lights and signs. These are *sources*, not *circuits*. This is usually done with a battery system. If the emergency lighting and sign lighting are on a separate circuit, they can come from a generator. Keep in mind that there must be lights in an emergency.

Aisles and Aisleways

Aisles between furniture, equipment, merchandise, or other obstructions must be at least 3 feet wide if serving one side or 3 feet

6 inches wide if serving both sides of the aisle. Regardless of the width of the aisle and whether or not it serves one or both sides, the distance to the nearest exit cannot be more than 150 feet based on the line of travel. Once again, sprinklered buildings have an advantage because you can increase the travel distance to 200 feet. Where permanent standard seating is used, there may not be more than six intervening seats between any seat and the nearest aisle.

Aisles must terminate in a cross aisle, foyer, or exit. Aisles can also terminate in a vomitory. The width of the cross aisle or vomitory must be at least the sum of the required width of the widest aisle plus 50% of the total width of the remaining aisles leading into it. This is shown in Figure 10-8.

Fixed Seating

For rooms with fixed seating, such as pews, booths and benches, it's easier to determine occupancy loads. The seats can be counted, or, if you have benches or pews, you're allowed so many people for so many feet of bench or pew. For booths in dining areas, the number of seats is based on one person for each 24 inches or major portion thereof of the length of the booth.

Basically, there are two types of fixed seating and they aren't easily identified. *Standard* seating consists of solid, fixed seats such as church pews, or benches. *Continental* seating apparently refers to seats that raise, because the code gives dimensions with the seat either up or down.

Here's what the code says about standard seating in Section 3316:

Section 3316. With standard seating the spacing of rows of seats shall provide a space of not less than 12 inches from the back of one seat to the front of the most forward projection of the seat immediately behind it as measured horizontally between vertical planes.

With continental seating the dimensions are with the seat either up or down. Measure in a horizontal line between the edge of the seat and the back of the seat in front. The following code dimensions apply:

18 inches clear between rows for 1-18 seats.
20 inches clear between rows for 19-35 seats.
21 inches clear between rows for 36-45 seats.
22 inches clear between rows for 46-59 seats.
24 inches clear between rows for 60 seats or more.

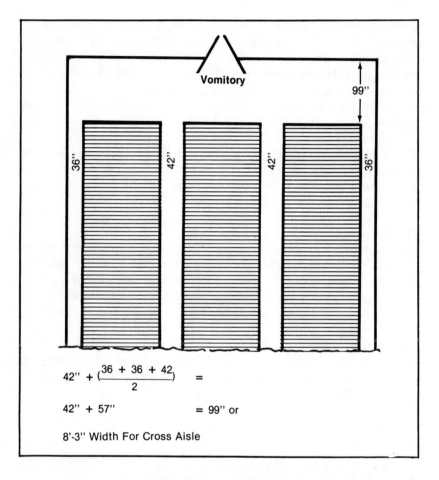

Figure 10-8 Here the designer followed the code. He put a 36-inch aisle along each wall of the auditorium (serving one side only) and two 42-inch aisles through the middle (serving both sides). In this case, as the math indicates, the cross-aisle, or vomitory, need only be **99** inches wide.

What we've said about fixed seating applies to seats inside of a building. Outdoor grandstands and bleachers are a whole new ballgame.

Grandstands and Bleachers

Regulations for grandstands and bleachers are similar to those for indoor seating. Very likely, the rash of bleacher collapses over the last few years has resulted in more stringent regulations. However, the construction of bleachers in the past has not been an area of general concern to the regulatory agencies—inspectors—because many of these structures are temporary. The code refers to temporary bleachers as "those which are intended for use at a location for not more than 90 days." With few exceptions the rules are the same for both temporary and permanent outdoor seating.

Exiting, of course, is based on the number of occupants, which is based on the number of seats. If chairs are used, a simple count of the chair backs will suffice. If benches are used, assume each person will occupy 18 inches of bench.

Stairs and ramps must still conform to Section 3305 and Section 3306. Aisles must be the same as those of interior auditoriums. But perimeter guardrails, which are not included in interior design, must be installed on all portions of elevated seating more than 30 inches above grade. The guardrails must be at least 42 inches high. On the edge of all walking platforms a 4-inch-high barrier must also be installed with each guardrail. Cross aisles and vomitories must be at least 54 inches wide and terminate at an exit, enclosed stairway, or exterior perimeter ramp.

Row Spacing

The spacing for rows of outdoor seating differs from that of indoor seating. Section 3323(e) states it a little differently than what we have previously discussed:

(e) Row Spacing. There shall be a clear space of not less than 12 inches measured horizontally between the back or backrest of each seat and the front of the seat immediately behind it. The minimum spacing of rows of seats measured from back to back shall be:
   A. Twenty-two inches for seats without backrests.
   B. Thirty inches for seats with backrests.
   C. Thirty-three inches for chair seating.

That's it in a nutshell. There's just one question left: "What's the difference between a bleacher and a grandstand?"

The Uniform Building Code isn't too clear on the subject:

Figure 10-9   When is a grandstand not a grandstand? Both of these structures could be considered
a grandstand by the code, but general acceptance
might say the playground model would be a
bleacher and the concrete one a grandstand.

Bleachers are tiered or stepped seating facilities without backrests in which an area of 3 square feet or less is assigned per person for computing the occupant load.

Grandstands are tiered or stepped seating facilities wherein an area of more than 3 square feet is provided for each person.

Perhaps Figure 10-9 will help show the difference between bleachers and grandstands.

Barrier-Free Design

There is a lack of uniformity from one state to another and with the Federal Government on this subject. Basically, buildings and their facilities must be accessible to the handicapped. As for the requirements of the building code, they're found in the following sections of the U.B.C. Beyond that I urge you to contact your local inspector:

Access to buildings — 3301(e), 3304(d), 1213
Access to toilet facilities — 511
Access to building uses — Table 33-A
Changes in floor elevations — 3304(h), 3305(f)
Handrails — 3306(j)
Landings — 3304(h), 3306(g)
Ramps — 3307
Water fountains — 511

Also, there are many important references in the Uniform Plumbing Code. Here in the State of Washington, following the lead of several other states, we've published a booklet entitled, *An Illustrated Handbook for Barrier Free Design.*

11
Keeping Your Building Warm and Dry

We're progressing nicely. We've covered foundations, walls, exits and occupancies. Now we need to discuss how to keep a building warm and dry. Right now we've got a box without a lid. So one of the things we'll need before we can go much further is a roof.

We'll also need a chimney. The chimney should be built so we can hook up a furnace or a fireplace. But first, let's discuss the roof.

Roof Construction

Chapter 32 of the U.B.C. deals with roof construction and covering. This chapter was completely rewritten for the 1979 edition. Many changes take place in construction each year because of new materials, methods, and facts. Periodically the International Conference of Building Officials (I.C.B.O.) rewrites certain chapters to be more effective and to reflect new trends. This makes the code easier to enforce because it eliminates redundancy and helps correct any errors and contradictions that might have resulted from previous amendments.

I'm going to reprint some of the basic pre-1979 requirements for roofs, however, because they are brief, clear, and still part of the current code:

1. Roof covering for all buildings shall be either fire-retardant or ordinary.
2. The roof coverings shall be securely fastened in an approved manner to the supporting roof construction.
3. The roof coverings shall provide weather protection for the building at the roof.

How does a roofing material qualify as fire-retardant? Fire-retardant roof coverings are classified in three groups: A, B or C. The classification is clearly marked on the material packages. The following tests are used to determine the classification of the materials:

1. Intermittent-flame test.
2. Spread of flames test.
3. Burning-brand test.
4. Flying-brand test.
5. Rain test.
6. Weathering test.

The last three tests are used only on treated wood shingles and shakes. Of all the tests, the weathering test takes the most time.

Testing Methods

For the burning-brand and intermittent-flame tests, the material is applied to a test deck just as it would be installed on the job. The only difference is that the edges of the deck are mortared with a mixture of asbestos-gypsum and water. This is to keep the heated gases produced by the testing from reaching both sides of the material at once. The test deck is 3⅓ feet wide by 4⅓ feet long. The roofing material to be used is all store-grade as defined in Section 32.703, U.B.C. Standards. The exact construction of the deck is also outlined, so that all tests are as near equal as possible.

Air is directed over the sample in a prescribed direction at twelve miles per hour. For shingle roofs the deck is inclined *at least* 5 inches per horizontal foot; for built-up roofs the *maximum* slope is 5 inches per horizontal foot. The test, which is done on duplicate samples, subjects the material to a luminous gas flame over the width of the deck at the bottom edge. It must heat the sample uniformly, except for the two upper corners.

The gas supply is regulated to develop a temperature of 1400 degrees for Class A and B roofing and 1300 degrees for Class C roofing. The flame is applied to the test sample for a specified time and then shut off for a specified time. This cycle is repeated throughout the prescribed length of the test.

The spread-of-flame test is conducted similarly. The amount of combustion is measured against flame spread, production of flaming or glowing brands, and the displacement of portions of the test sample. This is then compared to ratings for the three classes of material.

Ordinary Roofing

Now that you know a little about fire-retardant roofing, what about "ordinary" roofing? Ordinary roofing is just about all that's left. It consists of non-treated wood shingles and shakes, and roll roofing without mineral surfacing. Ordinary roofing is not permitted in Type I or II construction.

What about the architectural appendages such as marquees and pseudo-mansard designs, the ones with shakes and shingles? First, the code was referring to roofs, and although the mansard design may look like a roof, it's actually more of a decoration. Second, Chapter 17 of the U.B.C. allows mansards on the side of buildings facing a street or adequate adjoining space such as a parking lot. But they can only be attached to buildings of non-combustible construction.

What we're concerned with is fire resistance. The basic question is, what effect do these structures have on the fire resistance of a building?

Other than electrical wiring for lighting and signs, there is little in these marquees and mansards that can actually *cause* a fire. If added or attached to a non-combustible surface, they must be capable of containing a fire for a considerable time before causing damage to the rest of the building.

The inspector may require a layer of weather-resistant sheetrock between the roofing material and the sheathing, but otherwise they would be safe enough. Still, it's a good idea to check with the inspector before you begin.

Roofing Must Be Labeled

Each package of roofing material must be labeled to show the type of material and the name and address of the manufacturer. This applies to shakes, shingles, or manufactured roofing. The label should also include the grade and, in the case of manufactured roofing, the weight per roofing square.

Many areas used to have trouble with unlabeled material being used in construction work. It was usually labeled simply "approved," with no mention of the manufacturer, type of material, or even who had "approved" it. When I found this material on jobs, I'd look up the suppliers.

Often the material supplier would be aghast at my questions. He sold only "quality" material which, he assured me, was made by a "reputable" manufacturer. Unfortunately, he couldn't recall the manufacturer's name.

Roofing isn't the only product that is mislabeled or not labeled at all. It happens occasionally to all manufactured items. What really matters is that the material is often seconds or even thirds. It's often used to save money, but if you're going to use inferior material, what have you really saved? You'll probably wind up having to replace this shoddy material with quality brand-name products and usually spend more time and money doing so.

Roof Fasteners
We won't spend much time on how to fasten slate or tile shingles—that's quite a specialized job. Besides, most tile is kept in place by gravity, with only the top course fastened down.

Built-up roofing takes a little more work than most other roofing, but it's seldom used on anything other than flat or near-flat roofs. If you have a non-nailable roof, you must mop the base sheet with at least 20 pounds of hot asphalt for solid roofing, or at least 30 pounds of coal tar pitch per roofing square.

On nailable roofs, the base sheet must be nailed with at least one nail for each 1½ square feet, using nails specified by the roofing material manufacturer. Cement successive layers to the base sheets, using a type and amount of cementing material as specified for solidly-cemented base sheets.

Mineral-aggregate surfaced roofs must be surfaced with at least 50 pounds of hot asphalt or other cementing material embedded with at least 300 pounds of gravel or 250 pounds of crushed slag. Cap sheets are cemented to the base sheets with the same amount of cementing material used on other layers.

How Hot is Hot?
Hot asphalt must be at least 375 degrees F, but not more than 450 degrees. Never heat it over 475 degrees F. Coal tar must be at least 350 degrees F and not more than 400 degrees. It should never be heated more than that.

Applying heat to asphalt can be like putting a match to a dynamite fuse: it's okay if it doesn't go too far. This material should be heated only by experienced professionals under strictly controlled conditions. Heating the material beyond its "flash point"—the point at which it will ignite—creates a dangerous fire hazard. Most volatile materials have the flash point clearly printed on the label.

What Is A Roofing Square?
Roofs are measured by the *square* or *roofing square*. I mentioned earlier that certain substances should be put on the roof in certain amounts at different times. These materials were measured in pounds, tons, quarts, gallons or whatever, "per roofing square."

What is a roofing square? As far as I know, it's a term used only in roofing calculations. It's the amount of roofing material required to cover 100 square feet of roof surface. Normally, a roll of roofing material contains one square of roofing cover when laid to the manufacturer's specs. Composition shingles usually require three bundles to equal one roofing square.

Figure 11-1 is a sketch showing how to determine roof coverage. To calculate your roofing material needs, take the square footage of your roof and divide it by 100. This gives the number of squares required to cover your roof. If you have many ridges and valleys, add at least 15% to your total.

Applying Composition Shingles
Apply composition shingles only to solidly sheathed roofs with a slope of more than 4 inches to 12 inches.

Fasten composition shingles according to the manufacturer's instructions, using at least four nails for each strip shingle not more than 36 inches wide and two nails for each shingle not less than 20 inches wide. There must be an underlayment of not less than 15-pound felt unless your roof pitch exceeds 7 inches to 12 inches.

Many roofs are not the simple straight gable type. Whenever they differ, you'll find many ridges and valleys. These mean extra

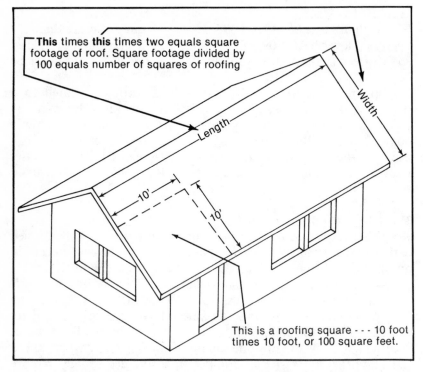

Figure 11-1 Method of Calculating Roof Coverage

work. Part of this work involves valley flashing. Valley flashing will vary according to the type of roofing. We'll explore that a little later in this chapter.

Wood Shingles or Shakes
Shingles may be applied to roofs with either solid sheathing or spaced sheathing. For spaced sheathing on wood roofs, the spaces must not exceed 6 inches, nor be more than the nominal width of the sheathing board. In any case, the sheathing board must be at least 1 inch by 4 inches, nominal dimensions. Wood shingles vary in width from 3 inches to 14 inches and in length from 16 inches to 24 inches. For laying regulations, refer to U.B.C. Table No. 32-A (Figure 11-2) and U.B.C. Table No. 32-B (Figure 11-3). Figure 11-4 shows a shingle laying diagram.

TABLE NO. 32-A—MAXIMUM WEATHER EXPOSURE

GRADE LENGTH	3" TO LESS THAN 4" IN 12"	4" IN 12" AND STEEPER
WOOD SHINGLES		
No. 1 16-inch	3¾"	5"
No. 2[1] 16-inch	3½"	4"
No. 3[1] 16-inch	3"	3½"
No. 1 18-inch	4¼"	5½"
No. 2[1] 18-inch	4"	4½"
No. 3[1] 18-inch	3½"	4"
No. 1 24-inch	5¾"	7½"
No. 2[1] 24-inch	5½"	6½"
No. 3[1] 24-inch	5"	5½"
WOOD SHAKES[2]		
18-inch	7½"[3]	7½"
24-inch	10"[3]	10"

[1]To be used only when specifically permitted by the building official.

[2]Exposure of the 24-inch by ⅜-inch resawn handsplit tapered shake type shall not exceed 7½ inches on roof slopes less than 8 inches in 12 inches to a minimum of 4 inches in 12 inches.

[3]See Exception 4 of Section 3203 (h) for restrictions.

From the Uniform Building Code, ©1982, ICBO.

Figure 11-2 Maximum Weather Exposure

There are similar requirements for shakes, except that the spacing between shakes can't be less than 3/8 inch or more than 5 inches. Because most shakes are split instead of sawed, their edges are not always straight. Therefore, the code merely states that the shakes must be parallel within one inch. The nails on shakes are placed within 1 inch of the edge of the shake and approximately 2 inches above the exposure line.

The beginning course of both the shingles and shakes must be doubled; but with shakes the bottom course can be shingles. Shakes must have a layer of Type 30 felt placed between each course in such a manner that no felt is exposed below the butts.

Snow

With shake roofs, snow presents another problem. If the inspector feels that you are in a snow area you must adhere to Section 3203(d)3H:

. . .In wind-driven snow areas sheathing shall be solid and the shakes shall be applied over an underlayment of not less than Type 15 felt.

TABLE NO. 32-B—ROOF COVERING APPLICATION [1]

ROOF COVERING MATERIAL	BUILT-UP ROOFING [See Section 3203 (d) 2]		
	ROOF SLOPE		APPLICATION TO CLEAN SOLID DECK
	Minimum	Maximum	
1. Base Sheet	0:12	1:12 [3]	Non-nailable deck cement per 3203 (d) 2 or nailable deck nail with at least one approved fastener for each 1½ square foot, Section 3203 (c) [4]
2. Felts	0:12	1:12 [3]	Cement each sheet with 20 lbs. per sq. asphalt or 30 lbs. per sq. pitch, Section 3203 (d) 2
3. Glass Fiber Felts	0:12	1:12 [3]	Cement each sheet with 25 lbs. per sq. asphalt, Section 3202 (d) 2
4. Cap Sheets	½:12	2:12 [3]	Cement with 20 lbs. per sq. asphalt, Section 3203 (d) 2
5. Gravel—400 lbs. per sq. [2]	0:12	3:12	Embed in 60 lbs. per sq. of asphalt or 70 lbs. per sq. of pitch [2]
6. Slag—300 lbs. per sq. [2]	0:12	3:12	Embed in 60 lbs. per sq. of asphalt or 70 lbs. per sq. of pitch [2]

[1] See text of Chapter 32 for specific details and for construction, definitions, materials, re-roofing, drainage and roof insulation.
[2] See Section 3203 (f) 3 for ordinary roof covering.
[3] See Section 3203 (h) for exceptions.

Figure 11-3 Roof Covering Application

TABLE NO. 32-B—ROOF COVERING APPLICATION¹—(Continued)

SHINGLES-SHAKES-TILE [See Section 3203 (d) 3 A for Ice Conditions]

ROOF MATERIAL	MINIMUM SLOPE	UNDERLAYMENT³	NUMBER OF FASTENERS	STAPLES	NAILS Minimum Gauge	NAILS Minimum Head
7. Asphalt Shingles	4:12³	One Type 15 felt applied per Section 3203 (d) 3 A	4 per 36 inch strip / 2 per 18 inch shingle	4	12	3/8
8. Asbestos-Cement Shingles	5:12³	One Type 15 asbestos felt applied per Section 3203 (d) 3 A	4 per shingle⁴	NP	11	3/8
9. Metal Shingles	3:12	One Type 30 felt applied per Section 3203 (d) 3 A	4	4	4	4
10. Slate Shingles	4:12	Two Type 15 or One Type 30 felt applied per Section 3203 (d) 3 A	2 per shingle or wire tie			
11. Noninterlocking Tile—Flat or Curved	3:12		2 per tile or wire tie⁷	NP	11	4
12. Interlocking Tile—Flat or Curved	3:12		2 per tile or wire tie⁵			3/16
13. Wood Shingles	4:12⁶	NR	2 per shingle Section 3203 (d) 3 G	4	14½	7/32
14. Wood Shakes	4:12³	One Type 30 felt interlayment Section 3203 (d) 3 H	2 per shake	4	13	7/32

NP—Not Permitted   NR—No Requirements

4. Approval of the building official required.
5. On slopes 7:12 and less, tiles with installed weight exceeding 7.5 pounds per square foot having a width no greater than 16 inches may have one fastener. Similar tiles with anchor lugs engaged over horizontal battens may have one fastener on slopes exceeding 7:12.
6. See Table No. 32-A for exposures on lesser slopes.
7. On slopes 7:12 and less, tiles with an installed weight exceeding 7.5 pounds per square foot having a width no greater than 16 inches may have one fastener.

From the Uniform Building Code, ©1982, ICBO.

Figure 11-3 (continued) Roof Covering Application

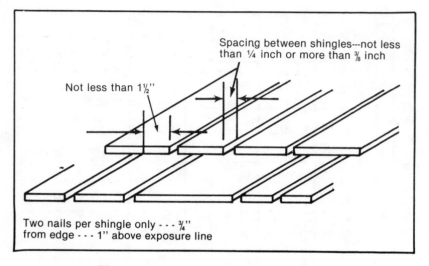

Figure 11-4   Shingle Laying Diagram

Valley Flashing

Flashing for all roofs is about the same. It must be underlaid with Type 15 felt, and the valley iron must be 28-gauge galvanized sheet metal.

There are, however, some variations:

Wood shingles and shakes: Sections of flashing must have an overlap of at least 4 inches and must extend 8 inches from the center line each way for shingles and 11 inches for shakes.

Asphalt shingles: Use metal flashing the same as for wood. Either laced asphalt shingles or a 90-pound mineral cap sheet may be used, if they are cemented together. The bottom layer should be 12 inches wide and laid face down, the top layer 24 inches wide and laid face up.

Metal shingles: Extend metal flashing 8 inches from the center line, with a splash diverter as part of the flashing. The flash diverter must be at least 3/4 inch high at the flow line.

Asbestos-cement shingles, slate shingles, clay and concrete tile: Extend metal flashing 11 inches from center line, with a splash diverter rib at the flow line at least 1 inch high formed as part of the flashing.

Attics

A house having an attic with more than 30 inches in vertical clear height (from the top of the joist to the underside of the rafter) must have an attic opening. This opening must be at least 22 inches by 30 inches, with at least 30 inches of clear headroom above the access opening. Here, the code (Section 3205(a)) throws in a teaser:

. . .and readily accessible in buildings of any height.

How would you define "readily accessible?" Many contractors put these openings in a closet to keep them out of sight. Is this "readily accessible?" The building inspector and the fire marshal probably wouldn't think so.

Roof Insulation

Today, insulation is used on many roofs. Section 3204 allows the use of combustible insulation, provided it is applied directly to an approved roof covering. Ordinary roof coverings other than Class A, B or C may be applied over foam plastic when the foam is separated from the interior of the building by plywood sheathing at least 1/2 inch thick. The edges must be supported by blocking, tongue-and-groove joints or other approved edge support.

If fire-retardant roof coverings are required, install insulation approved for the type of deck and the built-up roofing applied.

With built-up roofing you'll find a slightly different set of rules. A vapor barrier is required between the deck and the insulation in areas of the country where the average January temperature is below 45 degrees F or where excessive moisture is anticipated.

Draft Stops and Ventilation

You usually won't find this problem on the average home, but if there are more than 3,000 square feet in an enclosed attic, that space must be divided by partitions extending from the ceiling to the roof. The partitions cannot be less than 1/2-inch-thick gypsum wallboard, 1-inch nominal thickness of tight-fitting wood, or 3/8-inch-thick plywood. Other materials may be used, but check with the inspector first. If it's necessary to go from one section of the attic to another, you must install self-closing doors with the same fire resistance as the partition.

Be sure to thoroughly check attic ventilation. An allowable source of air to a vented attic is through the eaves or cornice of the building. When the insulation is blown in, it's easy for these areas to become plugged. A blocking strip placed between the rafters helps prevent this and assists in moving the air over the insulation.

The amount of venting required for an attic is computed on the basis of 1/150 of the area to be ventilated. For instance, if your attic contains 1,200 square feet, you need approximately 8 square feet of attic ventilation. The code states that 50% of this must come from the highest point of your attic—along the ridge, for instance—and the rest from screened "bird holes" along the eaves.

Smoke and Heat Venting
Single-story Group B, Division 2 and 4 occupancies (Mercantile Group) having more than 50,000 square feet in undivided area, and Group H occupancies (Hotels and Apartments) having over 15,000 square feet on a single floor, must have smoke and heat ventilation. These may be open or openable skylights, windows opening directly to the exterior of the building, or other types of openings.

Because smoke and heat ventilation is extremely important, the code goes into considerable detail to show how many vents are required and where they should go. Still, it's a good idea to contact your local inspector or fire marshal for advice.

Roof Drainage
If a roof isn't designed to support accumulated water, it must be sloped for drainage. These are a few do's and don't's:

- Install roof drains at the lowest point on the roof.
- Roof drains must be capable of handling the water flowing to them.
- In most areas, roof drains may not drain into the sanitary sewer.
- In many areas, roof drainage water is not permitted to flow over public property or onto adjacent property.
- Concealed roof drainage must conform to the plumbing code. Figure 11-5 shows a roof drain on a built-up roof.

Figure 11-5 Roof Drain on a Built-up Roof. Drains must be placed in such a manner that any water may be drained from the roof as rapidly as possible. The grated cover is a leaf strainer. Roof drainage, usually, may not go into the building sanitary plumbing system.

Heating

The U.B.C. doesn't say much about heating. That's pretty well covered under the Uniform Mechanical Code, except for electric heat, which is discussed in the National Electrical Code. What we will get into, however, are some of the ways buildings can be heated. Let's look at chimneys and fireplaces.

Chimneys

Not every house needs a chimney. Unless there's a fireplace in a house, many homes don't have chimneys at all. This, no doubt, gives many of the owners a cold feeling when the power company starts talking about power shortages.

Chapter 37 of the U.B.C. lists four classes of chimneys:

Residential Appliance-type, *is a factory-built or masonry chimney suitable for removing products of combustion from residential-type appliances producing combustion gases not in excess of 1000 degrees F measured at the appliance flue outlet.*

Low-heat Industrial Appliance-type, *is a factory-built, masonry or metal chimney suitable for removing the products of combustion from fuel-burning* *low-heat appliances producing combustion gases not in excess of 1000 degrees F under normal operating conditions but capable of producing combustion gases of 1400 degrees F during intermittent forced firing for periods up to one hour. All temperatures are measured at the appliance flue outlet.*

Medium-heat Industrial Appliance-type, is a factory-built, masonry or metal chimney suitable for removing the products of combustion from fuel-burning medium-heat appliances producing combustion gases not in excess of 2000 degrees F measured at the appliance flue outlet.

High-heat Industrial Appliance-type, is a factory-built, masonry or metal chimney suitable for removing the products of combustion from fuel-burning high-heat appliances producing combustion gases in excess of 2000 degrees F measured at the appliance flue outlet.

Remember, the temperatures listed above are measured at the appliance flue outlet.

Residential and low-heat chimneys are about the same. The only important difference is that the residential-type may have walls 4 inches thick and a flue liner, while the low-heat type requires 8-inch-thick walls and a flue liner. The liner in both cases must extend from a point 8 inches below the lowest inlet to a point above the enclosing walls. U.B.C. Tables Nos. 37-A and 37-B (see Figures 11-6 and 11-7) give dimensions and construction details for most chimneys.

Every chimney must rise from its own foundation, which must be on solid ground, to a point at least 2 feet higher than any point of a building within 10 feet horizontally. Bracket flues are no longer permitted. A chimney may not support any portion of the building unless the chimney was designed as a supporting member.

Construction Standards

The area of the chimney passageway must be at least the size of the vent connection. This is a cross-section dimension, not a linear dimension. Further, this measurement is made *after* the flue liner is installed. This liner, incidentally, may be omitted on residential chimneys with 8-inch solid masonry walls. This is an important consideration, derived from a footnote to U.B.C. Table No. 37-B:

Chimneys having walls 8 inches or more in thickness may be unlined.

Now, does that mean any old concrete block? Once mortared they appear to be quite solid. Here again, as shown in U.B.C. Table

TABLE NO. 37-A—MINIMUM PASSAGEWAY AREAS FOR MASONRY CHIMNEYS[1]

TYPE OF MASONRY CHIMNEY	MINIMUM CROSS-SECTIONAL AREA		
	ROUND	SQUARE OR RECTANGLE	LINED WITH FIREBRICK OR UNLINED
1. Residential	50 sq. in.	50 sq. in.	85 sq. in.
2. Fireplace [2]	$\frac{1}{12}$ of opening Minimum 50 sq. in.	$\frac{1}{10}$ of opening Minimum 64 sq. in.	$\frac{1}{8}$ of opening Minimum 100 sq. in.
3. Low heat	50 sq. in.	57 sq. in.	135 sq. in.
4. Incinerator Apartment type 1 opening 2 to 6 openings 7 to 14 openings 15 or more openings	196 sq. in. 324 sq. in. 484 sq. in. 484 sq. in. plus 10 sq. in. for each additional opening		Not applicable

[1]Areas for medium- and high-heat chimneys shall be determined using accepted engineering methods and as approved by the building official.

[2]Where fireplaces open on more than one side, the fireplace opening shall be measured along the greatest dimension.

Note: For altitudes over 2000 feet above sea level, the building official shall be consulted in determining the area of the property.

From the Uniform Building Code, ©1982, ICBO.

Figure 11-6   Minimum Passageway Areas for Masonry Chimneys

No. 37-B, the type of masonry unit determines the thickness of the chimney walls as well as the thickness of the liner.

Smoke doesn't go straight up a chimney, it spirals up. This is why a round chimney is the ideal shape. A square flue is good, since only the corners are dead space. A long, narrow, rectangular flue needs to have a much greater area to get the same results. It's a good idea to consider Section 3703(b) when designing a chimney:

(b) Construction. Each chimney shall be so constructed as to safely convey flue gases not exceeding the maximum temperatures for the type of construction as set forth in U.B.C. Table No. 37-B and shall be capable of producing a draft at the appliance not less than that required for safe operation.

Essentially, that's what we're concerned with and what all the above really means. If it doesn't work, you've wasted a lot of time.

TABLE NO. 37-B—CONSTRUCTION, CLEARANCE AND TERMINATION REQUIREMENTS FOR MASONRY AND CONCRETE CHIMNEYS

Chimneys Serving	Thickness (Min. Inches)		Height Above Roof Opening (Feet)	Height Above any Part of Building within (Feet)			Clearance to Combustible Construction (Inches)	
	Walls	Lining		10	25	50	Int. Inst.	Ext. Inst.
1. RESIDENTIAL-TYPE APPLIANCES [1][2] (Low Btu Input)								
Clay, Shale or Concrete Brick	4[3]	5/8 fire-clay tile or 2 fire-brick	2	2			1	1 or ½ gypsum[4]
Reinforced Concrete	4[3]							
Hollow Masonry Units	4[8]							
Stone	12							
Unburned Clay Units	8	4½ fire-brick						
2. BUILDING HEATING AND INDUSTRIAL-TYPE LOW-HEAT APPLIANCES[12] (1000°F. operating temp.—1400°F. Maximum)								
Clay, Shale or Concrete Brick	8	5/8 fire-clay tile or 2 fire-brick	3	2			2	2
Hollow Masonry Units	8[8]							
Reinforced Concrete	8							
Stone	12							

Figure 11-7 Requirements for Masonry and Concrete Chimneys

TABLE NO. 37-B—CONSTRUCTION, CLEARANCE AND TERMINATION REQUIREMENTS FOR MASONRY AND CONCRETE CHIMNEYS—(Continued)

Chimneys Serving	Thickness (Min. Inches)		Height Above Roof Opening (Feet)	Height Above any Part of Building within (Feet)			Clearance to Combustible Construction (Inches)	
	Walls	Lining		10	25	50	Int. Inst.	Ext. Inst.
3. MEDIUM-HEAT INDUSTRIAL-TYPE APPLIANCES[1][5] (2000°F. Maximum) Clay, Shale or Concrete Brick Hollow Masonry Units (Grouted Solid) Reinforced Concrete Stone	8 8 8 12	4½ Medium duty fire-brick	10		10		4	4
4. HIGH-HEAT INDUSTRIAL-TYPE APPLIANCES[1][2] (Over 2000°F.) Clay, Shale or Concrete Brick Hollow Masonry Units (Grouted Solid) Reinforced Concrete	16[6] 16[6] 16[6]	4½ High duty fire-brick	20			20	?	?
5. RESIDENTIAL-TYPE INCINERATORS	Same as for Residential-Type Appliances as shown above							
6. CHUTE-FED AND FLUE-FED INCINERATORS WITH COMBINED HEARTH AND GRATE AREA 7 SQ. FT. OR LESS Clay, Shale or Concrete Brick or Hollow Units Portion extending to 10 ft. above combustion chamber roof Portion more than 10 ft. above combustion chamber roof	4 8	4½ Medium duty fire-brick 5/8 fire-clay tile liner	3	2			2	2

(Continued on next page)

Figure 11-7 (continued) Requirements for Masonry and Concrete Chimneys

7. CHUTE-FED AND FLUE-FED INCINERATORS—COMBINED HEARTH AND GRATE AREAS LARGER THAN 7 SQ. FT.					
Clay, Shale or Concrete Brick or Hollow Units Grouted Solid or Reinforced Concrete					
Portion extending to 40 ft. above combustion chamber roof	4	4½ Medium duty fire-brick 5/8 fire-clay tile liner	10	2	2
Portion more than 40 ft. above combustion chamber roof	8	4½ Medium duty fire-brick			
Reinforced Concrete	8	laid in medium duty refract mortar			
8. COMMERCIAL OR INDUSTRIAL-TYPE INCINERATORS[2]					
Clay or Shale Solid Brick	8	4½ Medium duty fire-brick laid in medium duty refract mortar	10	4	4
Reinforced Concrete	8				

[1]See Table No. 9-A of the Mechanical Code for types of appliances to be used with each type of chimney.

[2]Lining shall extend from bottom to top of chimney.

[3]Chimneys having walls 8 inches or more in thickness may be unlined.

[4]Chimneys for residential-type appliances installed entirely on the exterior of the building.

[5]Lining to extend from 24 inches below connector to 25 feet above.

[6]Two 8-inch walls with 2-inch air space between walls. Outer and inner walls may be of solid masonry units or reinforced concrete or any combination thereof.

[7]Clearance shall be approved by the building official and shall be such that the temperature of combustible materials will not exceed 160°F.

[8]Equivalent thickness including grouted cells when grouted solid. The equivalent thickness may also include the grout thickness between the liner and masonry unit.

From the Uniform Building Code, ©1982, ICBO.

Figure 11-7 (continued) Requirements for Masonry and Concrete Chimneys

Fireplaces

Fireplaces have undergone many changes in the last few years, ever since the so-called "zero clearance" factory-built, metal fireplace inserts became popular. I'm not talking about "heatilators" that have been around for years, but pre-fabricated fireplaces that can be set in wood frames. These must have the I.C.B.O. stamp of approval and must be installed exactly as the manufacturer specifies. It's difficult to say if they'll be as durable as masonry fireplaces because they haven't been around very long. But there's no reason why the pre-fabricated models shouldn't last a long time. And they have the advantage of being much cheaper to install than a standard masonry fireplace.

If you're installing a masonry fireplace, there are a number of things to consider. (Many of these considerations have been incorporated into design of the factory-built jobs, making their installation that much easier and trouble-free.) The first of these is that the depth of the firebox may not be less than 20 inches. The width of the opening is not too important, but the height of the opening should not be higher than the size of the fire contemplated. Generally, the larger the fire, the higher the opening can be. However, a small fire in a large high firebox usually produces a smoking fireplace.

The shape of the back and sides of the firebox determines how well it will reflect the heat into the room. The shape of the smoke chamber, throat and smoke shelf is important, also. The damper, when fully opened, must not restrict the flue beyond the dimensions shown in U.B.C. Table No. 37-A (Figure 11-6). The damper blade, when fully opened, must not extend past the line of the inside of the flue.

Hearths

Masonry fireplaces must have hearths constructed of brick, concrete, stone or other approved noncombustible hearth slab. The hearth must be at least 4 inches thick and supported by noncombustible materials or reinforced to carry its own weight and all imposed loads. Hearth extensions must extend at least 16 inches from the front of the fireplace opening and at least 8 inches beyond the side of the opening. However, if your fireplace opening exceeds 6 square feet, the hearth extension must go 20 inches beyond the opening in front and 12 inches beyond the opening on each side.

Hearth extensions for factory-built fireplaces or fireplace stoves are a little different. These must be at least 3/8 inch thick and may be asbestos, concrete, hollow metal, stone, tile, or any other approved noncombustible material. They may be placed on the subflooring or finish flooring whether it is combustible or not. However, with the exception of fireplaces which open to the exterior of the building, the hearth slab must be readily distinguishable from the surrounding or adjacent floor.

Metal Damper Hoods

Most masonry fireplaces have metal damper hoods. These hoods usually come complete with smoke shelf, damper, and a properly sized flue outlet. According to the code, they must be made of 19-gauge corrosion-resistant metal. Copper, galvanized steel or other equivalent ferrous metal is acceptable. All seams must be smokeproof and unsoldered. Hoods must be sloped 45 degrees or less and extend horizontally at least 6 inches beyond the front of the firebox. They must be kept at least 18 inches from any combustible material unless they are of an approved design.

Line the top side of the hood with several inches of fiberglass to keep from losing heat into the chimney cavity. And always mortar the hood in place. In the past this wasn't always done, the claim being that expansion and contraction caused by heat eventually crack the mortar, allowing the hood to break away from the lintel. Therefore, it was common practice to stuff this space with fiberglass. After all, they reasoned, isn't fiberglass noncombustible?

While fiberglass is noncombustible, it does melt, leaving a space for flame to enter into the chimney cavity and go to work on the wood framing around the fireplace. Consequently, hoods must be mortared in.

By the way, combustible material should not be placed within one inch of a fireplace, smoke chamber or chimney wall. Neither can it be placed within six inches of the fireplace opening.

Fireplace Operation

In cold weather, when a fireplace has not been used for some time and the flue gets cold, there will be a reverse draft caused by cold air coming down the chimney. If you light a fire, the fireplace will smoke until the flue is warm enough to create a draft. To avoid this, burn a piece of rolled-up newspaper in the throat before you light the fire in the fireplace. This will warm the air in the flue and start a draft up the chimney. Of course, if the fireplace is not built correctly, it will smoke anyway.

Other causes of smokey fireplaces are discussed in Chapter Sixteen, "Combustion Air."

12
Concrete

In previous chapters we worked with concrete in a number of different ways, but little was said about what concrete really is. The average contractor constructing a small building—either a residence or a small commercial building—needs little more than a general knowledge of proper concrete handling procedures. That's because most concrete arrives at the site already mixed and ready to use.

Concrete and Cement

What's the difference between "concrete" and "cement"? Generally, "cement" is the powdered limestone used in the making of "concrete." Concrete is defined in Chapter 26 of the U.B.C:

Concrete. A mixture of portland cement, fine aggregate, coarse aggregate and water.

There are many types of concrete and concrete construction. These are covered in Chapter 26 of the U.B.C.

Definitions

I've already mentioned the distinction between concrete and cement, but there are a few other items that should be of interest to you, also. In fact, there are about 46 terms defined in Section 2602. Many of these, however, concern design only, so I'll just list a few of the most common items.

The following terms are defined for general use. Specialized definitions will appear as needed. These are reprinted from Section 2602 of the U.B.C:

Admixture. *A material other than portland cement, aggregate or water added to concrete to modify its properties.*

Aggregate. *Inert material which is mixed with portland cement and water to produce concrete.*

Deformed Reinforcement. *Deformed reinforcing bars, bar and rod mats, deformed wire, welded plain wire fabric and welded deformed wire fabric conforming to Section 2603(f)2.*

Embedment Length. *The length of embedded reinforcement provided beyond a critical section.*

Plain Concrete. *Concrete that does not conform to the definition for reinforced concrete.*

Precast Concrete. *A plain or reinforced concrete element cast in other than its final position in the structure.*

Prestressed Concrete. *Reinforced concrete in which there have been introduced internal stresses of such magnitude and distribution that the stresses resulting from loads are counteracted to a desired degree.*

Reinforced Concrete. *Concrete containing reinforcement, including prestressing steel, and designed with the assumption that the two materials act together in resisting forces.*

Surface Water. *Water carried by an aggregate except that held by absorption within the aggregate particles themselves.*

Of all construction materials, concrete is probably one of the most abused. It is mismatched, mismixed, and watered down. Products are added to slow or speed its hardening process. Yet in spite of the things done to it, concrete is one of the most reliable building products we have.

Weather will erode it, in time. However, it will not rust or rot, and even the poorest mixes will last long after the framing, wiring, and other components of a building have completely deteriorated.

Concrete is one of the most versatile of the manufactured building blocks, particularly during construction. It will adapt to nearly any design or building application, and will support greater loads than most other products.

Testing Concrete
With a few exceptions, concrete is difficult to inspect properly. Therefore, the inspector has the right to call for any tests he thinks are necessary. Many of these tests are spelled out in the job specs, so the contractor knows in advance—when he bids the job—what is expected. Often this is adequate, but if the inspector thinks the specified tests are inadequate, he can call for more sophisticated tests. Fortunately, most on-site concrete tests are easily performed. Two of the most common are the *slump* test and the *compression* or *compressive fracture* test.

Slump Test
The slump test is probably the simplest of all concrete tests. It involves a cone-shaped device made of sheet metal approximately 12 inches high with a base about 8 inches in diameter and a top about 4 inches in diameter. (See Figure 12-1.) This device is placed on a board or other flat surface and filled with concrete. The concrete is then settled by pushing a steel rod into it a prescribed number of times. The height of the settled concrete is then measured and the cone is removed from the wet concrete. After settling for several minutes the concrete is again measured; the difference between the first measurement and the second is the amount of slump in that batch.

Slump tests are usually made in a series of three, and the rate of slump is averaged out. This average is then compared with the slump allowed by the specs. If they don't agree within allowed percentages, the concrete should be disallowed.

Compressive Fracture Test
The compression test is a little more complicated. Unless a fracturing machine is taken to the job site, the test begins in the field but ends in a laboratory. A cylinder is cast using a round form varying from 2 inches in diameter by 4 inches in length to 10 inches in diameter and 18 inches in length. The usual size, where aggregate does not exceed 2 inches in diameter, is 6 inches by 12 inches. Unless required by the project specifications, cylinders smaller than 6 by 12 should not be made in the field.

The cylinder is placed on a flat surface where it won't be exposed to vibration or other disturbances, and filled with concrete. The concrete is then rodded a prescribed number of times for even

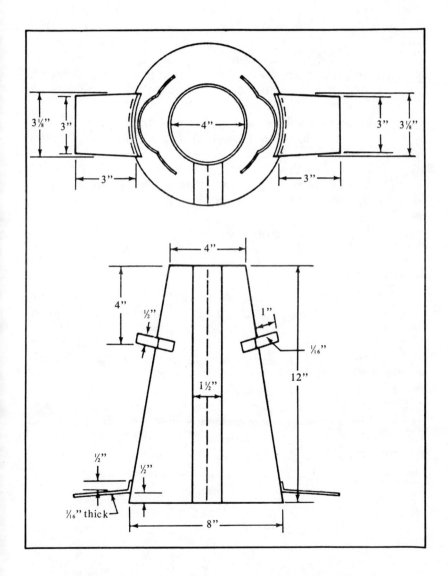

Figure 12-1 Details of Cone Used for Slump Tests. In making the test, the specimen is made in a mold or "slump cone" of 16 gauge galvanized metal in the form shown above. The base and top are open. The mold is provided with foot pieces and handles as shown.

distribution. Rodding requirements are given in U.B.C. Tables Nos. 26-10-A and 26-10-B (see Figure 12-2). The cylinders must be left undisturbed until the initial set-up, or hardening, has taken place. Movement after that should be minimal for the first 24 hours. Care should also be taken to protect the cylinders from unusually hot or cold weather.

The cylinders are then placed in a compression or breaking press. These presses have a calibrated dial that indicates the pressure at pounds per square inch (psi). Usually several cylinders are tested, one at a time, at specified intervals. Normal time between tests is 24 hours, 7 days, and 28 days. The results are checked with the specs. Usually, with transit-mixed concrete, compressive tests are run periodically by the company selling the concrete. Although there are times when the plant botches a load, the problems usually begin after the mix arrives at the job site.

Mixing The Batch

The cement must meet the requirements and specifications for the particular job at hand. U.B.C. Standards 26-1 lists eight types of concrete most commonly used in construction:

Type I — *For use in general concrete construction when the special properties specified for Types II, III, IV, and V are not required.*

Type IA — *Same use as Type I where air entrainment is desired.*

Type II — *For use in general concrete construction exposed to moderate sulfate action, or where moderated heat of hydration is desired.*

Type IIA — *Same use as Type II where air entrainment is desired.*

Type III — *For use when high early strength is required.*

Type IIIA — *Same use as Type III where air entrainment is desired.*

Type IV — *For use when a low heat of hydration is required.*

Type V — *For use when high sulfate resistance is required.*

As for the type you should be using, check with your supplier unless your specs call for something different. This should be determined by the engineer designing the job. Once you know the type of cement to use, you'll need to know the right proportions for the job at hand. Here again, this should be spelled out in the specs and will usually be noted in three figures, such as 1-3-5. This means "1 sack cement, 3 cubic feet of sand, 5 cubic feet of stone." To this you add the amount of water necessary to get the slump required by the specs.

TABLE NO. 26-10-A—NUMBER OF LAYERS REQUIRED FOR SPECIMENS

Specimen Type and Size, as Depth, in.	Mode of Compaction	Number of layers	Approximate Depth of Layer, in.
Cylinders:			
up to 12	rodding	3 equal	4
over 12	rodding	as required	4
up to 18	vibration	2 equal	8 as near as practicable
over 18	vibration	3 or more	8 as near as practicable
Prisms and horizontal creep cylinders:			
up to 8	rodding	2 equal	4
over 8	rodding	3 or more	4
up to 8	vibration	1	8 as near as practicable
over 8	vibration	2 or more	8 as near as practicable

TABLE NO. 26-10-B—DIAMETER OF ROD AND NUMBER OF RODDINGS TO BE USED IN MOLDING TEST SPECIMENS

Cylinders

Diameter of Cylinder, in.	Diameter of Rod, in.	Number of Strokes/Layer
2 to $<$6	3/8	25
6	5/8	25
8	5/8	50
10	5/8	75

Beams and Prisms

Top Surface Area of Specimen, in.	Diameter of Rod, in.	Number of Roddings/Layer
25 or less	3/8	25
26 to 49	3/8	one for each 1 in.^{2} of surface
50 or more	5/8	one for each 2 in.^{2} of surface

Horizontal Creep Cylinders

Diameter of Cylinder, in.	Diameter of Rod, in.	Number of Roddings/Layer
6	5/8	50 total, 25 along both sides of axis

Figure 12-2 Number of Layers and Rodding Requirements for Concrete Specimens

From the Uniform Building Code, ©1982, IBCO.

The aggregate must be clean and free of pollutants such as ash, dirt, grease, oil or wood chips. The nominal maximum size of aggregate should not be larger than 1/5 the narrowest dimension between the sides of the form, 1/3 the depth of the slabs, or 3/4 the minimum clear spacing between reinforcing steel. Check the workability of the mix and the methods of consolidation so the concrete can be placed without honeycombs or voids.

Use water free of oil, acids, alkalis, or organic materials that may affect either the concrete or the reinforcing steel.

All reinforcing material should conform to the specs, and placement should conform to the plans. U.B.C. Table No. 26-1 (Figure 12-3) shows the minimum bend point locations for rebar. U.B.C. Table No. 26-C-2 (Figure 12-4) shows the minimum diameters of bends.

Placing Concrete

To place concrete you need to know about forms. Formwork must produce a final structure that conforms to the shape, lines, dimensions and loading set forth by the architect or engineer. Because of the weight and fluidity of the concrete, the forms must be adequately braced to prevent collapse or leakage. I've worked on several jobs where the forms weren't braced right, and I can guarantee that it's a frustrating experience to see concrete seeping out where it shouldn't be. Figure 12-5 shows a formed foundation wall with metal clips on the top of the form to keep the boards from spreading. Forms for prestressed members must allow for any movement of the member without causing damage to the form.

Something else you should consider is whether your forms are accessible to the ready-mix truck. If they are, the truck can pour the concrete directly into the forms. If not, you'll have to transport the concrete to the forms by treemie, wheelbarrow, pump, or even by bucket and crane.

Regardless of the method used, don't let the concrete fall more than 48 inches from the chute to the form. If this distance exceeds 48 inches, use an extension chute. Prefabricated metal chute extensions are available or you can make your own from scrap wood at the job site. Just be careful to keep the ingredients in the batch from separating while pouring.

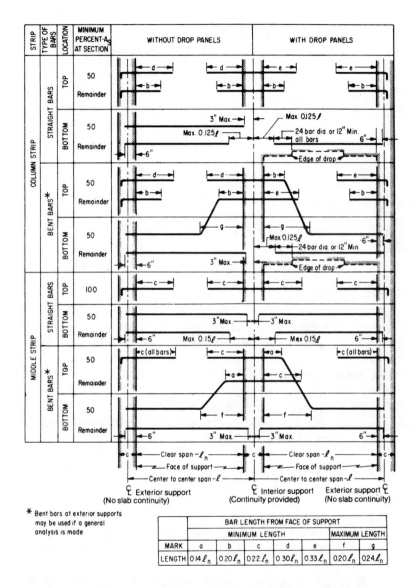

FIGURE NO. 26-1—MINIMUM BEND POINT LOCATIONS AND EXTENSIONS FOR REINFORCEMENT IN SLABS WITHOUT BEAMS
[See Section 2612 (m) 1 for reinforcement extension into supports.]

From the Uniform Building Code, ©1982, ICBO.

Figure 12-3 Minimum Bend Point Locations

TABLE NO. 26-C-2—MINIMUM DIAMETERS OF BEND

BAR SIZE	MINIMUM DIAMETER
Nos. 3 through 8	$6d_b$
Nos. 9, 10 and 11	$8d_b$
Nos. 14 and 18	$10d_b$

From the Uniform Building Code, ©1982, ICBO.

Figure 12-4   Minimum Diameters of Bend

When you're ready to remove the forms, be careful not to damage the green concrete. The only loads allowed on unshored portions during construction are the dead load and the live load. No construction can be supported by the new work until the concrete reaches adequate strength. This usually takes from 3 to 28 days. Generally, form removal can begin after 24 hours.

Curing
When it comes to concrete, time is of the essence. By using additives you can delay or increase the curing time, but generally it's just a matter of waiting. In about the first 24 hours, the concrete will acquire over half its strength. By the end of seven days you should have approximately 90% of the design strength; full strength won't be achieved until after 28 days.

If you've just poured a basement or foundation wall for a simple structure, you can probably work around the area in a day or two. This doesn't mean you can move a house onto a newly poured foundation. It's doubtful the inspector would allow such a load to be imposed on a new foundation within the 28-day period.

As for the actual curing, the code recommends that concrete be maintained above 50 degrees F and in a moist environment for at least the first seven days after placing. If you were using a high early-strength concrete, this time can be reduced to about three days. But what happens in the fall and winter, when temperatures fall below 50 degrees F?

Simply covering the concrete will help. The chemical reaction in the concrete itself—the interaction of the water, cement and other chemicals in the mix—creates a great deal of heat. If it appears that temperatures will fall below the safety point, a layer of straw, sawdust, or even polyethylene film will keep heat in and preserve the temperature needed.

Figure 12-5 Foundation Wall Ready to Have its Forms Stripped. Note the metal clips on the top of the form to keep it from spreading during pouring of the wall. Similar clips can be used on the bottom, or "form ties" can be used midway between the top and bottom of the form, depending on the height of the form. Note also that foundation bolts are already in place.

Increased Temperatures and Curing Time

In Section 2605(e)3, the code provides a method that will shorten curing time a great deal:

Curing by high-pressure steam, steam at atmospheric pressure, heat and moisture, or other accepted processes, may be employed to accelerate strength gain and reduce the time of curing. Accelerated curing shall provide the compressive strength of the concrete at the load stage considered at least equal to the design strength required at that load stage. The curing process shall produce concrete with a durability at least equivalent to the curing method of Section 2605(e)1.

How do you know when the concrete has reached proper strength? Remember those test cylinders I mentioned earlier? These cylinders contain samples of concrete taken from the same batch. Therefore, when the compression test shows that the samples have achieved the proper strength, the concrete used in the work should be at the right strength also.

Hot Weather

During hot weather, proper attention shall be given to ingredients, production methods, handling, placing, protection, and curing to prevent excessive concrete temperatures or water evaporation . . .

That's what Section 2605 (g) of the code says about hot weather, but it doesn't say how hot. That varies, depending on locale, humidity, and wind conditions. The key is to prevent the rapid evaporation of water from the fresh concrete.

Temperature is temperature as far as excessive temperature is concerned, but the degree of evaporation will vary widely, depending on the relative humidity. If you're in a humid part of the country, you'll have one set of values. If you're in an arid climate, you'll have another set of values. The Portland Cement Association reports that if the relative humidity decreases from 90% to 50%, the rate of evaporation increases five times; if the humidity is further reduced by 10%, evaporation is increased nine times.

When it's windy you'll find the same changes in the rate of evaporation. When the wind changes from 0 to 10 mph, the rate of evaporation increases four times; it's nine times greater when wind velocity increases to 25 mph.

Using cool materials and protecting the work from direct sunlight helps reduce evaporation. Spraying the concrete with a fine mist raises the relative humidity and helps slow down the evaporation.

Continuous Pour or Placement

Sometimes the pouring of a job must be interrupted. Although this should be avoided as much as possible, the code does provide for interruption of a pour in Section 2606(d):

(d) Construction Joints. Where a construction joint is to be made, the surface of the concrete shall be thoroughly cleaned and all laitance and standing water removed. Vertical joints also shall be thoroughly wetted immediately before placing of new concrete.

If you've ever tried to place a thin concrete slab over an existing one—raising the height of steps or a sidewalk, for example—then you're probably aware of how difficult it is to get a good seal or bond between the old concrete and the new.

The code calls for a "neat cement grout," meaning, generally, a mixture of water and cement spread over the surface. Several products do this job very well. The point is that you just can't pour new concrete over old without preparing the existing surface first. Ask your concrete supplier about the materials you'll need and how to use them.

Laitance

That last quote from the U.B.C. states that "all laitance and standing water be removed." Standing water is usually the result of sprinkling that was done to keep the previous pour from drying too rapidly. It may also be the result of rain or any number of reasons, but it should be mopped up. When standing water collects on the top of settled concrete, it brings with it a mixture of dust, impurities, small amounts of cement, and other foreign matter. When the water evaporates, it leaves a dusty, grayish-brown film on the surface of the concrete. This is *laitance*. On flat slabs where the surface is worked down and smoothed as part of the finishing process, laitance doesn't exist, or if it does, it is in such a small amount that it has little or no effect. Much of it is worked off when the slab is pre-finished. The rest is worked back into the concrete.

On formwork, however, laitance can be a real problem. It has no bonding ability. Therefore, if a pour is interrupted, the laitance must be removed before the job can proceed. This is usually done with sandblasting equipment.

Spacing of Reinforcement

The clear distance between parallel reinforcing bars in a layer should be at least the same as the nominal diameter of the bars. This distance should not be less than one inch. This is what the code specifies, but that doesn't pertain to splices, as defined in Figure 8-2 of Chapter 8, or to bundles when they are designed as part of an overall reinforcement plan. Do not use lap splices on bars larger than No. 11 except where larger bars are used as dowels in footings.

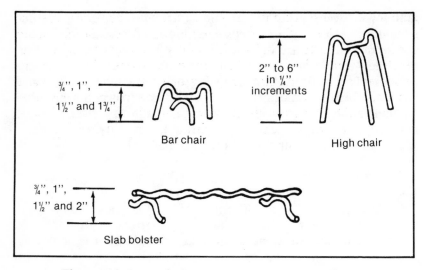

Figure 12-6 "Chairs" for Supporting Reinforcing Steel

Welded splices may be used. A full welded splice is one in which the bars are butted and welded to develop a tension of at least 125% of the specified yield strength of the bar.

Be sure to support all reinforcement. On vertical work, secure reinforcement so that it will not touch the sides of the forms or other reinforcement except as planned in the construction of the bundles or mats. In flatwork, such as slabs for floors or roofs, place reinforcement on *chairs* to keep it from touching the ground or form below. A chair is a metal device usually constructed of a heavy gauge wire (see Figure 12-6).

I've mentioned that on slabs—particularly basement floors or patios—reinforcing steel, either bars or mats, will be laid on the ground. After the pour is made, the steel is "hooked" in such a way that the finisher can pull it up into the concrete. This is *not* an acceptable method of placing the reinforcement, however, because the steel is not placed evenly within the slab and much of its effectiveness may be lost.

Settling or Consolidating Concrete

The amount of *settling*, or *consolidating*, depends largely on the amount of slump in a mix. A high slump mix requires little consolidation. There are two methods of consolidating—hand spading or vibration. Mechanical vibrators do the work of settling much easier than hand-spading, and they allow for the placement of stiffer mixes. But don't use vibrators if the mix can be hand spaded. There's always the possibility of the material separating too much. This is also why vibrators should not be used to move concrete horizontally.

13
Fire Safety

Despite the heroic efforts of fire fighters, people are going to die in fires. Many buildings are not entirely fire safe; some could even be called "fire traps." And, all too often people are responsible for creating the flammable conditions around them. Consequently, it's impossible to prevent all fires.

The idea, then, is to reduce the damage caused by fires that do break out. This can be done in several ways. The best is to build as much fire resistiveness into a structure as possible or is economically feasible. In Chapter Three we discussed the types of construction that provide a high degree of fire resistiveness based on occupancy. This should be the first line of defense in reducing damage caused by fire. However, construction can only reduce the damage done to a building; it cannot, in most cases, prevent the start of fires. And fire-resistive construction can be costly, though this is an area where cost should not be an influence.

But fires usually don't start by themselves. And no building is completely fire resistive. So the next step is to provide adequate fire detection and control systems.

Fire Detection and Control Systems
Many types of fire detection and control equipment and systems

are available. There are simple smoke detectors placed near bedroom doors, multiple interconnected smoke detectors placed throughout a building, automatic sprinklers, and wet and dry standpipes. Some businesses even maintain their own fire suppression teams.

Each of these has its benefits and limitations, and no system is 100% effective in all situations. Smoke detectors or alarms detect smoke and signal the occupants. But unless they also signal a fire station, these devices can't put out a fire.

Automatic sprinklers detect fire through heat sensors which trigger the system to spray the fire. To be truly effective they should be wired to a fire station. But automatic sprinklers are subject to false alarms and can cause a great deal of water damage.

Standpipes provide a source of water for extinguishing a fire but not the actual means of putting one out. In-house fire-suppression teams can be effective but are expensive to maintain and often are not properly trained in all aspects of fire fighting.

These are just some of the considerations to keep in mind regarding fire detection and control systems. There are many others. If your smoke detectors are electrically operated, what will happen if the power source is cut off or ineffective? Also, what would happen to your automatic sprinklers if a fire breaks out the day that water is shut off because the city is repairing a line in the street? Are back-up systems available?

Automatic Sprinkler Systems

There are many regulations covering the installation of fire sprinkler systems. The code doesn't cover Group R-3 (single family residential) and Group M (miscellaneous and agricultural) occupancies. But all other occupancies, with certain exceptions, must have automatic sprinklers. According to Chapter 38, U.B.C., a building of 1500 square feet or more will need an automatic sprinkler system. First, let's take a look at the code's general requirement. Section 3802(b) states that automatic sprinkler systems must be installed:

In every story or basement of all buildings when the floor area exceeds 1500 square feet and there is not provided at least 20 square feet of opening entirely above the adjoining ground level in each 50 lineal feet or fraction thereof of exterior wall in the story or basement on at least one side of the building. Openings shall have a minimum dimension of not less than 30 inches. Such openings shall be accessible to the fire department from the exterior and shall not be obstructed in a manner that fire fighting or rescue cannot be accomplished from the exterior.

When openings in a story are provided on only one side and the opposite wall of such story is more than 75 feet from such openings, the story shall be provided with an approved automatic sprinkler system, or openings as specified above shall be provided on at least two sides of an exterior wall of the story.

If any portion of a basement is located more than 75 feet from openings required in this section, the basement shall be provided with an approved automatic sprinkler system.

It then goes on to define specific areas in certain occupancies where sprinklers are required, and provides exceptions where conditions can alter the requirement or need. For instance, in a cold storage building you should have a "dry" system or you might wind up with a "frozen" one. A "dry" system is just like a regular system in which the heads are controlled by a fusible link. When a fire occurs the link melts. It releases a pressure controlled switch which floods the line and puts out the flames.

Sometimes antifreeze can be used to prime the lines, as set forth in the U.B.C. Standards. However, this should be done carefully because the antifreeze solution could be harmful to products stored in the area, doing more damage than a conventional system might cause.

There are some areas where sprinklers can be reduced or omitted completely. An example is a communications center or a power house. Can you imagine what would happen if a sprinkler system went off over a bank of telephone relays? But that doesn't mean that fire alarms or controls aren't required.

Sprinklers aren't the only source of fire suppression, but they are, in most cases, the least costly. There are many chemical systems on the market, but check with the inspector as to what is allowable.

Because of a recent rash of fires in nightclubs and discos, the '82 edition of the U.B.C. has an added section specifically dealing with the problems. Section 3802(c) states:

Group A Occupancies. 1. Nightclubs, discos. An automatic sprinkler system shall be installed in rooms primarily used for entertaining occupants who are drinking or dining and unseparated accessory uses where the total area of such unseparated rooms and assembly uses exceeds 5000 square feet. For uses to be considered as separated, the separation shall be not less than as required for a one-hour occupancy separation. The area of other uses shall be included unless separated by at least a one-hour occupancy separation.

Section 3802(d)2 considers permissible omissions this way:

Sprinklers shall not be installed when the application of water or flame and water to the contents may constitute a serious life or fire hazard, as in the manufacture or storage of quantities of aluminum powder, calcium carbide, calcium phosphide, metallic sodium and potassium, quicklime, magnesium powder and sodium peroxide.

Sprinklers are provided, first, for early suppression of any flame or fire, and second, to create a safe period for the early and rapid escape of the building's occupants. That's why the need for sprinklers decreases as the normal human occupancy of an area decreases. In most cases, an automatic sprinkling system is all that's needed. They often put a fire out before the fire fighters can arrive. But what happens in the event of a flash fire or a smoldering fire which does not create enough heat to immediately set off a sprinkler but which can fill an area with deadly fumes?

In certain occupancies smoke detectors are required in addition to the automatic sprinklers and in some cases must be photo-eye controlled. All Group R-3 occupancies are now required to have small detectors next to sleeping areas.

As for the flash fire, sprinklers work—but do they work in time? For that you have to refer to your type of occupancy and area separations to keep the high danger areas remote from the areas of high human loads.

Standpipes

Few homes have standpipes but most large apartment and office buildings do. U.B.C. Table No. 38-A (Figure 13-1) explains types and locations of standpipes. Section 3801(c) tells you what they are and how they're used:

Standpipe System is a wet or dry system of piping, valves, outlets, and related equipment designed to provide water at specified pressures and installed exclusively for the fighting of fires and classified as follows:

Class I is a dry standpipe system without a directly connected water supply and equipped with 2½-inch outlets for use by the fire department or trained personnel.

Class II is a wet standpipe system directly connected to a water supply and equipped with 1½-inch outlets intended for use by the building occupants.

Class III is a combination standpipe system directly connected to a water supply and equipped with both 1½-inch outlets for use by the building occupants and 2½-inch outlets for use by the fire department or trained personnel.

TABLE NO. 38-A—STANDPIPE REQUIREMENTS

OCCUPANCY[1]	NONSPRINKLERED BUILDING[2]		SPRINKLERED BUILDING[3][4]	
	Standpipe Class	Hose Requirement	Standpipe Class	Hose Requirement
1. Occupancies exceeding 150 ft. in height and more than one story	III	Yes	III	No
2. Occupancies 4 stories or more but less than 150 ft. in height, except Group R, Div. 3	[I and II[5]] (or III)	[6] Yes	I (or III)	No
3. Group A Occupancies with occupant load exceeding 1000	II	Yes	No requirement	No
4. Group A, Div. 2.1 Occupancies over 5000 square feet in area used for exhibition	II	Yes	II	Yes
5. Groups I, H, B, Div. 1, 2 or 3 Occupancies less than 4 stories in height but greater than 20,000 square feet per floor	II[5]	Yes	No requirement	No

[1]Class II standpipes need not be provided in assembly areas used solely for worship.

[2]Except as otherwise specified in Item No. 4 of this table, Class II standpipes need not be provided in basements having an automatic fire-extinguishing system throughout.

[3]Combined systems with their related water supplies may be used in sprinklered buildings.

[4]Portions of otherwise sprinklered buildings which are not protected by automatic sprinklers shall have Class II standpipes installed as required for the unsprinklered portions.

[5]In open structures where Class II standpipes may be damaged by freezing, the building official may authorize the use of Class I standpipes which are located as required for Class II standpipes.

[6]Hose is required for Class II standpipes only.

From the Uniform Building Code, ©1982, ICBO.

Figure 13-1   Standpipe Requirements

Knowing what standpipes are is one thing, but knowing how they should be placed is something else. U.B.C. Table No. 38-A will help you with this. Figure 13-2 illustrates a typical standpipe location.

There's one big disadvantage to the standpipe system that causes a great deal of concern among fire fighters. The occupants will often delay calling the fire department. Instead, they'll try to put out the fire themselves. Most fire fighters will tell you that the first few moments of a fire are critical. The first thing anyone should do is call the fire department—then do as much as you can.

Of course, if your building or company is organized to fight fire—and many industrial plants are—that casts a different light

Figure 13-2   Typical Standpipe Location

on the subject. In that case, chances are the local department would not be called unless they were really needed.

According to the U.B.C., every building six stories or more must have at least one Class I standpipe for use during construction. This standpipe must be in place before the building is more than 50 feet above grade. If the standpipe is not connected to a water main, there must be provisions for fire department inlet connections at accessible locations.

What Should Fire-safety Requirements Accomplish?
The primary goal of any fire control or fire-safety system is to save lives. Second to that is reducing property damage. That's why fire resistance is built into structures. Most structural materials and building components will either burn or melt. The objective is to suppress this condition long enough for the occupants to get out and to safety and to give additional time for fire crews and equipment to arrive.

That's why the building code covers construction and exits. All exits, as explained in Chapter Ten, must be designed to get people outdoors and to safety by the quickest and most direct route. Don't assume that the occupants know where all the exits are or that they know what to do in an emergency. You must make sure they get out easily and quickly.

Exit Size
According to Chapter 33 of the U.B.C., a required exit is 3'0" by 6'8". That figures out to be 20 square feet for a standard exit doorway as was indicated in Section 3802(b), mentioned above.

One thing that really concerns me is the "minimum dimension" of the opening. Section 3802(b) states that "Such openings shall have a minimum dimension of not less than 30 inches." However, going back to Section 1204 we find that:

All escape or rescue windows from sleeping rooms shall have a minimum net clear opening of 5.7 square feet. The minimum net clear opening height dimension shall be 24 inches. The minimum net clear opening width dimension shall be 20 inches.

Why the difference? My interpretation is that we're adding apples and oranges. The reference to "All egress or rescue windows from sleeping rooms . . ." means sleeping rooms in any kind of structure, *whether sprinklered or not*. The other reference, "Openings . . . of not less than 30 inches," pertains to *all* openings in *all* types of buildings *subject to the automatic sprinkler requirement*.

Will The Opening Be Large Enough?
When a fireman puts a ladder up to a window, the ladder must penetrate the window enough so that it cannot slip sideways. The average fire ladder is between 16 and 20 inches wide. Thus, it will fit easily into the 30-inch opening.

Let's say that the window is 44 inches above the floor, the maximum allowable distance. In the event of a fire, a healthy able-bodied person shouldn't have too much trouble getting up to the window and out to the ladder. But suppose we have four people in the room. One is the fire fighter with a bulky air pack on his back; one is a woman eight months pregnant; one is obese and in poor health; and one is an elderly man riddled with arthritis. Will they all be able to escape? It makes you stop and think, doesn't it? Perhaps it would be advisable to make the window a little larger and lower.

What Should Be Done?

Perhaps the safest building is one made from reinforced concrete, has no doors or windows, is completely sprinklered, has smoke detectors, has nothing stored in it, and has no occupants. That might be a safe building, but it sure wouldn't be very economical or practical. Therefore, we must consider economy, practicality, and fire safety.

City officials, primarily the fire marshal and the building official, must take a good look at their city and ask themselves some questions:

• Has the city experienced many fires over the years?

• How many lives have been lost in the last three years due to fire? What percentage is this of the total population of the city?

• Will more stringent rules reduce this figure?

• What will be the ratio of cost to benefits?

• Are most of the buildings in town relatively new? That is, have they been built in the last twenty years? If so, they may be fairly fire resistant.

Fire extinguishing systems are expensive. To be effective they must be installed properly. The big problem is that, unless you're constructing a residential building, you have little idea what the building will be used for a few years from now. The system installed today may by inadequate in ten years. If you have a borderline-size building (by code standards) with a low-hazard occupancy, should you install sprinklers now or wait until the occupancy needs of the building require it?

From an insurance standpoint, a good automatic sprinkler system will pay for itself in premium savings in five to ten years. In fact, you'll probably find the average time to amortize a good system is about seven years. Yet, it's understandable that many owners are hesitant to install a sprinkler system. If they're building on speculation the concern isn't over savings a few years from now but the money that must be spent today.

Still, the best fire suppression is not nearly as good as fire prevention. Good construction, clean working areas, reduced fire hazards and informed occupants are your best bet to control fire danger.

14

Skylights, Glass, and Miscellaneous Components

Every structure has hundreds of smaller miscellaneous components. The code covers many of these quite thoroughly. But it can't cover everything. Some items are specially designed for highly complex projects. And there are always new methods and materials, composite structures and job site conditions to consider. The inspector can't answer every question raised by referring to the code. If he's on his toes he'll take a flexible approach to interpreting the code where no specific guidance is given. This first item we'll discuss requires such an approach.

Theaters and Stages

Stages and platforms are covered in Chapter 39 of the U.B.C. Fly galleries and proscenium walls were covered in the section on occupancy groups and won't be repeated here. However, there are a few pertinent items that should be explored in more detail.

Proper ventilation is one of the first and most important considerations in designing a stage. Almost half of Chapter 39 of the U.B.C. is on ventilation. Lights and human activity on the stage generate a great deal of heat. Most stages have a lot of flammable material. The two together create a very volatile situation. For that reason most permanent items on a stage must be as fire resistive as possible.

The ventilators serve two purposes in a theater. The first is obviously ventilation—drawing off excess hot air. Modern air conditioning has greatly reduced the need for ventilation alone. The second purpose is fire venting. The code requires special vents to release heat and smoke in case of a fire. Skylights are used for this purpose. They must be readily opened, either by spring action, or force of gravity sufficient to overcome the effects of neglect, rust, dirt, frost, snow, or expansion and warping of the framework. They must be controlled by a fusible link so they open automatically in case of fire.

Section 3903 requires that dressing room sections, workshops, and storerooms be separated from each other and from the stage by a one-hour fire-resistive separation. Section 3907 requires one 36-inch exit from each side of the stage directly (or through an exit passageway) to a street or exit court.

Projection Rooms

Motion picture projection rooms are not covered in the same chapter as stages and platforms. Originally, theaters were for stage productions. When movies became popular, theaters were built primarily for movies but had facilities for stage productions as well. Gradually, as vaudeville began to ebb, the large stage areas became a costly addition that seldom was used. The stage began to disappear from movie theaters and many movie theaters or "cinemas" as they are more correctly called, have no stage at all. However, stages without movie facilities have become common again.

U.B.C. Chapter 40 covers projection rooms. Projection rooms have separate rules even if they are in a building with stages or platforms. The section on projection rooms applies to school projections rooms and drive-in theaters that do not have a stage.

Every projection room must have a sign with one-inch block letters stating: "Safety Film Only Permitted In This Room."

Motion picture projection rooms must have floor area of at least 80 square feet for one projection machine and 40 square feet for each additional machine. A 7'6" ceiling height is the minimum allowed. The ceiling must be of the same construction as required for the rest of the building. Exits must conform to Chapter 33 of the U.B.C., but don't have to be surfaced with fire-rated materials.

Openings in the wall between the projection room and the auditorium can't exceed 24% of the wall area. The openings must be framed with fire-rated materials.

In a drive-in theater, many inspectors will waive this 25% maximum. Also, ventilation isn't too important because most projection rooms are now air conditioned. But I would follow the code and require that each projection room have a lavatory and a water closet. Also, fire requirements for the snack bar and its connection with the projection room are important. Check to be sure the exits are adequate. Between shows these places get quite crowded.

Skylights

The title of this chapter included the word *skylight*. You probably know exactly what a skylight is. But skylights are covered under two different sections of the U.B.C. Chapter 34 gives the basic information about skylights and this is reinforced by Section 5207 in Chapter 52. Why two chapters? Chapter 34 covers glass skylights; Chapter 52 looks at the plastic skylights.

Pre-formed skylights are almost entirely plexi-glass or similar plastic. But how would you classify the corrugated plastic panels used in most modern metal buildings? Would you consider these translucent panels a form of skylight? The code looks at them that way and covers the subject under Section 5206.

In other than Types III, IV and V buildings, all skylight frames have to be built of noncombustible materials. Skylights must be designed to carry any roof load that is channeled to it. Skylights set at an angle of less than 45 degrees, must be mounted at least 4 inches above the plane of the roof on a curb constructed suitable for the frame. Figure 14-1 shows this very well. In fact, curbing is a good idea on any skylight because it provides a neater, more leak-resistant roof construction at that point. However, if your roof pitch is 3:12 or greater, a curbing is not required if a self-flashing skylight is used.

Glass or Plastic?

U.B.C. Chapter 34 covers glass skylights. Glass specifications in general are in Chapter 54 and windows are in Chapter 15. Chapter

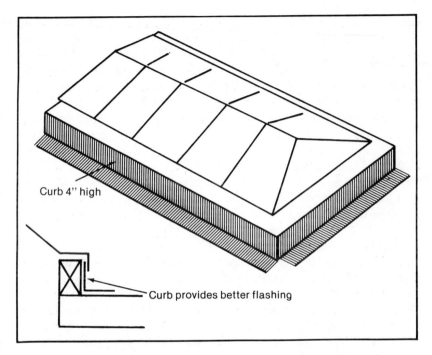

Figure 14-1 Construction of a Glass Skylight

34 covers only miscellaneous uses of glass. Any discussion of glass in skylights is probably wasted because I haven't seen anything but plastic used in skylights for a long time. But just on the off chance that glass isn't dead yet, and recent looks at large hotels with covered atriums indicate that glass may not be, let's proceed with the discussion.

The code says all glass in skylights must be wired glass, laminated glass, or tempered, with a minimum thickness of 7/32 inch. But watch the exception. Skylights over vertical shafts extending through two or more stories must have plain glass. But wired glass is allowed if the top of the shaft has a ventilation area of at least one-eighth the cross-section of the shaft. (The ventilated area can never be less than 4 square feet.)

If plain glass is used, you need a wire screen not smaller than 12-gauge with a mesh not larger than one inch supported above and below the skylight.

Greenhouses

Chapter 34 also governs the construction of greenhouses. Ordinary glass is permitted if the height of the greenhouse at the ridge is not over 20 feet above grade. That same 20 foot mark controls framework construction of the greenhouse also. If your greenhouse is less than 20 feet above grade, a wood framework is allowed. Otherwise metal frames and sash bars are required.

Sidewalk Light Ports

A long time ago it was common to place glass panels in sidewalks so that light was admitted to basements below. I haven't seen any glass sidewalk light ports lately. The ones I remember were tinted green, and were somewhat chipped. At night the light from underneath would make the glass sparkle like emeralds. However, the code still permits them, but only if they are in a metal frame and at least 1/2 inch thick. If the area of the glass goes over 16 square inches, it must be wire reinforced.

Floor lights or sidewalk lights must be able to carry the floor or sidewalk load unless protected by a railing at least 42 inches high. If you have this railing, the design load need be no more than the roof design load.

On private property, basements may be built under sidewalks. But building a basement under a public sidewalk usually requires a special permit. Basements are extended under public walks so sidewalk freight elevators can take deliveries directly to the basement. Usually you can't extend a basement under public property without getting the proper easement and zoning relaxation.

The Word "Plastic" May Be Misleading

Now, let's get back to the use of plastic. The word *plastic* is a broad term that covers many materials. Chapter 53 of the U.B.C. at one time covered only "plastic glazing material." The chapter now uses the term "light transmitting plastics." Rapid changes in plastics in the last several decades has kept the code-writing people on their toes. Many materials will form a "plastic" under some condition. Even concrete in its liquid state is referred to as being plastic. Webster's definition includes an interesting note, however. It says:

The form "plastics" is preferred by some technical authorities for use as the singular (as, there is no one plastics that will meet all these requirements) to distinguish it from plastic meaning any substance capable of being molded.

Chapter 52 of the U.B.C. also includes exterior wall panels, roof panels, skylights, light diffusing systems, diffusers in electrical systems, partitions, awnings, patio covers, greenhouses and canopies. Installation requirements for plastics are somewhat loose in the code. The main requirement is that it must have strength and durability to withstand design loads dictated in the code.

Fastenings, too, are left somewhat in limbo. They must be able to withstand design load and include space for expansion and contraction of the materials. Here the main requirement is that you satisfy the inspector of the quality of your material. If you are using one of the many standard brands on the market, this shouldn't be any problem. He's probably already familiar with them.

Plastic Glazing Material

In a Type V-N building, doors, sash and framed openings that don't have to be fire protected may be glazed or equipped with any approved plastic material. However, in the other more heavily regulated buildings, use of plastics is more regulated. For instance, the aggregate area of plastic glazing may not exceed 25% of any wall surface on a story. The area of a single pane of glazing material above the first story may not exceed 16 square feet. And the vertical dimension of a single pane may not exceed 4 feet. You can increase this area by 50% in a sprinklered building.

There is one unusual requirement in plastic glazing and that is the installation of an approved flame barrier extending 30 inches beyond the exterior wall in the plane of the floor, or vertical panel not less than 4 feet high shall be installed between the glazed units located in adjacent stories. This is to slow down the melting effect of any flames from below. Also, you can't go above 65 feet from grade with any plastic glazing.

Use of Public Property

Permanent use of public property is restricted in the building code as well as in your own local zoning ordinances. Permanent use, of course, is the construction of any structure that is going to stay

TABLE NO. 44-A—TYPE OF PROTECTION REQUIRED FOR PEDESTRIANS

HEIGHT OF CONSTRUCTION	DISTANCE FROM CONSTRUCTION	PROTECTION REQUIRED
8 feet or less	Less than 6 feet 6 feet or more	Railing None
More than 8 feet	Less than 6 feet	Fence and canopy
	6 feet or more but not more than one-fourth the height of construction	Fence and canopy
	6 feet or more, but between one-fourth to one-half the height of construction	Fence
	6 feet or more but exceeding one-half the construction height	None

From the Uniform Building Code, ©1982, ICBO.

Figure 14-2   Protection Required for Pedestrians

where it is built. Temporary use could be considered as the fences, barricades and shelters used during construction or demolition. These may require special permits from your jurisdiction but they are allowed by the code. Other temporary uses would be any structure erected for fairs, exhibitions, carnivals, and so forth.

Temporary construction used during erection or demolition of another building is usually for the protection of the public. Sidewalk area in front of a jobsite can be used if you provide a pedestrian walkway four feet wide. If you need to use the entire walkway, pedestrians can be detoured into the street. But a 4-foot walkway is required here also and you must provide a railing on the traffic side and a fence on the construction side. Lights are required during darkness. U.B.C. Table No. 44-A (Figure 14-2) shows the protection needed for pedestrians.

Be careful when mixing or handling mortar, concrete, or other material on public property. The code says this work can't deface public property or create a nuisance. All utility lines and their frames, standards, and catch basins must be protected so that you don't interfere with these devices. Incidentally, any opening in a fence or shield must be protected by doors that may be kept closed.

Install adequate signs and railings to direct pedestrians. Railings must be built of new 2 x 4's or larger lumber and be at least 42 inches high. Railings adjacent to excavations must have a mid-rail.

All fences must be solid, substantial and at least 8 feet high. They are to be built between the walkway and the site and must extend the full length of the site. Plywood fences must be made of exterior grade plywood. Plywood 1/4 to 5/16-inch-thick must have studding no more than 2 feet o.c. unless a horizontal stiffener is added at mid-height. Plywood thicker than 5/8 inch can span 8 feet.

Sidewalk canopies (to protect pedestrians from overhead work) must have a clear height of 8 feet, have a tightly sheathed roof of 2-inch nominal wood plankings, and must be lighted during hours of darkness.

Permanent Use of Public Property

The permanent use of public property is usually restricted to projections over the property line. Cornices, architectural projections, eave overhangs, exterior private balconies and similar projections extending beyond the floor area are governed by Section 1710 of the U.B.C. Projections in Type I or II buildings must be of noncombustible material. Projections in other buildings can be either noncombustible or combustible. However, combustible materials used where protected openings are required must be of one-hour fire-resistiveness or heavy timber.

Chapter 45, Section 4504 discusses some of those projections as follows:

Section 4504. Oriel windows, balconies, unroofed porches, cornices, belt courses and appendages such as water tables, sills, capitals, bases and architectural projections may project over the public property of the building site a distance as determined by the clearance of the lowest point of the projection above the grade immediately below, as follows:

    Clearance above grade less than 8 feet—no projection is permitted.

    Clearance above grade over 8 feet—1 inch of projection is permitted for each additional inch of clearance, provided that no such projections shall exceed a distance of 4 feet.

That almost sounds too easy, doesn't it? Near the end of section 1710 of the U.B.C. is this little-known item:

Projections shall not extend more than 12 inches into the areas where openings are prohibited.

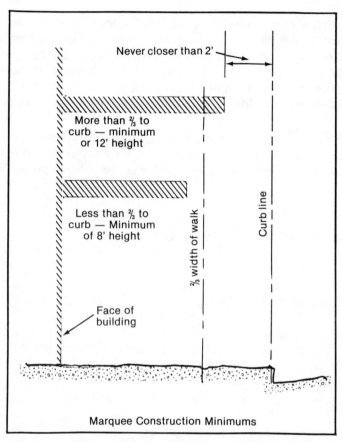

Figure 14-3 Marquee Construction Measurements. The primary reason for the two foot setback from the curb is to avoid problems that might occur from tall trucks parking at curbside.

This is one of those things that you may have forgotten about. What is a protected opening? Where are openings in walls prohibited? Chapter Four of this book will help you find out if the wall you're looking at will permit an opening. Consider carefully the street width. And check the local zoning ordinance. Even if the code lets you build that balcony, your local zoning ordinance may not.

Awnings and Marquees

Remember the old fashioned striped canvas awnings that used to grace main street? For many years they were in disrepute and not recognized by the U.B.C. because they were considered a fire hazard. Now they are back and honorable again. However, they can't encroach on public property further than 7 feet from the face of the building or within 2 feet of the face of the curb. The main awning has to be at least 8 feet high. The frames must be noncombustible but the covers do not need not be.

Marquees are a little different. They must be solid construction and attached to the building. They cannot be more than 3 feet thick when the marquee extends more than 2/3 the distance to the curb. If they are less than 2/3 of that distance they can go to 9 feet thick. As for the height above the walk, see Figure 14-3. This illustrates both the height above the walk and the distance to the curb.

Doors, either fully opened or when opening must not project more than 1 foot beyond the property line. In alleys no projection is allowed.

Grade

A number of times in the previous chapters we've rubbed our noses into the word *grade*. You should understand what grade means in the code. In recent years the U.B.C. has simplified the definition:

Grade (Adjacent Ground Elevation) is the lowest point of elevation of the finished surface of the ground, paving or sidewalk within the area between the building and the property line or, when the property line is more than 5 feet from the building, between the building and a line 5 feet from the building.

15

Finish Materials and Installation Procedures

U.B.C. Chapter 47 is entitled "Installation of Wall and Ceiling Coverings." It covers plaster, lath, softwood, plywood paneling, exposed aggregate plaster (stucco) and pneumatically placed cement plaster (gunite).

Before continuing, let me make an important distinction. A *vertical* assembly is any assembly of building materials rising vertically. This means walls. A *horizontal* assembly refers to any assembly of building materials laid and used in a flat or horizontal position. This means floors and ceilings.

Suspended Ceilings

Ceiling members are not always attached. Sometimes they're laid in place and held there by gravity. A suspended ceiling is a good example. The panels are laid in runners suspended from the structural framing above. These panels may be light diffusers where lighting is installed above the ceiling, or they may be solid panels.

Sometimes the space between the suspended ceiling and the structural framing above is used for an "extended plenum" or "plenum chamber" to circulate either heated or cooled air. In this case, air diffusers are placed at designed locations. The air is "dumped" under pressure into the space between the two ceilings and then forced out through the diffusers. The hangers must be saddle-tied around the main runner to develop their full strength. U.B.C. Table No. 47-A (Figure 15-1) gives specifications for suspended ceilings weighing less than 10 pounds per square foot.

Lath

The U.B.C. no longer covers wood lath. U.B.C. Table No. 47-B (Figure 15-2) lists types of lath; wood is not among them. This signals the end of an era.

The main difference between interior and exterior lath is the types of gypsum lath which may be used. Also, interior lath should not be installed until weather protection is completed. Apply gypsum lath with the long dimension perpendicular to the supports. Stagger end joints in successive courses. However, you can have end joints on one support if joint stripping is applied to the full length of the joint. If the lath joints don't touch or if the space between them is greater than 3/8 inch, the joint must be stripped.

If metal lath or wire fabric lath is used, it must be attached with at least 18-gauge wire ties spaced not more than 6 inches apart or with an approved fastener. Apply metal lath with the long dimension of the sheets perpendicular to the supports. Lap joints at least one mesh at the sides and ends, but not less than 1 inch. Metal rib lath with edge ribs greater than 1/8 inch are lapped by nesting the outside ribs. If the edge ribs are less than 1/8 inch, metal rib lath must be lapped 1/2 inch at the sides or the outside ribs may be nested. If laps aren't over supports, tie them with 18-gauge wire.

The type and weight of metal lath, the gauge and spacing of wire in welded or woven lath, the spacing of supports and the methods of attachment to wood supports are given in U.B.C. Tables Nos. 47-B (Figure 15-2) and 47-C (Figure 15-3).

A major difference between interior and exterior lathing is that a "weep screed" is required at or below the foundation line on all exterior stud walls. Place the screed at least 4 inches above grade. It allows water to drain to the exterior of the building.

Weather-Resistive Barriers

Section 4706(d) states that a weather-resistant barrier must be installed as required in Section 1707(a); below, but also includes,

TABLE NO. 47-A—SUSPENDED AND FURRED CEILINGS[1]
(For Support of Ceilings Weighing Not More than 10 Pounds per Square Foot)

	SIZE AND TYPE		MAXIMUM AREA SUPPORTED (In Square Feet)	SIZE
Minimum Sizes for Wire and Rigid Hangers				
Hangers for Suspended Ceilings			12.5	No. 9 gauge wire
			16	No. 8 gauge wire
			18	3/16" diameter, mild steel rod [2]
			20	7/32" diameter, mild steel rod [2]
			22.5	1/4" diameter, mild steel rod [2]
			25.0	1" x 3/16" mild steel flats [3]
	For Supporting Runners	Single Hangers Between Beams[4]	8	No. 12 gauge wire
			12	No. 10 gauge wire
			16	No. 8 gauge wire
		Double Wire Loops at Beams or Joists[3]	8	No. 14 gauge wire
			12	No. 12 gauge wire
			16	No. 11 gauge wire
Hangers for Attaching Runners and Furring Directly to Beams and Joists	For Supporting Furring without Runners[4] (Wire Loops at Supports)	Type of Support: Concrete	8	No. 14 gauge wire
		Steel		No. 16 gauge wire (2 loops)[5]
		Wood		No. 16 gauge wire (2 loops)[5]

[1]Metal suspension systems for acoustical tile and lay-in panel ceiling systems weighing not more than 4 pounds per square foot, including light fixtures and all ceiling-supported equipment and conforming to U.B.C. Standard No. 47-18, are exempt from Table No. 47-A.

For furred and suspended ceilings with metal lath construction, see U.B.C. Standard No. 47-4.

[2]All rod hangers shall be protected with a zinc or cadmium coating or with a rust-inhibitive paint.

[3]All flat hangers shall be protected with a zinc or cadmium coating or with a rust-inhibitive paint.

Figure 15-1   Suspended and Furred Ceilings

Minimum Sizes and Maximum Spans for Main Runners [6] [7]

SIZE AND TYPE	MAXIMUM SPACING OF HANGERS OR SUPPORTS (ALONG RUNNERS)	MAXIMUM SPACING OF RUNNERS (TRANSVERSE)
¾" – .3 pound per foot, cold- or hot-rolled channel	2'0"	3'0"
1½"– .475 pound per foot, cold-rolled channel	3'0"	4'0"
1½"– .475 pound per foot, cold-rolled channel	3'6"	3'6"
1½"– .475 pound per foot, cold-rolled channel	4'0"	3'0"
1½"–1.12 pounds per foot, hot-rolled channel	4'0"	5'0"
2" –1.28 pounds per foot, hot-rolled channel	5'0"	5'0"
2" – .59 pound per foot, cold-rolled channel	5'0"	3'6"
1½" x 1½" x 3/16" angle	5'0"	3'6"

Minimum Sizes and Maximum Spans for Cross Furring [6] [7]

SIZE AND TYPE OF CROSS FURRING	MAXIMUM SPACING OF RUNNERS OR SUPPORTS	MAXIMUM SPACING OF CROSS FURRING MEMBERS (TRANSVERSE)
¼" diameter pencil rods	2'0"	12"
⅜" diameter pencil rods	2'0"	19"
⅜" diameter pencil rods	2'6"	12"
¾"–.3 pound per foot, cold- or hot-rolled channel	3'0"	24"
	3'6"	16"
	4'0"	12"
1"–.410 pound per foot, hot-rolled channel	4'0"	24"
	4'6"	19"
	5'0"	12"

[4]Inserts, special clips or other devices of equal strength may be substituted for those specified.
[5]Two loops of No. 18 gauge wire may be substituted for each loop of No. 16 gauge wire for attaching steel furring to steel or wood joists.
[6]Spans are based on webs of channels being erected vertically.
[7]Other sections of hot- or cold-rolled members of equivalent strength may be substituted for those specified.

From the Uniform Building Code, ©1982, ICBO.

Figure 15-1 (continued) Suspended and Furred Ceilings

TABLE NO. 47-B¹—TYPES OF LATH—MAXIMUM SPACING OF SUPPORTS

TYPE OF LATH²	MINIMUM WEIGHT (Per Square Yard) GAUGE AND MESH SIZE	VERTICAL (In Inches)			HORIZONTAL (In Inches)	
		Wood	Metal — Solid Plaster Partitions	Metal — Other	Wood or Concrete	Metal
1. Expanded Metal Lath (Diamond Mesh)	2.5 3.4	16^3 16^3	16^3 16^3	12 16	12 16	12 16
2. Flat Rib Expanded Metal Lath	2.75 3.4	16 19	16 24	16 19	16 19	16 19
3. Stucco Mesh Expanded Metal Lath	1.8 and 3.6	16^4	—	—	—	—
4. ⅜" Rib Expanded Metal Lath	3.4 4.0	24 24	24^5 24^5	24 24	24 24	24 24
5. Sheet Lath	4.5	24	5	24	24	24
6. Wire Fabric Lath — Welded	1.95 pounds, No. 11 gauge, 2" x 2" 1.16 pounds, No. 16 gauge, 2" x 2" 1.4 pounds, No. 18 gauge, 1" x 1"⁶	24 16 16^4	24 16 —	24 16 —	24 16 —	24 16 —
6. Wire Fabric Lath — Woven⁴	1.1 pounds, No. 18 gauge, 1½" Hexagonal⁶ 1.4 pounds, No. 17 gauge, 1½" Hexagonal⁶ 1.4 pounds, No. 18 gauge, 1" Hexagonal⁶	24 24 24	16 16 16	16 16 16	16 24 24	24 16 16

Figure 15-2   Maximum Spacing of Supports for Lath

7. ⅜" Gypsum Lath (perforated)	16	—	16[7]	16	16
8. ⅜" Gypsum Lath (plain)	16	—	16[7]	16	16
9. ½" Gypsum Lath (perforated)	16	—	16[7]	16	16
10. ½" Gypsum Lath (plain)	24	—	24	24	24

[1]For fire-resistive construction, see Tables No. 43-A, No. 43-B and No. 43-C. For shear-resisting elements, see Table No. 47-I. Metal lath, wire lath, wire fabric lath and metal accessories shall conform with the provisions of U.B.C. Standard No. 47-4. Gypsum lath shall conform with the provisions of U.B.C. Standard No. 47-8.

[2]Metal lath and wire fabric lath used as reinforcement for portland cement plaster shall be furred out away from vertical supports at least ¼ inch. Self-furring lath meets furring requirements. Exception: Furring of expanded metal lath is not required on supports having a bearing surface width of 1⅝ inches or less.

[3]Span may be increased to 24 inches with self-furred metal lath over solid sheathing assemblies approved for this use.

[4]Wire backing required on open vertical frame construction except under expanded metal lath and paperbacked wire fabric lath.

[5]May be used for studless solid partitions.

[6]Woven wire or welded wire fabric lath, not to be used as base for gypsum plaster without absorbent paperbacking or slot-perforated separator.

[7]Span may be increased to 24 inches on vertical screw or approved nailable assemblies.

From the Uniform Building Code, ©1982, ICBO.

Figure 15-2 (continued) Maximum Spacing of Supports for Lath

TABLE NO. 47-C—TYPES OF LATH-ATTACHMENT TO WOOD AND METAL[1] SUPPORTS

TYPE OF LATH	NAILS[2,3] Type and Size	MAXIMUM SPACING[5] Vertical (In Inches)	MAXIMUM SPACING[5] Horizontal (In Inches)	SCREWS[3,6] MAX. SPACING[5] Vertical (In Inches)	SCREWS[3,6] MAX. SPACING[5] Horizontal (In Inches)	STAPLES[3,4] Round or Flattened Wire: Wire Gauge No.	STAPLES Crown (In Inches)	STAPLES Leg[7] (In Inches)	STAPLES MAX. SPACING[5,6] Vertical (In Inches)	STAPLES MAX. SPACING[5,6] Horizontal (In Inches)
1. Diamond Mesh Expanded Metal Lath and Flat Rib Metal Lath	4d blued smooth box 1½ No. 14 gauge $\frac{7}{32}$" head (clinched)[7] 1" No. 11 gauge $\frac{7}{16}$" head, barbed 1½" No. 11 gauge $\frac{7}{16}$" head, barbed	6 6 6	— — 6	6	6	16	¾	⅞	6	6
2. ⅜" Rib Metal Lath and Sheet Lath	1½" No. 11 ga. $\frac{7}{16}$" head, barbed	6	6	6	6	16	¾	1¼	At Ribs	At Ribs
3. ¾" Rib Metal Lath	4d common 1½" No. 12½ gauge ¼" head 2" No. 11 gauge $\frac{7}{16}$" head, barbed	At Ribs	— At Ribs	At Ribs	At Ribs	16	¾	1⅝	At Ribs	At Ribs

[1]Metal lath, wire lath, wire fabric lath and metal accessories shall conform with the provisions of U.B.C. Standard No. 47-4.

[2]For nailable nonload-bearing metal supports, use annular threaded nails or approved staples.

[3]For fire-resistive construction, see Tables No. 43-B and No. 43-C. For shear-resisting elements, see Table No. 47-I. Approved wire and sheet metal attachment clips may be used.

[4]With chisel or divergent points.

Figure 15-3 Attachment to Wood and Metal Supports

4. Wire Fabric Lath[9]	4d blued smooth box (clinched)[8] 1" No. 11 gauge $\frac{7}{16}$" head, barbed	6 6	– –	6	6	16	¾	⅞	6	6
	1½" No. 11 gauge 7/16" head, barbed 1¼" No. 12 gauge ⅜" head, furring 1" No. 12 gauge ⅜" head	6 6 6	6 6			16	7/16 [9]	⅞	6	6
5. ⅜"Gypsum Lath	1⅛" No. 13 gauge $\frac{19}{64}$" head, blued	8[10]	8[10]	8[10]	8[10]	16	¾	⅞	8[10]	8[10]
6. ½"Gypsum Lath	1¼" No. 13 gauge 19/64" head, blued	8	8[10] 6[11]	8[10]	8[10] 6[11]	16	¾	1⅛	8[10]	8[10] 6[11]

[5]Maximum spacing of attachments from longitudinal edges shall not exceed 2 inches.

[6]Screws shall be an approved type long enough to penetrate into wood framing not less than ⅝ inch and through metal supports adaptable for screw attachment not less than ¼ inch.

[7]When lath and stripping are stapled simultaneously, increase leg length of staple ⅛ inch.

[8]For interiors only.

[9]Attach self-furring wire fabric lath to supports at furring device.

[10]Three attachments per 16-inch-wide lath per bearing. Four attachments per 24-inch-wide lath per bearing.

[11]Supports spaced 24 inches o.c. Four attachments per 16-inch-wide lath per bearing. Five attachments per 24-inch-wide lath per bearing.

From the Uniform Building Code, ©1982, ICBO.

Figure 15-3 (continued) Attachment to Wood and Metal Supports

"the added requirement that, when applied over wood base sheathing, shall include two layers of Grade D paper."

Section 1707 (a) Weather-Resistive Barriers. All weather-exposed surfaces shall have a weather-resistive barrier to protect the interior wall covering. Such barrier shall be equal to that provided for in U.B.C. Standard No. 17-1 for kraft water-proof building paper or U.B.C. Standard No. 32-1 for asphalt-saturated rag felt. Building paper and felt shall be free from holes and breaks other than those created by fasteners and construction system due to attaching of the building paper, and shall be applied over studs or sheathing of all exterior walls. Such felt or paper shall be applied weatherboard fashion, lapped not less than 2 inches at horizontal joints and not less than 6 inches at vertical joints.

Weather-protective barriers may be omitted in the following cases:

1. When exterior covering is of approved weatherproof panels.

2. In back-plastered construction.

3. When there is no human occupancy.

4. Over water-repellent panel sheathing.

5. Under approved paperbacked metal or wire fabric lath.

6. Behind lath and portland cement plaster applied to the underside of roof and eave projections.

Plaster

Basically, two types of plaster are used in construction today. *Portland cement plaster* is used for both outdoor or indoor work. *Gypsum plaster* is used only on interior work. Both require three coats when applied over metal lath or wire fabric lath. You must apply at least two coats over any other material allowed by the code. However, you can never apply plaster directly to fiber insulation board. Plaster thickness is measured from the face of the lath and other bases.

Three tables tell the story of plaster. U.B.C. Table No. 47-D (Figure 15-4) gives the minimum thickness of both kinds of plaster over plaster bases. Table 47-E (Figure 15-5) shows the proportions of aggregate to cementitious materials in the creation of gypsum plaster. Table 47-F (Figure 15-6) does the same thing for portland cement plaster and portland cement-lime plaster.

Curing times for portland cement or cement-lime plaster are shown in U.B.C. Table No. 47-F. These times can be modified under certain conditions. Concrete or masonry surfaces must be clean and free from efflorescence, sufficiently damp, and rough to ensure proper bonding. If the surface isn't rough, apply bonding agents or a portland cement dash bond coat. Mix the dash bond coat in the proportions of 1½ cubic feet of sand to 1 cubic foot of portland cement.

TABLE NO 47-D—THICKNESS OF PLASTER[1]

PLASTER BASE	FINISHED THICKNESS OF PLASTER FROM FACE OF LATH, MASONRY, CONCRETE	
	Gypsum Plaster	Portland Cement Plaster
1. Expanded Metal Lath	5/8 " minimum[2]	5/8 " minimum[2]
2. Wire Fabric Lath	5/8 " minimum[2]	3/4 " minimum (interior)[3] 7/8 " minimum (exterior)[3]
3. Gypsum Lath	1/2 " minimum	
4. Masonry Walls[4]	1/2 " minimum	1/2 " minimum
5. Monolithic Concrete Walls[4,5]	5/8 " maximum	7/8 " maximum
6. Monolithic Concrete Ceilings[4,5]	3/8 " maximum[6,7,8]	1/2 " maximum[7,8]

[1]For fire-resistive construction, see Tables No. 43-A, No. 43-B and No. 43-C.

[2]When measured from back plane of expanded metal lath, exclusive of ribs, or self-furring lath, plaster thickness shall be 3/4-inch minimum.

[3]When measured from face of support or backing.

[4]Because masonry and concrete surfaces may vary in plane, thickness of plaster need not be uniform.

[5]When applied over a liquid bonding agent, finish coat may be applied directly to concrete surface.

[6]Approved acoustical plaster may be applied directly to concrete, or over base coat plaster, beyond the maximum plaster thickness shown.

[7]On concrete ceilings, where the base coat plaster thickness exceeds the maximum thickness shown, metal lath or wire fabric lath shall be attached to the concrete.

[8]An approved skim-coat plaster 1/16 inch thick may be applied directly to concrete.

From the Uniform Building Code, ©1982, ICBO.

Figure 15-4 Thickness of Plaster

TABLE NO. 47-E—GYPSUM PLASTER PROPORTIONS[1]

NUMBER	COAT	PLASTER BASE OR LATH	MAXIMUM VOLUME AGGREGATE PER 100 POUNDS NEAT PLASTER[2,3] (Cubic Feet)	
			Damp Loose Sand[4]	Perlite or Vermiculite[4]
1. Two-coat Work	Base Coat	Gypsum Lath	2½	2
	Base Coat	Masonry	3	3
2. Three-coat Work	First Coat	Lath	2[5]	2
	Second Coat	Lath	3[5]	2[6]
	First and Second Coats	Masonry	3	3

[1]Wood-fibered gypsum plaster may be mixed in the proportions of 100 pounds of gypsum to not more than 1 cubic foot of sand where applied on masonry or concrete.

Gypsum plasters shall conform with the provisions of U.B.C. Standard No. 47-9.

[2]For fire-resistive construction, see Tables No. 43-A, No. 43-B and No. 43-C.

[3]When determining the amount of aggregate in set plaster, a tolerance of 10 percent shall be allowed.

[4]Combinations of sand and lightweight aggregate may be used, provided the volume and weight relationship of the combined aggregate to gypsum plaster is maintained. Sand and lightweight aggregate shall conform with U.B.C. Standard No. 47-3.

[5]If used for both first and second coats, the volume of aggregate may be 2½ cubic feet.

[6]Where plaster is 1 inch or more in total thickness, the proportions for the second coat may be increased to 3 cubic feet.

Figure 15-5   Gypsum Plaster Proportions

TABLE NO. 47-F—PORTLAND CEMENT PLASTERS[1]

PORTLAND CEMENT PLASTER

COAT	VOLUME CEMENT	MAXIMUM WEIGHT (OR VOLUME) LIME PER VOLUME CEMENT[2]	MAXIMUM VOLUME SAND PER VOLUME CEMENT[3]	APPROXIMATE MINIMUM THICKNESS[4]	MINIMUM PERIOD MOIST CURING	MINIMUM INTERVAL BETWEEN COATS
First	1	20 lbs.	4	3/8"[5]	48[6] Hours	48[7] Hours
Second	1	20 lbs.	5	1st and 2nd Coats total 3/4"	48 hours	7 Days[8]
Finish	1	1[9]	3	1st, 2nd and Finish Coats 7/8"	—	8

PORTLAND CEMENT-LIME PLASTER[10]

COAT	VOLUME CEMENT[11]	MAXIMUM VOLUME LIME PER VOLUME CEMENT	MAXIMUM VOLUME SAND PER COMBINED VOLUMES CEMENT AND LIME	APPROXIMATE MINIMUM THICKNESS[4]	MINIMUM PERIOD MOIST CURING	MINIMUM INTERVAL BETWEEN COATS
First	1	1	4	3/8"[5]	48[6] Hours	48[7] Hours
Second	1	1	4½	1st and 2nd Coats total 3/4"	48 hours	7 Days[8]
Finish	1	1[9]	3	1st, 2nd and Finish Coats 7/8"	—	8

[1]Exposed aggregate plaster shall be applied in accordance with Section 4709. Minimum overall thickness shall be 3/4 inch.

[2]Up to 20 pounds of dry hydrated lime (or an equivalent amount of lime putty) may be used as a plasticizing agent in proportion to each sack (cubic foot) of Type I and Type II standard portland cement in first and second coats of plaster. See Section 4708 (a) for use of plastic cement.

[3]When determining the amount of sand in set plaster, a tolerance of 10 percent may be allowed.

[4]See Table No. 47-D.

[5]Measured from face of support of backing to crest of scored plaster.

[6]See Section 4707 (c) 2.

[7]Twenty-four hours minimum interval between coats of interior portland cement plaster. For alternate method of application, see Section 4708 (e).

[8]Finish coat plaster may be applied to interior portland cement base coats after a 48-hour period.

[9]For finish coat plaster, up to an equal part of dry hydrated lime by weight (or an equivalent volume of lime putty) may be added to Types I, II and III standard portland cement.

[10]No additions of plasticizing agents shall be made.

[11]Type I, II or III standard portland cement. See Section 4708 (a) for use of plastic cement.

From the Uniform Building Code, ©1982, ICBO.

Figure 15-6 Portland Cement Plasters

Exposed Aggregate Plaster
Section 4709 covers this subject:

> *(a) General.* Exposed natural or integrally colored aggregate may be partially embedded in a natural or colored bedding coat of portland cement or gypsum plaster, subject to the provisions of this section.
>
> *(b) Aggregate.* The aggregate may be applied manually or mechanically and shall consist of marble chips, pebbles, or similar durable, nonreactive materials, moderately hard (three or more on the MOH scale.)

You probably know this material as *stucco.* It's used in almost the same way as standard exterior plaster except that the aggregate is added to a "bedding" coat. For exterior work, this bedding coat consists of one part portland cement, one part Type S lime and a maximum three parts of graded white or natural sand by volume. It must have a minimum compressive strength of 1000 pounds per square inch. The composition of the interior bedding coat is 100 pounds of neat gypsum plaster and a maximum 200 pounds of graded white sand.

Pneumatically Placed Plaster
Section 4710 describes pneumatically placed plaster, which we know as *gunite:*

> Pneumatically placed portland cement plaster shall be a mixture of portland cement and sand, mixed dry, conveyed by air through a pipe or flexible tube, hydrated at the nozzle at the end of the conveyor and deposited by air pressure in its final position.

By "hydrated at the nozzle," all they mean is that water is added to the dry gunite mixture at the point where it leaves the tube.

At least two coats of gunite must be applied. Together, these coats must be at least 7/8 inch thick. Curing time between coats is specified in U.B.C. Table No. 47-F (Figure 15-6).

There's one refinement that doesn't apply to other types of plaster. The rebound material may be screened and reused as sand. But it may not exceed 25% of the total sand used in any batch.

Gypsum Wallboard
I've seen sheetrock put up almost every way possible. Some installers would probably sew it on if they could.

Fastening sheetrock seems to be the biggest problem. I think that one of the reasons is that most installers are paid by the unit rather than by the hour. If they take shortcuts or omit a few nails here and there, they can put up more material and make more money.

It's for reasons such as this that the code regulates sheetrock. It must be inspected, as outlined in Section 305:

4. Lath and/or Gypsum Board Inspection: To be made after all lathing and gypsum board, interior and exterior, is in place but before any plastering is applied or before gypsum board joints and fasteners are taped and finished.

Fastening Sheetrock

There are three methods commonly used for laying up sheetrock. The most common is nailing, second is attaching with screws, and third is using adhesives. About the only difference between using nails and using screws is that nails have 7- or 8-inch spacing while screws have 12-inch spacing. Usually screws are used in commercial areas for Type I construction with steel studding. For this type of construction, the sheetrock is usually thicker to get the required fire-resistiveness.

There are two other methods of laying up sheetrock to get fire-resistiveness: single-ply and two-ply application. Specifications are given in U.B.C. Table No. 47-G (Figure 15-7) for single-ply and Table 47-H (Figure 15-8) for two-ply application.

The Gypsum Institute, which wrote most of the section on sheetrock application, lists twelve steps to properly apply sheetrock. Although this pertains mostly to nailing, many of the same rules also apply to screws.

Nailing: The footnotes on U.B.C. Table No. 47-G mention two methods of nailing. The first is outlined in the table itself where it indicates that spacing of single nails will be generally 7 inches both on the edge or in the field. Footnote 3 mentions the "double-nailing" pattern:

Two nails spaced 2 inches to 2½ inches apart may be used where the pairs are spaced 12 inches on center except around the perimeter of the sheets.

TABLE NO. 47-G—APPLICATION OF SINGLE-PLY GYPSUM WALLBOARD

THICKNESS OF GYPSUM WALLBOARD (Inch)	PLANE OF FRAMING SURFACE	LONG DIMENSION OF GYPSUM WALLBOARD SHEETS IN RELATION TO DIRECTION OF FRAMING MEMBERS	MAXIMUM SPACING OF FRAMING MEMBERS[1] (Center to Center) (In Inches)	MAXIMUM SPACING OF FASTENERS[1] (Center to Center) (In Inches)		NAILS[2]—TO WOOD
				Nails[3]	Screws[4]	
½	Horizontal	Either Direction	16	7	12	No. 13 gauge, 1⅜″ long, 19/64″ head; 0.98″ diameter; 1¼″ long, Annular ringed; 5d, cooler nail (0.86″ dia., 1⅝″ long, 15/64″ head)
	Horizontal	Perpendicular	24	7	12	
	Vertical	Either Direction	24	8	12	
⅝	Horizontal	Either Direction	16	7	12	No. 13 gauge, 1⅜″ long, 19/64″ head; 0.98″ diameter; 1¼″ long, Annular ringed; 5d, cooler nail (0.86″ dia., 1⅝″ long, 15/64″ head)
	Horizontal	Perpendicular	24	7	12	
	Vertical	Either Direction	24	8	12	

Nail or Screw Fastenings With Adhesives (Maximum Center to Center in Inches)

(Column headings as above)				End	Edges	Field	
½ or ⅝	Horizontal	Either Direction	16	16	16	24	As required for ½″ and ⅝″ gypsum wallboard, see above
	Horizontal	Perpendicular	24	16	24	24	
	Vertical	Either Direction	24	16	24	[5]	

[1]For fire-resistive construction, see Tables No. 43-B and No. 43-C. For shear-resisting elements, see Table No. 47-I.

[2]Where the metal framing has a clinching design formed to receive the nails by two edges of metal, the nails shall be not less than ⅝ inch longer than the wallboard thickness, and shall have ringed shanks. Where the metal framing has a nailing groove formed to receive the nails, the nails shall have barbed shanks or be 5d, No. 13½ gauge, 1⅝ inch long, 15/64-inch head for ½-inch gypsum wallboard; 6d, No. 13 gauge, 1⅞ inch long, 15/64-inch head for ⅝-inch gypsum wallboard.

[3]Two nails spaced 2 inches to 2½ inches apart may be used where the pairs are spaced 12 inches on center except around the perimeter of the sheets.

[4]Screws shall conform with U.B.C. Standard No. 47-5 and be long enough to penetrate into wood framing not less than ⅝ inch and through metal framing not less than ¼ inch.

[5]Not required.

From the Uniform Building Code, ©1982, ICBO.

Figure 15-7 Application of Single-Ply Gypsum Wallboard

TABLE NO. 47-H—APPLICATION OF TWO-PLY GYPSUM WALLBOARD[1]

FASTENERS ONLY

THICKNESS OF GYPSUM WALLBOARD (Each Ply) (inch)	PLANE OF FRAMING SURFACE	LONG DIMENSION OF GYPSUM WALLBOARD SHEETS	MAXIMUM SPACING OF FRAMING MEMBERS (Center to Center) (In Inches)	MAXIMUM SPACING OF FASTENERS (Center to Center) (In Inches)				
				Base Ply			Face Ply	
				Nails[2]	Screws[3]	Staples[4]	Nails[2]	Screws[3]
3/8	Horizontal	Perpendicular only	16	16	24	16	7	12
	Vertical	Either Direction	16				8	
1/2	Horizontal	Perpendicular only	24				7	
	Vertical	Either Direction	24				8	
5/8	Horizontal	Perpendicular only	24				7	
	Vertical	Either Direction	24				8	

Fasteners and Adhesives

3/8 Base Ply	Horizontal	Perpendicular only	16	7	12	5	Temporary Nailing or Shoring to Comply with Section 4711 (d)	
	Vertical	Either Direction	24	8		7		
1/2 Base Ply	Horizontal	Perpendicular only	24	7		5		
	Vertical	Either Direction	24	8		7		
5/8 Base Ply	Horizontal	Perpendicular only	24	7		5		
	Vertical	Either Direction	24	8		7		

[1]For fire-resistive construction, see Tables No. 43-B and No. 43-C. For shear-resisting elements, see Table No. 47-I.

[2]Nails for wood framing shall be long enough to penetrate into wood members not less than ½ inch and the sizes shall conform with the provisions of Table No. 47-G. For nails not included in Table No. 47-G, use the appropriate size cooler nail as set forth in Table No. 25-17-I of U.B.C. Standard No. 25-17. Nails for metal framing shall conform with the provisions of Table No. 47-G.

[3]Screws shall conform with the provisions of Table No. 47-G.

[4]Staples shall be not less than No. 16 gauge by ⅞-inch crown width with leg length of ⅞ inch, 1⅛ inches and 1⅜ inches for gypsum wallboard thicknesses of ⅜ inch, ½ inch and ⅝ inch, respectively.

From the Uniform Building Code, ©1982, ICBO.

Figure 15-8 Application of Two-Ply Gypsum Wallboard

I mentioned the nailing requirements set forth by the Gypsum Institute. These are found in their handbook. Although these requirements are not directly in the code, many are presented in various forms. It's good advice to follow. This is what the Institute says about nailing:

1. Drive nails at least 3/8 inch from ends and edges of sheetrock.

2. Position nails on adjacent ends or edges opposite each other.

3. Begin nailing from *center* of wallboard and proceed toward edges or outer ends.

4. When nailing, apply pressure on wallboard adjacent to nail being driven to ensure that wallboard is secured tightly on framing member.

5. Drive nails with shank perpendicular to face of board.

6. Use crown-head hammer.

7. With the last blow of the hammer, seat nail so head is in a slight uniform dimple formed by the last blow of the hammer.

8. Do not break paper at nail head or around circumference of dimple by over-driving it. A nail set should not be used. Maximum depth of dimple should not exceed 1/32 inch.

9. If face paper is fractured, an additional nail or fastener must be set not more than 2 inches from fracture.

10. Above nailing schedule must be used whether or not adhesives are used.

11. Screws may be used provided they are approved sizes. Spacing may be altered if screws are used. Check with Building Official.

12. Gypsum wallboard may be applied parallel or perpendicular to studs.

Screws: Both U.B.C. Tables Nos. 47-G and 47-H give the proper spacing when using screws as fasteners for sheetrock. Footnote 4 in Table No. 47-G mentions that screws "shall conform with U.B.C. Standard 47-5 and be long enough to penetrate into wood framing not less than 5/8 inch and through metal framing not less than 1/4 inch." There aren't too many surprises in U.B.C. Standards about the screws. Here are some of the main requirements:

• The head of the screw must be at least .315 inch in diameter.

• The driving recess must be a No. 2 "Phillips" design with a minimum depth of .105 inch.

• Screws must be self drilling and drive into the stud in less than five seconds.

• Screw threads must be capable of pulling the head of the screw below the surface of the wallboard through four layers of .010-inch-thick kraft paper over 5/8-inch Type X gypsum wallboard.

Adhesives: As a building inspector I made a few people unhappy by not allowing the use of adhesives on sheetrock unless a full-time inspector was there to check each step of the job. To do a good job, you must apply the adhesive according to the manufacturer's recommendations. According to the code, that means you must put down a bead of adhesive that when spread will be at least 1 inch wide and 1/16 inch thick. This calls for a continuous bead at least 1/4 inch to 3/8 inch for all studs and cross members.

I found that some installers were only putting down spots or thin beads of adhesive, especially when the tube was about to run out (after all, adhesives cost money). Once the rock was in place, there was no easy way of telling how wide, thick or continuous the adhesive was. That's why I wanted constant supervision.

It really wasn't a very big deal. The installers found they didn't save a lot of time, anyway. For practical reasons they had to apply the adhesive on the reverse side of the panel. That meant marking the panel for the stud locations. Then the panel had to be held in place while the adhesive dried. Back then the code didn't require nailing. But as you can see in U.B.C. Table No. 47-G, the code now requires a certain amount of nailing on single-ply applications.

Two-ply installation: Two-ply is usually used where extra thickness is required for fire-resistiveness. Sheetrock is heavy. It's much easier to lay up two pieces of 3/8-inch sheetrock than one piece 3/4 inch thick. And, if you need 1 or 1½ inches of sheetrock thickness, it's even easier to see the advantage.

A second advantage is that you get a smoother wall. The first layer is laid up like a single layer. The second layer is applied over the first, using adhesives without nailing. You'll have to hold this layer in place until the adhesive sets up, but that usually doesn't take long. The amount of taping is reduced, and the overall effect and finish are neater. To get the required fire-resistiveness, the second layer must be applied perpendicular to the base layer.

How is Sheetrock Fire Resistive?

At first it's difficult to understand how a white powder encased in two layers of paper could be fire resistive. It's all due to a chemical reaction. As fire burns through the paper and reaches the gypsum, the heat causes a thin layer of water vapor to form over the surface. This repels the fire and cools the surface. But the effect doesn't last long. That's the reason for the additional thickness: to get longer fire-resistiveness. The water vapor will evaporate in time, but it does slow down the fire.

Glass and Glazing

You and I might call it glass and glazing, but architects and engineers call it *fenestration.* The word is derived from the Latin *fenestra*, which means window. Along with it comes *fenestrate,* to furnish with windows.

Chapter 54 of the U.B.C. covers windows. Glass and glazing entered the code as a separate item in 1967. Since then there have been a few changes. The chapter defines the limitations of glass by area and type. This is shown in U.B.C. Table No. 54-A (Figure 15-9), which defines the allowable area of glass in relation to the thickness of the glass and the wind load. (Use U.B.C. Table No. 23-G (Figure 7-4, Chapter 7) to determine wind load. Pay particular attention to the height above grade in determining this load.)

U.B.C. Table No. 54-B (Figure 15-10) contains adjustment factors for the wind load. Be sure to read the footnotes. They explain how to apply this factor to your particular situation.

Glass firmly supported on all four edges must be glazed with minimum laps and edge clearances given in U.B.C. Table No. 54-C (Figure 15-11). The design for glass not firmly supported on all four edges must be approved by the inspector. Glass supports are considered firm when support deflections at design load do not exceed 1/175 of the span. Determining deflection in the field may be difficult. Here's what I suggest. Lean on the support. If you feel any give, the support won't pass inspection.

Human Impact

Section 5406 is one of the most important sections in Chapter 54. It covers the type of glazing to be used for areas subject to "human impact." This means the glazing next to glass doors, the glass doors themselves, and glazing near any walking surfaces, sliding glass doors, shower doors, tub enclosures and storm doors.

TABLE NO. 54-A—MAXIMUM ALLOWABLE AREA OF GLASS[1]
(In Square Feet)

WIND LOAD (In Pounds per Square Foot)	PLATE OR FLOAT GLASS THICKNESS (In Inches)													SHEET GLASS THICKNESS (In Inches)								
	1/8	3/16	7/32	1/4	5/16	3/8	7/16	1/2	5/8	3/4	7/8	1	1 1/4	SS	DS	3/16	1/4	5/16	3/8	1/2	5/8	3/4
10	41	72	81	89	107	144	185	275	351	465	525	656	956	41	56	95	109	128	186	213	243	311
15	27	48	54	60	71	96	123	183	234	310	350	438	637	27	38	63	73	86	124	142	162	207
20	21	36	40	45	53	72	92	137	176	232	262	328	478	20	28	47	55	64	93	107	122	155
25	16	29	32	36	43	58	74	110	140	186	210	262	382	16	23	38	44	51	74	85	97	124
30	14	24	27	30	36	48	62	92	117	155	175	219	319	14	19	32	36	43	62	71	81	104
35	12	21	23	26	31	41	53	79	100	133	150	188	273	12	16	27	31	37	53	61	69	89
40	10	18	20	22	27	36	46	69	88	116	131	164	239	10	14	24	27	32	46	53	61	78
45	9	16	18	20	24	32	41	61	78	103	117	146	212	9	13	21	24	29	41	47	54	69
50	8	14	16	18	21	29	37	55	70	93	105	131	191	8	11	19	22	26	37	43	49	62
60	7	12	13	15	18	24	31	46	59	77	88	109	159	7	9	16	18	21	31	36	41	52
70	6	10	12	13	15	21	26	39	50	66	75	94	137	6	8	14	16	18	27	30	35	44
80	5	9	10	11	13	18	23	34	44	58	66	82	120	5	7	12	14	16	23	27	30	39
90	4.5	8	9	10	12	16	21	31	39	52	58	73	106	4.5	6	11	12	14	21	24	27	35
100	4	7	8	9	11	14	18	27	35	46	52	66	96	4	5.5	9	11	13	19	21	24	31

[1]Maximum areas apply for rectangular lights of plate, float or sheet glass firmly supported on all four sides in a vertical position. Glass mounted at a slope not to exceed one horizontal to five verticals may be considered vertical. Maximum areas based on minimum thicknesses set forth in Table No. 54-1-C, Uniform Building Code Standard No. 54-1.

From the Uniform Building Code, © 1982, ICBO.

Figure 15-9   Maximum Allowable Area of Glass

**TABLE NO. 54-B—ADJUSTMENT FACTORS—RELATIVE
RESISTANCE TO WIND LOAD[1]**

GLASS TYPE	APPROXIMATE RELATIONSHIP
1. Laminated	0.6
2. Wired	0.5
3. Heat-strengthened	2.0
4. Fully tempered	4.0
5. Factory-fabricated Double Glazing[2]	1.5
6. Rough Rolled Plate	1.0
7. Sandblasted	Varies[3]
8. Regular Plate, Float or Sheet	1.0

[1]To determine the maximum allowable area for glass types listed in Table No. 54-B multiply the allowable area established in Table No. 54-A by the appropriate adjustment factor. Example: For ¼-inch heat-strengthened glass determine the maximum allowable area for a 30-pound-per-square-foot wind load requirement. Solution procedure: Use Table No. 54-A to determine the established allowable area for ¼-inch plate or float glass. Answer: 36 square feet, then multiply 36 by 2—the heat-strengthened glass adjustment factor. Answer: 72.

[2]Use thickness of the thinner of the two lights, not thickness of the unit.

[3]To be approved by the building official since adjustment factor varies with amount of depreciation and type of glass.

From the Uniform Building Code, ©1982, ICBO.

Figure 15-10   Relative Resistance to Wind Load

The code also lists certain exceptions. Instead of listing areas where protection from human impact is essential, the code excludes areas where there's little danger of human impact:

Exceptions: 1. Openings in doors through which a 3-inch sphere is unable to pass.
2. Assemblies of leaded glass or faceted glass and items of carved glass when used for decorative purposes indoors or in locations described in Section 5406(d), Item No. 6 or 7.
3. Glazing materials used as curved glazed panels in revolving doors.
4. Commercial refrigerated cabinet glazed doors.

Glass for bathtub and shower enclosures must be laminated safety glass or approved plastic. How do you know if a piece of glass has been tempered? The manufacturer's brand name must be on the corner of each piece. On other than single- or double-strength glass, look for that brand name if you're thinking about cutting any glass. It might save you the embarrassment and cost of shattering a perfectly good piece of tempered glass, because those are purchased in design sizes only.

TABLE NO. 54-C—MINIMUM GLAZING REQUIREMENTS

Fixed Windows and Openable Windows Other Than Horizontal Sliding					
GLASS AREA	UP TO 6 SQ. FT.	6 TO 14 SQ. FT.	14 TO 32 SQ. FT.	32 TO 50 SQ. FT.	OVER 50 SQ. FT.
1. Minimum Frame Lap . .	¼ "	¼ "	⁵⁄₁₆ "	³⁄₈ "	½ "
2. Minimum Glass Edge Clearance	⅛ " ¹˒²	⅛ " ¹˒²	³⁄₁₆ " ¹	¼ "	¼ " ¹
3. Continuous Glazing Rabbet and Glass Retainer³ . .	Required				
4. Resilient Setting Material⁴.	Not Required	Required			

Sliding Doors and Horizontal Sliding Windows				
GLASS AREA	UP TO 14 SQ. FT.	14 TO 32 SQ. FT.	32 TO 50 SQ. FT.	OVER 50 SQ. FT.
5. Minimum Glass Frame Lap	¼ "	⁵⁄₁₆ "	³⁄₈ "	½ "
6. Minimum Glass Edge Clearance .	⅛ " ²	³⁄₁₆ "	¼ "	¼ "
7. Continuous Glazing Rabbet and Glass Retainer³	Required above third story	Required		
8. Resilient Setting Material⁴	Not Required	Required		

[1] Glass edge clearance in fixed openings shall be not less than required to provide for wind and earthquake drift.

[2] Glass edge clearance at all sides of pane shall be a minimum of ³⁄₁₆ inch where height of glass exceeds 3 feet.

[3] Glass retainers such as metal, wood or vinyl face stops, glazing beads, gaskets, glazing clips and glazing channels shall be of sufficient strength and fixation to serve this purpose.

[4] Resilient setting material shall include preformed rubber or vinyl plastic gaskets or other materials which are proved to the satisfaction of the building official to remain resilient.

From the Uniform Building Code, ©1982, ICBO.

Figure 15-11   Minimum Glazing Requirements

Patio Covers

Patio covers hit the market in so many different styles, colors and materials that the 1970 Edition of U.B.C. placed them in a separate chapter. This was Chapter 49 in the Appendix. In the 1973 Edition this chapter was completely rewritten.

Section 4901 defines patio covers:

Patio covers are one-story structures not exceeding 12 feet in height. Enclosure walls may have any configuration, provided the open area of the longer wall and one additional wall is equal to at least 65 percent of the area below a minimum of 6 feet 8 inches of each wall, measured from the floor. Openings may be enclosed with insect screening or plastic.

In the next paragraph it states what they can and cannot be used for:

Patio covers shall be used only for recreational, outdoor living purposes and not as carports, garages, storage rooms or habitable rooms.

This last item is very important. Many manufacturers claim their patio covers can be used for carports. That's wrong. A pre-manufactured carport may be used as a patio cover, but a pre-manufactured patio cover may *not* be used as a carport.

To determine which is which (especially when you're facing a fast-talking salesman) get the make and model number, the manufacturer's name, and any other information. Then call the inspector. It will only take him a minute or two to check his Research Recommendations and find out if the cover is even approved for *any* application. If it's a common national brand he'll have the information on hand. He can also tell you whether it's a carport or a patio cover. You'll need his blessing anyway when you apply for a permit, so you might as well start off on the right foot.

Patio covers and carports are exposed to many stresses and strains that are not common with other structures. They must be designed to withstand the stress limits of the code, all dead loads, and a minimum vertical live load of 10 pounds per square inch, as well as one other very critical load. This is the *uplift load*. Because of their construction, patio covers and carports are probably more susceptible to this load than most structures. They must be designed to support a minimum wind uplift load equal to the horizontal wind load pushing upward against the roof surface. However, if your patio is less than 10 feet above grade, the uplift load may be 3/4 the horizontal wind load.

Agricultural Buildings
Recognizing that the code would eventually be used in most rural and agricultural areas, the I.C.B.O. added Chapter 15, "Agricultural Buildings," to the code in 1973. In the 1979 Edition

it became Chapter 11 of the Appendix. Section 1107 states the following:

The provisions of this chapter shall apply exclusively to agricultural buildings. Such buildings shall be classified as a Group M, Division 3 Occupancy and shall include the following uses:
1. *Storage, livestock and poultry.*
2. *Milking barns.*
3. *Shade structures.*
4. *Horticultural structures (greenhouse and crop protection).*

The allowable height and area of agricultural buildings are greatly increased and exit requirements are generally relaxed. U.B.C. Table No. 11-A (Figure 3-8 in Chapter 3) shows basic allowable areas. Because of their lower occupancy rate, setbacks, occupancy separations and most other restrictions are vastly different from other types of buildings. However, residences, private garages and commercial or quasi-commercial buildings are not affected by this chapter; the sections of the main code applying to them prevail.

Sound Transmission Control

Standards for sound transmission control appear in Chapter 35 of the Appendix. What is new is that now Group R occupancies have some protection from noisy neighbors.

After reading through that chapter and the standards that go with it, I'm afraid it's still going to be difficult to enforce compliance, especially in apartment buildings. To do so you'd need a sound engineer with a battery of equipment.

Prefabricated Buildings

These could include everything from small metal tool sheds to barns and equipment storage facilities. Most of the smaller structures are exempt from permit requirements. Section 301(b) of the U.B.C. exempts detached accessory buildings under 120 square feet. That's where the prefabbed buildings start. Chapter 50 of the U.B.C. covers them under "Purpose" and "Definition":

Section 5001(a) Purpose. The purpose of this chapter is to regulate materials and establish methods of safe construction where any structure or portion thereof is wholly or partially prefabricated.

(c) Definition. **Prefabricated Assembly** *is a structural unit, the integral parts of which have been built up or assembled prior to incorporation in the building.*

That raises the question of whether or not you could prefab a building you would use later for a house and do it, let's say, in your back yard. It might work except for some sneaky little provisions in Chapter 50. One is that a certificate of approval must be obtained for each structure, and the approval can only be given by an approved agency. However, it does open the door for the use of these buildings. Usually the ones you find complying with this chapter are the standard steel and aluminum structures that are assembled like giant erector sets. Other than checking the interior facilities of these structures, (sanitation, insulation, interior finish) all there is to inspect are the footings and foundations.

16

Combustion Air

As a building inspector I was constantly running into problems over "combustion air." Here's what Section 601 of the Uniform Mechanical Code has to say about it:

Section 601. (a) Air Supply. All fuel-burning equipment shall be assured a sufficient supply of air for proper fuel combustion, ventilation, and draft hood dilution.

Exception: The method of providing combustion air in this chapter shall not apply to direct vent appliances, enclosed furnaces, listed cooking appliances, refrigerators, and clothes dryers.

In new or recently remodeled buildings, combustion air is seldom a problem. But in older buildings or those that have been occupied for a while, conditions can deteriorate. For instance, louvered vents that provide air can become blocked by dampers or by goods stored in front of them. Rooms may be remodeled in such a way that the supply of combustion air is completely cut off. Section 601(b) of the U.M.C. offers the following guidelines:

. . . if the volume (in cubic feet) of the room or space in which a fuel-burning appliance is installed is less than 1/20 of the maximum hourly fuel output rate in

Btu's of all appliances, provision shall be made to supply the deficiency in combustion and ventilating air for all fuel-burning appliances in such room other than listed cooking appliances, refrigerators or dryers.

Btu's (British Thermal Units)

You'll hear a lot about Btu's whenever you get involved with heat-producing appliances such as furnaces, water heaters, ovens or hot plates. Webster's has this to say about Btu's:

British thermal unit. *The amount of heat required to raise the temperature of one pound of water one degree Fahrenheit at or near its point of maximum density.*

Size of Enclosure

Let's convert what we've discussed so far into common, everyday figures. If your home measures 24 feet by 36 feet and you have the usual 8-foot ceilings, you've got about 7,000 cubic feet of space. Let's say your furnace is in an unfinished basement with the same dimensions as the house. Therefore, we can assume your fuel-burning appliance is located in a space of about 7,000 cubic feet.

Let's further assume that your fuel needs are 150,000 Btu's per hour. 1/20 of 150,000 Btu's is 7,500, so your unfinished basement will be less than the 1/20 requirement of the code and would be adequate for the location of your furnace.

But, you may have another problem. An unfinished basement simply screams for the family handyman to finish it. When this is done the furnace usually ends up in a furnace room or a corner of the utility room. That means the furnace will be squeezed into a smaller area, but you'll still have to furnish an adequate supply of air.

Say, for example, your utility room is 8 feet by 10 feet. This amounts to about 640 cubic feet. By dividing this into the 150,000 Btu figure, we find that your area is only about 1/236, and on that basis you will need to admit some combustion air into the enclosure.

Air Required

Here again we must go back to the size of the area in which your fuel-burning appliance is located. We decided that the utility room would be about 8 feet by 10 feet, or 640 cubic feet. Let's assume you have a gas furnace. Section 601(d)of the U.M.C. has this to say on the subject:

TABLE NO. 6-A—OPENING REQUIREMENTS FOR ROOMS OR ENCLOSURES CONTAINING GAS- OR LIQUID-FUEL-BURNING EQUIPMENT[1]

INPUT	MINIMUM TOTAL FREE AREA OF DUCTS OR OPENINGS, WHERE FLOOR AREA OF COMPARTMENT IS LESS THAN TWICE THE FLOOR AREA OF THE APPLIANCES THEREIN	MINIMUM TOTAL FREE AREA OF DUCTS OR OPENINGS, WHERE FLOOR AREA OF COMPARTMENT IS MORE THAN TWICE THE FLOOR AREA OF THE APPLIANCES THEREIN
0 through 500,000 Btu/h	2 sq. in. for each 1000 Btu/h	1 sq. in. for each 1000 Btu/h
500,000 through 1,000,000 Btu/h	1000 sq. in. plus 2 sq. in. for each 1500 Btu/h over 500,000 Btu/h	500 sq. in. plus 1 sq. in. for each 1500 Btu/h over 500,000 Btu/h
Over 1,000,000 Btu/h	1666 sq. in. plus 2 sq. in. for each 2000 Btu/h over 1,000,000 Btu/h	833 sq. in. plus 1 sq. in. for each 2000 Btu/h over 1,000,000 Btu/h

[1]This table shall not apply when Section 607 is used.

From the Uniform Mechanical Code, ©1982, ICBO.

Figure 16-1 Opening Requirements for Furnace Enclosures

(d) Insufficient Space—Gas and Liquid. Except as otherwise provided for in this Chapter, rooms or spaces that do not have the volume as specified in subsection (b) of this Section in which a gas or liquid fuel-burning appliance or appliances are installed shall be provided with minimum unobstructed combustion air openings equal to that set forth in Table 6-A and in Section 603 of this Code.

Where the floor area of the appliance compartment is less than twice the floor area of the appliances therein, the minimum total free area shall be not less than 200 square inches.

Where the floor area of the appliance compartment is more than twice the floor area of the appliances therein, the minimum total free area shall be not less than 100 square inches.

My tape measure shows the furnace to be 22 inches by 26 inches, almost four square feet in area. Therefore, according to Section 601(d) you'd only need 100 square inches of free space to admit combustion air into the room. Is this enough? Let's take a look at U.M.C. Table No. 6-A (see Figure 16-1).

Column 1 lists the input rating in Btu's. The first item has a rating of "0 to 500,000 Btu's". That's the range in which your furnace will be operating, so that's the rating we'll be working with. As for the other two columns, the first is for appliances in a space where the floor area is less than twice the area of the appliance, and the other is where it is more. Because your room is 80 square feet compared with only 4 square feet for the appliance, we'll be working in the third column. This column indicates we must compute the combustion air opening on the basis of 1 square inch for each 1,000 Btu's. That means we must have a minimum of 150 square inches (150,000 divided by 1,000) and not the amount set forth as a minimum in Section 601(d).

Supplying the Air

According to Section 602 of the U.M.C., half of the required air must come from an opening located within the upper 12 inches of the room or enclosure. The other half must come from an opening not more than 12 inches above the base of the lowest appliance. That would mean two louvered openings, one at the top and one at the bottom of the door.

Door? No, the code doesn't require the louvers to be placed in a door, but that's the way it's usually done. Most contractors I know prefer this method because it's cheaper than cutting grillwork into the wall. Also, according to the heating contractors, it's safer. If the openings are placed in the door, there's little likelihood they'll ever be blocked.

Of course, there are other ways to supply combustion air. The second paragraph of Section 602 says that if the enclosure is not less than 50 square feet, "all" the air may come from a supply opening within the upper 12 inches of the enclosure. But there must be an equivalent supply opening extending directly to the firebox.

Sources of Air

Where the air comes from and its condition are important. Not long ago, a hospital near me converted its furnaces and boilers from oil to natural gas. Because of other remodeling, the combustion air duct was closed off and another opened through a hole in the wall of the furnace room directly to the outside of the building. This was properly fitted with a louvered vent electrically interlocked with the gas burner. So, when the thermostat called for heat, the louvers were electrically opened at the same time ignition took place.

This had been designed by a heating engineer who did a beautiful job. When the boiler fired, I was on hand to check the system and the louvers responded perfectly. The job was approved.

About the middle of January I received calls from both the contractor and the hospital. Everything in the boiler room was frozen. Why? Several steam lines and a main water line passed in front of the combustion air vent. With below-freezing weather outside and the boiler calling for heat, the icy wind blowing through the vent had frozen all the pipes in front of it. The problem was solved by placing heaters in the passageway where the cold wind entered. But it took a freeze-up to point out the problem. I couldn't find anything about it in the code except a warning that exposed pipes should be protected—inside a room with two boilers.

Section 603(c) of the Uniform Mechanical Code offers several sources of combustion air:

Prohibited Sources. Combustion air supply shall not be obtained from any hazardous location or from any area in which objectionable quantities of flammable vapor, lint, or dust are given off. Combustion air shall not be taken from a machinery room.

Combustion air openings or ducts cannot be used where fire dampers are required. Volume dampers can't be installed in combustion air openings or ducts.

That leaves you with three primary sources of combustion air:
1. Outside of the building.
2. The underfloor area, provided there is sufficient ventilation.
3. Inside the building or conditioned space.

Outside: To use outside air you must screen your entry duct with a corrosion-resistant screen of not more than 1/2-inch mesh. You should also size your duct to the volume of air needed because dampering is not allowed. For some reason attic space is included under "outside air" instead of in a category of its own. However, the attic can only be used if there are sufficient openings to the outside. You must have a minimum clear space of 30 inches at the maximum height of the attic.

Underfloor: Underfloor space may be used if there is sufficient ventilation either through special vents or openings through the foundation vents. In any event, make sure the screens have been cleaned. That also applies in the attic. All screened openings must be kept free of dust, leaves, and other debris that may restrict the opening.

Inside: Using air from inside a building opens up another can of worms. Section 601 of the U.M.C. gives specifications for obtaining combustion air solely from this source. The main consideration is that the Btu rating must not exceed 1/20 the gross cubic feet of the structure. But I prefer to go by "available space." That is, the area that can't be closed off by doors. In most homes you'll probably have enough space, even if several bedroom doors are closed.

Other Air Users

There are many other air users in your house—common household items such as fireplaces, kitchen fans and bathroom vents. Each removes air from a confined space. I doubt seriously if many people are aware of how great this removal is. Perhaps you have a recirculating kitchen fan. These draw air across a charcoal filter to remove cooking odors and grease, then discharge the air back into the room. This type of fan is okay because it puts air back into the room. But if your fan discharges to the exterior of the building, then it's *reducing* the amount of available combustion air.

While we're at it, here's a little advice. Check the attic through the attic crawl hole. The duct from your fan might be dumping kitchen grease into the attic. The same thing goes for the bath vent. Make sure these vents discharge outside.

Section 606 of the U.M.C. states:

Operation of exhaust fans, kitchen ventilation systems, clothes dryers, or fireplaces shall be considered in determining combustion air requirements to avoid unsatisfactory operation of installed gas appliances.

Notice that it says ". . .to avoid unsatisfactory operation of installed gas appliances." This undoubtedly was included because gas furnaces are probably the biggest combustion air users. Electric furnaces don't need the combustion air required by fuel-burning appliances.

Fireplaces

As an inspector I was often called out to investigate smoking fireplaces, especially in new homes. There are many reasons for a smoky fireplace. But fireplace construction is seldom the culprit. Houses today are more airtight than they used to be. Single-wall construction of solid wood or fiber panels is one reason. It doesn't allow as much air leakage as diagonal shiplap construction. Storm windows, weatherstripping and plastic vapor barriers further reduce air leakage.

What you've got is a situation where furnaces, kitchen and bath fans and fireplaces are competing for whatever air is trapped inside the house. During the day when windows are open and doors are being opened and closed, this isn't a problem. There's a lot of air coming into the house. But it can be a problem at night, when the windows and doors are shut.

I usually found that a fireplace was smoking because it was starved for oxygen. The flames were licking out for any available air.

Many fireplaces are now designed with vents and tubes to provide combustion air from the outside.

Commercial Air Users
Commercial establishments such as restaurants also have combustion air problems. The vent hoods (and many are required) take a lot of air out of most kitchens. And there are gas-flame grills, water heaters and other items gobbling up air.

In winter, the problem usually becomes worse. Windows are kept shut and air conditioning units are plugged. But venting of kitchen vapor and steam continues. The kitchen becomes an airless box until someone opens a door and momentarily relieves the condition.

The same thing can happen in your home. If, some windless night after everyone has settled down for the evening, you open a door or window and a gust of air blows in, you've got a problem. You're living in a vacuum created by your fireplace, furnace and other air-consuming devices. A properly designed house, and one that doesn't draw cold air, is one with a slightly positive pressure.

Combustion air is probably the least considered of all of a house's ills. But, with the many devices competing for air, it's something that can't be ignored.

Index

Practical References For Builders

National Construction Estimator
Current building costs in dollars and cents for residential, commercial and industrial construction. Prices for every commonly used building material, and the proper labor cost associated with installation of the material. Everything figured out to give you the "in place" cost in seconds. Many time-saving rules of thumb, waste and coverage factors and estimating tables are included. **512 pages, 8½ x 11, $16.00. Revised annually.**

Rough Carpentry
All rough carpentry is covered in detail: sills, girders, columns, joists, sheathing, ceiling, roof and wall framing, roof trusses, dormers, bay windows, furring and grounds, stairs and insulation. Many of the 24 chapters explain practical code approved methods for saving lumber and time without sacrificing quality. Chapters on columns, headers, rafters, joists and girders show how to use simple engineering principles to select the right lumber dimension for whatever species and grade you are using. **288 pages, 8½ x 11, $14.50**

Wood-Frame House Construction
From the layout of the outer walls, excavation and formwork, to finish carpentry, and painting, every step of construction is covered in detail with clear illustrations and explanations. Everything the builder needs to know about framing, roofing, siding, insulation and vapor barrier, interior finishing, floor coverings, and stairs. . .complete step by step "how to" information on what goes into building a frame house. **240 pages, 8½ x 11, $11.25. Revised edition**

Building Layout
Shows how to use a transit to locate the building on the lot correctly, plan proper grades with minimum excavation, find utility lines and easements, establish correct elevations, lay out accurate foundations and set correct floor heights. Explains planning sewer connections, leveling a foundation out of level, using a story pole and batterboards, working on steep sites, and minimizing excavation costs. **240 pages, 5½ x 8½, $11.75**

Spec Builder's Guide
Explains how to plan and build a home, control your construction costs, and then sell the house at a price that earns a decent return on the time and money you've invested. Includes professional tips to ensure success as a spec builder: how government statistics help you judge the housing market, cutting costs at every opportunity without sacrificing quality, and taking advantage of construction cycles. Every chapter includes checklists, diagrams, charts, figures, and estimating tables. **448 pages, 8½ x 11, $24.00**

Manual of Electrical Contracting

From the tools you need for installing electrical work in new construction and remodeling work to developing the finances you need to run your business. Shows how to draw up an electrical plan and design the correct lighting within the budget you have to work with. How to calculate service and feeder loads, service entrance capacity, demand factors, and install wiring in residential, commercial, and agricultural buildings. Covers how to make sure your business will succeed before you start it, and how to keep it running profitably. **224 pages, 8½ x 11, $17.00**

Masonry & Concrete Construction

Every aspect of masonry construction is covered, from laying out the building with a transit to constructing chimneys and fireplaces. Explains footing construction, building foundations, laying out a block wall, reinforcing masonry, pouring slabs and sidewalks, coloring concrete, selecting and maintaining forms, using the Jahn Forming System and steel ply forms, and much more. **224 pages, 8½ x 11, $13.50**

Residential Electrical Design

Explains what every builder needs to know about designing electrical systems for residential construction. Shows how to draw up an electrical plan from the blueprints, including the service entrance, grounding, lighting requirements for kitchen, bedroom and bath and how to lay them out. Explains how to plan electrical heating systems and what equipment you'll need, how to plan outdoor lighting, and much more. If you are a builder who ever has to plan an electrical system, you should have this book. **194 pages, 8½ x 11, $11.50**

Building Cost Manual

Square foot costs for residential, commercial, industrial, and farm buildings. In a few minutes you work up a reliable budget estimate based on the actual materials and design features, area, shape, wall height, number of floors and support requirements. Most important, you include all the important variables that can make any building unique from a cost standpoint. **240 pages, 8½ x 11, $12.00. Revised annually**

Reducing Home Building Costs

Explains where significant cost savings are possible and shows how to take advantage of these opportunities. Six chapters show how to reduce foundation, floor, exterior wall, roof, interior and finishing costs. Three chapters show effective ways to avoid problems usually associated with bad weather at the jobsite. Explains how to increase labor productivity. **224 pages, 8½ x 11, $10.25**

Estimating Home Building Costs

Estimate every phase of residential construction from site costs to the profit margin you should include in your bid. Shows how to keep track of manhours and make accurate labor cost estimates for footings, foundations, framing and sheathing finishes, electrical, plumbing and more. Explains the work being estimated and provides sample cost estimate worksheets with complete instructions for each job phase. **320 pages, 5½ x 8½, $14.00**

Construction Estimating Reference Data

Collected in this single volume are the building estimator's 300 most useful estimating reference tables. Labor requirements for nearly every type of construction are included: sitework, concrete work, masonry, steel, carpentry, thermal & moisture protection, doors and windows, finishes, mechanical and electrical. Each section explains in detail the work being estimated and gives the appropriate crew size and equipment needed. Many pages of illustrations, estimating pointers and explanations of the work being estimated are also included. This is an essential reference for every professional construction estimator. **368 pages, 11 x 8½, $18.00**

Construction Superintending

Explains what the "super" should do during every job phase from taking bids to project completion on both heavy and light construction: excavation, foundations, pilings, steelwork, concrete and masonry, carpentry, plumbing, and electrical. Explains scheduling, preparing estimates, record keeping, dealing with subcontractors, and change orders. Includes the charts, forms, and established guidelines every superintendent needs. **240 pages, 8½ x 11, $22.00**

Manual of Professional Remodeling

This is the practical manual of professional remodeling written by an experienced and successful remodeling contractor. Shows how to evaluate a job and avoid 30-minute jobs that take all day, what to fix and what to leave alone, and what to watch for in dealing with subcontractors. Includes chapters on calculating space requirements, repairing structural defects, remodeling kitchens, baths, walls and ceilings, doors and windows, floors, roofs, installing fireplaces and chimneys (including built-ins), skylights, and exterior siding. Includes blank forms, checklists, sample contracts, and proposals you can copy and use. **400 pages, 8½ x 11, $18.75**

Planning and Designing Plumbing Systems

Explains in clear language, with detailed illustrations, basic drafting principles for plumbing construction needs. Covers basic drafting fundamentals: isometric pipe drawing, sectional drawings and details, how to use a plot plan, and how to convert it into a working drawing. Gives instructions and examples for water supply systems, drainage and venting, pipe, valves and fixtures, and has a special section covering heating systems, refrigeration, gas, oil, and compressed air piping, storm, roof and building drains, fire hydrants, and more. **224 pages, 8½ x 11, $13.00**

Plumbers Handbook Revised

This new edition shows what will and what will not pass inspection in drainage, vent, and waste piping, septic tanks, water supply, fire protection, and gas piping systems. All tables, standards, and specifications are completely up-to-date with recent changes in the plumbing code. Covers common layouts for residential work, how to size piping, selecting and hanging fixtures, practical recommendations and trade tips. This book is the approved reference for the plumbing contractors exam in many states. **240 pages, 8½ x 11, $16.75**

How to Sell Remodeling
Proven, effective sales methods for repair and remodeling contractors: finding qualified leads, making the sales call, identifying what your prospects really need, pricing the job, arranging financing, and closing the sale. Explains how to organize and staff a sales team, how to bring in the work to keep your crews busy and your business growing, and much more. Includes blank forms, tables, and charts. **240 pages, 8½ x 11, $17.50**

Paint Contractor's Manual
How to start and run a profitable paint contracting company: getting set up and organized to handle volume work, avoiding the mistakes most painters make when starting out, getting top production from your crews and the most value from your advertising dollar. Shows how to estimate all prep and painting. (including the manhour figures the author uses when estimating residential, commercial or industrial jobs). Suggests pricing strategies when bidding custom residential, tract and apartment painting. Includes sample estimating forms and checklists so your estimates cover all costs on every job. **224 pages, 8½ x 11, $19.25**